TERRORIST SUICIDE BOMBINGS

Attack Interdiction, Mitigation, and Response

TERRORIST SUICIDE BOMBINGS

Attack Interdiction, Mitigation, and Response

Mordecai Dzikansky ∎ Gil Kleiman ∎ Robert Slater

CRC Press
Taylor & Francis Group
Boca Raton London New York

CRC Press is an imprint of the
Taylor & Francis Group, an **Informa** business

CRC Press
Taylor & Francis Group
6000 Broken Sound Parkway NW, Suite 300
Boca Raton, FL 33487-2742

First issued in paperback 2021

Version Date: 20110816

ISBN-13: 978-0-367-77902-3 (pbk)
ISBN-13: 978-1-4398-7131-7 (hbk)

Visit the Taylor & Francis Web site at
http://www.taylorandfrancis.com

and the CRC Press Web site at
http://www.crcpress.com

CONTENTS

SECTION II   A Suicide Bomber's Motives

SECTION III   Evaluating Suicide Bombing

SECTION IV　*Defending against Suicide Bombings*

SECTION V   *Key Players*

SEPTEMBER 10, 2010
STATEMENT OF
PRESIDENT BARACK OBAMA

I think that in this day and age,...there is always going to be the potential for an individual or a small group of individuals, if they are willing to die, to kill other people. Some of them are going to be very well organized and some of them are going to be random. That threat is there. And it's important, I think, for the American people to understand that, and not to live in fear. It's just a reality of today's world that there are going to be threats out there.

We go about our business. We are tougher than them. Our families and our businesses and our churches and mosques and synagogues and our Constitution, our values, that's what give us strength. And we are going to have this problem out there for a long time to come. But it doesn't have to completely distort us. And it doesn't have to dominate our foreign policy. What we can do is to constantly fight against it. And I think ultimately, we are going to be able to stamp it out. But it's going to take some time.

News conference, East Room, The White House, September 10, 2010

FOREWORD: A SUICIDE BOMBER IN ACTION

The following description of what the final hours are like for someone about to go on a suicide bombing mission is a composite portrait of numerous bombers. The composite is drawn from conversations that co-authors Mordecai Dzikansky and Gil Kleiman have had with Israeli intelligence officers, investigators, and bomb technicians as well as from their reading media interviews with Palestinian would-be suicide bombers caught before they could blow themselves up.

It is 5:33 a.m. The young man had spent the past six hours sleeping, fitfully to be sure, but sleeping. When he had gone to bed, he had been excited, nervous of course, but definitely on a high, though he had taken no drugs. Drugs might numb his mind. He definitely wanted all of his senses alive and functioning. Waking up with the same joyful feeling that he had experienced the mornings of his past birthdays, he was pleased that he had slept well. He wanted to be conscious of every moment during the next three hours.

Can he truly say why he agreed to the deed he will perform at 8 a.m.? Why was he was willing to place himself in a crowd and, with no hesitation at all, detonate explosives strapped to his waist?

Was it purely the glory that would surely come to him and to his family? Certainly that was an important motive. On their trees neighbors were sure to hang pictures of him holding sticks of dynamite.

Spray-painted graffiti would praise him as the latest Palestinian Arab martyr. His photograph would adorn the wall of local stores. The image that gave him greatest pride was of heart-shaped flowers, with a picture of a bomb on the flowers, on display outside his parents' front door.

As he rose from his bed, his mind focused on his father, so proud of him, and so jealous. "What more could a father want?" his father would ask when the deed was done. In all honesty, we cannot say for sure what motivates the young man the most. Might it be the financial stability promised to his parents? Or perhaps it is the prospect of becoming an eternal martyr? Or the 72 virgins he will meet upon arriving in heaven?

Though the Koran does state that the righteous will find 'full-breasted "maidens," upon reaching paradise, nothing in Islam's holy book specifically states that the faithful will receive 72 virgins apiece. One reference in the Hadith, traditional sayings that have been traced to Mohammed, notes that the smallest reward for those in Heaven is, among other things, 72 wives.*

The young man had not done such a thing but he had heard stories of past suicide bombers who had wrapped their penises into fireproof aluminum foil to save them for the pleasures to come.

To be sure, most young suicide bombers were obsessed with sex; but many suicide bombers were vengeful over the enemy's killing of a brother or father, others were frustrated and angry over the poverty in their midst. Yet, the promise of eternal martyrdom appeared to be their key motive. Feeling a total devotion to God, a wish to die with Jewish blood on their hands, the Palestinian–Arab suicide bombers thought of themselves as holy and heroic.

After he had blown himself up, when people began digging into the young man's background, they would discover his motive of revenge: the enemy had gunned down his brother a month earlier. But he had lost other family members and friends and never asked the militant organizations for such an assignment.

Oddly enough, considering that he would not be around to enjoy the plaudits, he specifically asked to go on the "sacrifice mission," in order to gain honor as a martyr, and in doing so, to become the equivalent of a rock star to his friends and family. His photo would adorn walls of local stores; it would be on key chains and the equivalent of baseball cards. A band would sing a song praising him for carrying out the suicide bombing. In his honor, children would play a game, which included a mock funeral for a suicide bomber.

Throughout his childhood, he had not felt a need for fame, but now with this opportunity, he yearned to make his parents, other close

---

* In the Koran we find: 76: 12-21 Verily, for the Muttaqun, there will be a success (Paradise); Gardens and grapeyards; and young full-breasted (mature) maidens of equal age; and a full cup (of wine). http://www.muslimtents.com/aminahsworld/Verses_on_paradise.html

In the Hadith, traditional sayings traced to Muhammad. Hadith number 2,562, the Prophet says: "The smallest reward for the people of Paradise is an abode where there are 80,000 servants and 72 wives, over which stands a dome decorated with pearls, aquamarine, and ruby, as wide as the distance from Al-Jabiyyah [a Damascus suburb] to Sana'a [Yemen]. http://answers.yahoo.com/question/index?qid=20100329114456AAEX34I

relatives and friends proud of him. He did not feel desperate. He and his family were not poor. Both his parents had decent jobs. The young man himself had been training to become a lawyer. The family lived in reasonable quarters. Food was never an issue. He seemingly had much to live for. But he felt he had even more reason to die.

Why, he asked himself, did his sponsors plan and execute these suicide bombings? It was not to subdue the enemy State of Israel. That was unrealistic; and anyway it was not what the suicide bombing was all about. It was to instill fear in the enemy, to terrorize them; it was to gain headlines around the world. The suicide missions were meant to shine light on their cause.

His one act alone did not smite an enemy, but at least he and his people would have taken the initiative, and seized control if only for moments or hours.

From his bed he could see the faintest hint of light emerging from the window to his right. In a few hours, hundreds of early-morning shoppers would begin streaming into the open-air vegetable and fruit market a few miles from his home, a market where his enemies shopped every day. Meeting with his terrorist sponsors—two older men with short beards and obvious expertise in explosives—the night before for final instructions, he learned for the first time that those shoppers would be his targets.

Until then, he had been told nothing about the dramatic action—only that he had been expected to carry out the task and would be told his ultimate destination the night before. The secrecy excited him; it made him feel that he was doing something special.

Three weeks earlier when a friend mentioned to him casually that men in his village were looking for volunteers for a very special task to harm the enemy, his ears perked up. He thought of his dead brother; he thought of how much he hated the enemy. He was willing to do anything he would be asked to do. Nothing could be too dangerous. Yet he carried on with his normal life, not offering himself for the mission. He assumed that the task was for older men only. He was 18 years old. But a few days later, he returned to his friend and asked how to contact these men from the village; he wanted to volunteer for the task. He hoped that an exception might be made for him. It was.

His sponsors had seemed pleased that he had volunteered for the mission without knowing what he would be asked to do. Meeting daily, they talked with him about the cause, the enemy, Islam, the concept of martyrdom—but they did not reveal what they wanted him to do. They wanted to assess whether he was really up to it. Sensing that he was sincere, they finally explained what they were planning for him to do, showing him the equipment he would need, telling him that once he agreed to the mission he would no longer be able to see his parents, other close relatives or friends. Secrecy had to be preserved. He said he understood what they were saying. He showed no fear and shed no tears.

For the past two weeks, he had been training for this moment. He was put through many exercises to prepare him for the big day: he was asked to write a will, to write letters to his family and friends. He had been put through activities testing his will. Once, he was asked to deliver a gun to someone and he did. On another occasion, his sponsors had taken him to a cemetery where one handler asked him to put on a white shroud routinely used to cover bodies for burial. He was then buried in a mock grave. Offering no explanation for the request, his sponsors, he surmised, were trying to get him used to the idea of his death.

It seemed that his sponsors had thought of everything. He was promised that if, in retaliation for his suicide bombing, his family's home was destroyed they would pay to replace it. In addition, his family would receive nearly $1,000 a month; his siblings would receive scholarships—all by way of expressing gratitude to the young man.

As part of his training, he had been taken to a safe house where his sponsors made a video recording in which he indicated his consent to becoming a suicide bomber as well as his utter devotion to Islam. In the video, he bade farewell to his family and encouraged others to follow in his footsteps as a suicide bomber. Soon after he had blown himself up, the video would be turned over to the media. The video might have been entitled, The Making of a Rock Star.

His sponsors also took a still photo of him that would be displayed throughout the West Bank and the Gaza Strip, the territories that his enemy, the Israelis, had been occupying since the 1967 war. By distributing this photo all over the occupied territories, his sponsors would begin the process of turning the young man into a martyr.

The night before the young man was to carry out his mission, his sponsors had showed him the equipment he would take into "battle": the suicide belt he would place around his waist; the explosives that would be fastened on to the belt; the detonator switch; a blue T-shirt with no writing on it; jeans, socks, and sneakers. He would wear no disguise. He had no need for one. To others in the market, he would seem like one of many young men, Israeli as well as Arab, who were shopping that morning. He was fascinated with the belt, the explosives, the secrecy, the importance his sponsors placed on the mission.

Until this point his mission had seemed far off, not real. But now, as the time approached, he began to focus on it, feeling a growing sense of pride and purpose. He said to himself: "This is the day I have longed for. I will not be around; but the world will sit up and take notice of me—if only for a fleeting moment." With the mission less than 12 hours away, his sponsors gave him important advice: make sure to eat something before he set out on the task. Hunger could distract him; it could keep him from focusing on every single instruction he had to follow.

Remembering that advice soon after waking, he walked over to a small fridge nearby, and took out some cheese and a yogurt. Though no day for smiles, he let a slight smile crease his face: prisoners on death row, offered a final meal, surely had a heartier repast. But he made due with light fare.

Though soon the concept of time would be meaningless, the seconds now ticking off were crucial to him. In an hour, he was to meet his sponsors at the safe house a half-mile away from his home. He must not tarry though the irony was clear: he was rushing to his demise. Did he not want to stretch out his last hours on Earth? Of course he did. Did he not want to say goodbye to family and friends? Certainly.

But the two sponsors had forbidden him to talk to anyone during the next three hours. Upon meeting him, they would provide him with his lethal tools and final encouragement. They would hand him a map with the precise place marked where he would stand when he blew himself up.

A few moments later, he closed his door behind him, and headed for the safe house, feeling no fear. His body did not shake. His mind remained clear and focused. He knew exactly what he was doing. Not for a single second did he think of retreating from the deed.

The time was approaching and he was ready.

ACKNOWLEDGMENTS

MORDECAI DZIKANSKY

I became an expert on suicide bombing. In a *Sunday New York Daily News* interview (April 18, 2004), New York Police Department (NYPD) Commissioner Raymond Kelly said: "We have in-depth information on suicide bombings in Israel within three hours. Morty goes there, he works with Israeli authorities. It helps us, enables us to adjust, position our cops here differently."

In 1983, when I first put on the uniform at the age of 20, I never imagined that my career would take this direction. Traditional policing was my goal: locking up the bad guys. In my worst nightmares, I never imagined a terror attack on my city like that of 9/11 and how the events of that day would change me, New York, and the NYPD; how that day would change the responsibility of law enforcement, first responders, and the general public and lead to the writing of this manual.

I would like to acknowledge and honor the heroic first responders who gave their lives on 9/11 and those who are still fighting the illnesses they suffered from working the rescue and recovery missions that ensued.

I thank my NYPD family for their vision and support and for allowing me to be part of a unique organization that truly lives up to its name "New York's Finest."

I offer a heartfelt thank you to the Israel National Police for admitting me into its inner circles and helping maximize the safety of New York City. With this manual, the Israel Police's lessons and my experiences will be shared with readers as part of our global fight against suicide bombings.

A special thank you to the Israel Police Bomb Squad: Your dedication, knowledge, and perseverance are awe-inspiring.

To my coauthors:

Robert Slater: I knew that I had met a truly gifted author and professional journalist when we worked together on our first book, *Terrorist Cop*. It has been a true privilege to work with you again on this project, and

I greatly appreciate your stewardship and passion for this difficult but important topic.

Gil Kleiman: I learned very early on in my police career how invaluable having a good partner can be. When I was posted as the first NYPD overseas liaison in Israel, for the first time in my career I was on my own and in a most challenging environment. Once we met, I knew right off the bat that I had found a "partner" who would become one of my closest friends. Your commitment and dedication to being the voice of truth are most admirable. I am grateful that we have been able to translate our difficult experiences into information that other first responders can use in battling the evil of terror.

To my family:

It has been three years since I retired from the NYPD and three years since the last bombing in Israel; then, on March 23, 2011, as we were in the final days of completing this book, a bomb exploded at a crowded bus stop in Jerusalem, killing one and injuring over 30. During my liaison days in Israel, my children, Zachary, Jake, and Talia, were too young to comprehend terms like "suicide bombing" or to watch the horror of a suicide bombing scene unfold live on the news. Sitting with my wife Meryl and our children on the afternoon of March 23, we watched the live feed from the Jerusalem bombing scene and shared the pain of the victims and of the country. Meryl and I realized that though they are still merely children, our children now appear to understand the realities of terror and the importance of alertness and vigilance in fighting it. I would like to thank Meryl and our children for their encouragement and support throughout this much-needed book project.

Mordecai Z. Dzikansky
Ra'anana, Israel
March 27, 2011

GIL KLEIMAN

I decided to write this book six years ago upon learning that someone I knew was giving a speech on suicide bombings to a police organization in the United States. My mouth dropped. My "partner" Mordecai Dzikansky and I had been to more suicide bombings than anyone else in the world. Yet neither of us had ever seen this man (we called him "Sleek") at any single suicide bombing. I was livid; "Sleek" had no credentials. In my view, he had no right to discuss this topic. With his lack of personal experience, he had only theoretical knowledge, just enough to get his "students" killed.

I decided right then and there that I was going to write a book that told it like it was, the way I had experienced it. It was a book that would keep first responders alive.

I could not have done the book without my coauthor Robert Slater, who replaced my inability to write a legible sentence with the flowing words of a *New York Times* best-selling author. I can talk, but not write. I like to say I was a spokesman, not a "writer man." Without Bob, this book would never have been written, period.

To Morty (my other coauthor Mordecai Dzikansky), it has been a long journey.... We met in Israel in late 2002 soon after I had lectured to intelligence officers from various Israeli-based embassies, essentially a "spy" convention. Morty had just arrived from the New York Police Department (NYPD) to analyze Israel's wave of suicide bombings. I was Israel Police spokesman for the foreign media.

After the lecture, we learned that we grew up 13 blocks from one another in Brooklyn, and that fact of geography led to the strongest friendship imaginable. He was the only one in Israel who knew what to answer when I asked him, "Djeet?" Sharing the agonizing up-front witnessing of countless suicide bombing sites, we found comfort before and after these events in just "hanging out," in discussing "police gossip," in being there for one another, especially once we both developed posttraumatic stress disorder (PTSD).

To my children Mary Lee, Liam Jonac, and Shane Murray, I want to thank you for taking care of one another, making dinner, getting yourselves ready for bed, while your mother and I were out "fighting terror." I thank you too for turning out normal and intelligent and for abiding your mother and I talking "police talk" at the dinner table.

I thank my father, Murray Kleiman, a lawyer, mathematician, and renaissance man who at the age of 20 was already a mathematics instructor at City College in New York. He taught me that the key to a happy life is to plan ahead as if you were going to live forever, but to enjoy each day as if you were going to die tomorrow.

I thank my mother, Jennie Reiss Kleiman, an accountant and school teacher but always a full-time mother who protected me the way a lioness would protect her cub, never giving in to any teacher or principal who had the "audacity" to say anything bad about me. She taught me, "Who dares wins." Without your teaching me not to be afraid, I would not have had the courage to do all the things that I did.

I thank also my birth mother, Karen Jordan Good, who at the age of 15 had the strength and courage to pass me over for adoption to a family who would provide for my every need. Because of her wishes, I was placed in an Orthodox Jewish home, which led me to move to Israel, which led me to serve in the Israel Police, and which eventually led me to write this book. Without her decision 53 years ago, all those things would not have occurred. She wanted me placed in an Orthodox Jewish home because, as she put it, "Orthodox Jewish families always seemed to be happy, and I wanted you to be happy."

Finally, to my wife Israel Police Superintendent Ilanit Kleiman: you helped me have a future. You helped me live. I recall, in my darkest days of suffering from PTSD, how you doggedly entered the Disabled Veterans Administration building. Despite a security man informing us that the building was closed to the public, you refused to leave the premises until someone came down and gave me a referral to a psychiatrist. Getting that appointment, you said to me, "Now we can go home and start living." It was my personal "turning point," and I thank you for helping me through my recovery—and for all other things.

Gil Kleiman
Modi'in, Israel
March 28, 2011

ROBERT SLATER

This seems the appropriate place to acknowledge:

- That whenever we told friends and family that we were writing a manual on suicide bombing, they suddenly looked bemused and seemed to ask themselves: "For or against?" We assured them: "It's actually a manual that teaches how to defend against suicide bombings."
- That this was the first manual we were writing and we would have to think long and hard on how one wrote a manual. After all, when—as students—we last focused on manuals, we were studying the contents, not concerned with how a manual should

be written. So we asked ourselves one crucial question: "What would first responders want to learn from this manual and what should they know to deal with suicide bombing?" Then we made our selections of subject matter.

- That we wrestled with a few technical issues: First, do we refer to suicide bombers always with the "he/she" phrase? After all, there were a number of female suicide bombers, and we write a chapter about them. Finding the "female suicide bombers" cumbersome, we settled on identifying suicide bombers in the masculine unless it was clear we were writing of a female suicide bomber.

- That we wrestled with how we refer to the three coauthors in the text. Writing "we" all the time, as in "we think," or "we believe," seemed confusing to us. It might not always be clear to whom the "we" referred—two of us or three of us? We decided to identify each of us by our last names in the text when we wanted to identify just one of us, but not the others. When we do employ the word "we," we mean all three of us.

- That we grappled with how graphic the photos we use in the manual should be. As this book is meant to be a teaching tool for first responders, we decided not to hold back. So readers will find photos that are difficult to look at, but that give a much better idea of what a suicide bombing looks like than any words we could have written or than any of the frequently sanitized newspaper photos and TV footage could show.

- That we worried, in sections where we describe how suicide bombers behave and what weapons they employ, that we might be divulging information that could help suicide bombers in their missions. Coauthors Gil Kleiman, a former bomb technician, and Mordecai Dzikansky, who knew precisely what information could help a suicide bomber, took great care not to provide such information. We three coauthors made sure that anything we wrote on these sensitive subjects came from public sources. We refused to reveal anything new to potential suicide bombers. We firmly believe that we have held to that standard.

The idea for this manual grew out of a book that Mordecai Dzikansky and Robert Slater wrote called *Terrorist Cop: The NYPD Jewish Cop Who Traveled the World to Stop Terrorists* (Barricade Books, 2010). In that book, Dzikansky told his personal story of rising through the ranks of the NYPD, one of the first Orthodox Jewish police officers in the department;

later, becoming a worldwide expert on suicide bombing through numerous visits to suicide bombing sites in Israel and elsewhere. Happily, Mark Listewnik, our editor at Taylor & Francis, asked us, as we had just finished the manuscript for *Terrorist Cop*, to produce a manual on suicide bombing that would fill a gap on the learning side for first responders. We wish to thank Mark Listewnik, as well as Stephanie Morkert, project coordinator, and Prudy Taylor Board, project editor. Gil Kleiman, a former senior official with the Israel National Police, joined as a coauthor. As the writer, I met with Mordecai and Gil frequently to decide what should go into the manual, and then turning our decisions into text. For me, though the subject matter was often gruesome, it was a joyful experience working with my coauthors. Their knowledge of the subject was remarkable. They had facts in their heads from their personal experiences that helped enormously in the writing. We wish to extend our gratitude to our agent-attorney, Lloyd J. Jassin, who had the original insight that, after *Terrorist Cop*, it would be fitting and timely for Dzikansky, Kleiman and I to undertake a textbook on suicide bombings. Lloyd has been a great "partner" in this effort, offering excellent advice, and simply being there, watching out for us. Thanks, Lloyd.

I wish to thank Judith Resnik and Kermit Roosevelt for their help in clarifying portions of the text. I thank Ed Rock for his help with parts of the text. I want to thank my wife, Elinor Slater, who once again used her skills as a professional editor to polish the manuscript into a much better form. I thank my children: Miriam and her husband Shimi, Adam and his wife Tal, and Rachel, for being close by, expressing love and deep interest in what I was doing that made it all worthwhile. Those of my six grandchildren who are old enough to speak and form questions peppered me with queries about the topic, truly making me feel that I was doing something that mattered to them. And so I thank Edo, Maya, Shai, Shani, Matan, and Ben.

Robert Slater
Jerusalem, Israel
March 27, 2011

ABOUT THE AUTHORS

Mordecai Dzikansky stands at French Hill (Jerusalem) bus stop near where suicide bombings occurred several times during the Second Intifada. An Israeli
border policeman looks on. (*Credit*: Mordecai Dzikansky photo collection)

Mordecai Z. Dzikansky spent his 25-year police career (1983–2008) with
the New York City Police Department (NYPD). Appointed to the NYPD
in 1983, he served as a uniformed patrolman for two years in Brooklyn
North. In 1985 he began his career in investigations, ultimately rising
to the NYPD's highest detective rank—detective first grade. Through
2002 he served in various units, including the Organized Crime Control

Bureau, Midtown North Detective Squad, and the elite Manhattan South Homicide Squad. In addition, Dzikansky was selected to work on terror-related investigations, including the murders of Israeli Knesset member Meir Kahane (1990) and Ari Halberstam (Brooklyn Bridge murder, 1994). In the aftermath of 9/11, seeking ways to defend New York City against terror, NYPD Police Commissioner Raymond W. Kelly appointed Dzikansky as the first NYPD Intelligence Division overseas liaison to the Israel National Police (INP) to provide on-site intelligence analysis of suicide bombings in Israel and elsewhere. That analysis helped shape the NYPD's efforts to detect potential suicide bombers and to reduce casualties in the event of a suicide bombing attack. From 2003 to 2006, Dzikansky responded in person and analyzed 21 suicide bombing sites in Israel and attacks globally in Russia, Egypt, Spain, and Turkey. David Cohen, deputy commissioner of intelligence for the NYPD, said of Dzikansky: "No U.S. law enforcement person has been on site at more suicide bombings." Dzikansky also worked with senior members of the Israeli intelligence community on joint investigations related to New York City and the State of Israel.

Dzikansky retired from the NYPD in 2008. In 2009, his essay, "The Phenomenon of Suicide Bombings in Israel: Lessons Learned and Transportation System Vulnerabilities," was published in *Countering Terrorism, National Academy of Sciences*, a summary of a U.S.–Russian workshop. His first book, *Terrorist Cop: The NYPD Jewish Cop Who Traveled the World to Stop Terrorists*, his memoir coauthored with Robert Slater, was published in 2010. Dzikansky is an associate of the International Institute for Counter-Terrorism, Herzliya, Israel, and has appeared as a featured speaker at its annual international conferences on global terrorism.

Gil Kleiman talking to press in Jerusalem at a bus suicide bombing on January 29, 2004. (*Credit***: Gil Kleiman photo collection)**

Gil Kleiman spent 23 years (1983–2006) with Israel's national police force as a bomb squad technician, attorney, security-training officer, homicide detective, and police spokesman. In 1980 he received his undergraduate degree with a major in history from George Washington University and a law degree from Bar Ilan University in Israel in 1991. From 1983 to 1987 Kleiman was a Tel Aviv-based bomb disposal technician and an instructor in the Israel Police Bomb Squad training school. From 1997 to 2001, while working in the Security Division of the Israel Police, he advised officials at government installations on security preparations, including target hardening. As Israel Police spokesman for the foreign press from 2001 to 2006, he spent hundreds of hours at an untold number of terror attacks, including 48 suicide bombings, all in Israel. He quickly became Israel's face and voice to the rest of the world as Israel's suicide bomb spokesperson. Since retiring from the police in 2006, Kleiman has provided background explanations, information, and professional technical briefings to hundreds of law enforcement agencies around the world.

Dzikansky and Kleiman currently work together lecturing and consulting on global security and policing topics and are called upon by various law enforcement agencies, universities, academic think tanks, and community organizations to provide first-hand analysis of current terror trends, lessons learned, and worldwide applications in preventing and responding to terrorism.

Robert Slater, who worked on the research and writing of this book, is the author of 31 books. He has written about such major business personalities as George Soros, Jack Welch, and Bill Gates. His books have appeared on the *New York Times*, *BusinessWeek*, and *Wall Street Journal* best-seller lists. Working for United Press International and *Time Magazine* from 1973 until 1996 in Israel, he covered numerous suicide bombings.

Section I

The Suicide Bomber in a Western Urban Environment

1

Introduction
The Phenomenon of Suicide Bombing

Make no mistake about it: Western urban environments in the United States and Western Europe are prime targets for suicide bombings over the next decade, whether in New York, Chicago, Los Angeles, Paris, London, Rome, or other major cities. For that reason alone, the phenomenon of suicide bombing takes on a new urgency [1].

Few suicide bombings occurred in the West during 2010: One occurred in Moscow on March 29 against two Metro stations, killing 40 and wounding 100; another took place in Stockholm on December 11, killing the suicide bomber and injuring several others. There had been none in Israel that year, the last occurring in February 2008.

Western intelligence officers, however, monitored much "chatter" that year indicating that plans for suicide bombings were under way: Terrorist cells were purchasing materials for explosives, reviewing maps of potential targets, and holding conversations on cell phones and the Internet. It is clear that time is running out for law enforcement authorities. They must step up their preparations for what is bound to be a long and complicated process: the effort to prevent as many suicide bombings as possible and, if that fails, to mitigate the effects of those bombings by reducing the number of dead and wounded.

Suicide bombings against civilian targets, essentially the weapon of choice of radical Islamist terrorist organizations, have emerged with a dramatic impact due in part to a coordinated set of suicide bombings known as 9/11 and to several waves of Palestinian suicide bombings against Israel from 1994 to 1999 and from 2000 to 2007.

In the worst case of modern suicide bombing, over 3,000 people were killed in the September 11, 2001, attacks on New York City's World Trade Center, on Washington D.C.'s Pentagon, and in the abortive attack on either the White House or the U.S. Capitol Building. Of the 3,214 killed, 266 were on the four planes (no one survived); 2,823 were in and around the World Trade Center; and 125 were at the Pentagon. Almost all deaths were civilians and first responders [2].

In a continuous string of 140 suicide bombings from 2000 to 2008, Palestinians from the Israeli-occupied territories of the West Bank and the Gaza Strip, assisted at times by local Israeli Arabs, killed 543 victims [3]. This figure was small compared to the nation's 7.7 million residents, but the deaths and the wounding of many others had an enormous psychological effect on the nation—fear tinged with frustration [4].

Suicide attacks against Israeli targets did not discriminate among the old, the young, the wealthy, or the poor. These attacks impacted all sectors of the civilian population and were carried out in crowded public venues, including train stations, bus terminals, buses, restaurants, shopping malls, nightclubs, and outdoor markets. This method of attack was designed to maximize casualties; it was inexpensive; and it instilled fear in the general public, forcing civilians to make burdensome adjustments in their behavior.

Soon after the second and more intense wave of Palestinian suicide bombings against Israeli targets that began in 2000, people avoided dining out despite a law that required restaurants of a certain size to have security guards posted at their entrances. Parents drove children to school instead of sending them on buses. Citizens altered their schedules to avoid being in crowds. But in time, Israelis understood that it was important to resume normal life in order to avoid giving the terrorists a victory.

For instance, after a suicide bombing on a city bus, within three to four hours, the bus was removed from the scene and people lined up for the next bus. But despite such efforts to return life to normal quickly, the overall effect of those bombings was to traumatize an entire population. Eventually, Israel launched a major military operation, targeted Palestinian terrorist leaders for assassination, and built a fence to secure the Israeli population from suicide bombers.

SUICIDE BOMBING: CAPTIVATING THE PUBLIC

Suicide bombing has fascinated much of the world, some sympathetic with the tactic, many against it. Sympathizers justify the practice by noting that it is sanctioned in the Koran, arguing that suicide bombing is neither sinful nor evil, but a legitimate weapon in trying to inflict harm on a far more powerful enemy.

Opponents of suicide bombing are appalled that anyone would knowingly take his life in order to kill innocent men, women, and children. Many belittle bombers as sick, weak-minded, or crazy. However, to accept such myths—that suicide bombers are crazy and that nothing can be done to stop crazies bent on killing themselves—is to throw in the towel before the battle against these suicide bombers has even begun. Western law enforcement officials cannot simply dismiss suicide bombers as unfathomable. They must recognize that these bombers have motives and agendas that indicate a degree of rationality to their lethal deeds. Once that rationality is acknowledged, it becomes possible to figure out how to mitigate the lethal, anguishing, and dramatic effects of suicide bombings.

Though ending the phenomenon of suicide bombing is all but impossible, the measures advocated in this manual can empower law enforcement personnel to reduce the number of killed and wounded.

The authors do not overlook the fact that, since 9/11, the federal government—along with such major American cities as New York, Denver, Seattle, and Los Angeles—have sought to improve their defensive capabilities against terror in general, and specifically against suicide bombings. Airport security has been strengthened. Intelligence agencies have greater latitude in searching for and arresting potential suicide bombers. Significant financial resources have been allocated to counterterrorist efforts. Most importantly, preparing for possible suicide bombings has become a growing priority among Western law enforcement agencies.

It is tempting to conclude that these measures have played a significant role in the total lack of mega terror on American soil since 9/11. It is, however, worth keeping in mind that terror on a lesser scale has been carried out successfully in major Western cities such as London, Madrid, Istanbul, and Moscow. Increased financial resources and greater latitude provided to law enforcement officers may be keeping suicide bombers from carrying out numerous deadly missions, big and small. Or, suicide bombers may simply be "laying low," convinced that undertaking a new wave of suicide bombings might diminish the awesome "victory" they gained from the events of 9/11.

Whatever the case, there is every reason for Western law enforcement to refrain from resting on its laurels. Danger still lurks—great danger. Our purpose on these pages is not to scare the wits out of law enforcement and other first responders. Rather, our purpose is to sound the alarm and to note that, despite the continuing danger, it is not too late to learn what to do specifically if and when a wave of suicide bombings occurs.

WHY A MANUAL?

Other books on suicide bombing have been published, but their authors are generally academic observers whose second-hand knowledge comes primarily from books, newspapers, and magazine articles. In contrast, the authors of this book—Mordecai Dzikansky and Gil Kleiman—draw upon their lengthy, direct, hands-on experience with suicide bombings, largely in the State of Israel, a veritable laboratory for this topic. This manual is the first on suicide bombings written by senior police officers with experience at suicide bombing sites. As part of their combined 48 years of law enforcement experience, they have visited 74 suicide bombing sites: 21 in Israel and 5 elsewhere for Dzikansky and 48 sites, all in Israel, for Kleiman. Their records attest to the authority they bring to this manual:

Mordecai Dzikansky spent his entire police career with the New York City Police Department (NYPD). Starting as a patrolman in 1983, he became a homicide detective, rising to the rank of detective first grade in 2004. In the aftermath of 9/11, it was Israel's counterterror experience that led NYPD police commissioner Raymond W. Kelly to appoint Dzikansky as the first NYPD Intelligence Division overseas liaison to the Israel National Police with the primary purpose of analyzing suicide bombings in Israel.

Gil Kleiman spent 23 years (1983–2006) with Israel's national police force as a bomb squad technician, attorney, security-training officer, homicide detective, and spokesman for the Israel Police. From 1983 to 1987 he was a bomb technician based in Tel Aviv and an instructor in the Israel Bomb Squad training school. From 1997 to 2001, he advised officials at government installations on security preparations, including target hardening. As spokesman for the foreign press from 2001 to 2006, he visited all major Israeli-based terror attack sites.

In this manual, using their expertise, Dzikansky and Kleiman help first responders and homeland security professionals grapple with the subject of suicide bombings by demystifying the false assumptions that have grown up around this favored terrorist tactic. First responders and homeland security professionals clearly need a teaching tool that explains suicide bombing in all its aspects, a tool that, thus far, has been missing from their course work.

Dzikansky and Kleiman offer advice on
the accepted best practices in the field and on
what lessons have been learned that can help in
defending against suicide bombers. Through this
manual, they help first responders reprioritize so
that their efforts with regard to suicide bombing
or any other form of terror have as much priority
in their minds as other more traditional crimes.

First responders:

Police PR/media
Bomb technicians
Intelligence officers
Investigative officers
Forensics officers
Firefighters
Emergency medical services (EMS)
Media

The main part of the book is a hands-on
look at the phenomenon of suicide bombing and the possible defenses
against such terror tactics. The authors also examine and evaluate theo-
ries of academic scholars about the motives, tactics, and strategies of suicide bombers.

The first part of the book explains what suicide bombings look like;
examines the advantages, limitations, and effectiveness of suicide bombing
as a terror tactic; and looks at the bombers' motives, tactics, agendas, and tools
of their trade. There is a chapter devoted to what happened on 9/11, the worst
suicide bombing in history and the event that shaped perceptions and counterterror strategies toward suicide bombers in the decade after that attack.

The second half of the book discusses various ways of defending
against suicide bombings that will, if adopted, help reduce casualties. The
authors show how the federal government and New York City reacted to
9/11 and prepared for future terror. They look at case studies of suicide
bombings that were thwarted or not thwarted—successes and failures
of law enforcement authorities in the West in trying to defend against
these bombings. The discussion also considers how Israel defended itself
against suicide bombings, fully aware that only some of what it did might
be applicable to other parts of the West.

The authors give advice on how to identify a suicide bomber and
examine measures that can be adopted to reduce suicide bombing casualties. They also review the roles of the key players—the first responders—in defending against suicide bombers: law enforcement personnel,
including bomb technicians and intelligence, investigative, and forensics
officers; firefighters; and emergency medical service (EMS) personnel.

The concluding chapters examine two key issues that grow out of
the dramatic, gruesome nature of these bombings: The first is the way
that suicide bombers and their facilitators seek to exploit the media and
how governments and the media seek to defuse the bombers' efforts at
self-promotion. The second issue is the little-discussed but crucial role
that posttraumatic stress disorder (PTSD) plays in the careers of first

responders. The book closes with recommendations aimed at helping law enforcement defend against suicide bombers.

It is reasonable to assume that suicide bombers, if and when they decide to launch a wave of bombings in America or elsewhere in the West, will target major cities. Consequently, police departments in those cities receive much attention in this book, but not to the exclusion of law enforcement officers in smaller towns. Their needs are also addressed.

Most police departments do not have intelligence units. Only those in major American cities do. But almost every police department has a detective squad that engages in forensics investigations and general investigative work, staying in touch with informants and encompassing all other aspects of law enforcement. From forensics officers to investigators, the men and women performing these tasks know that they are unlikely to run across a suicide bomber. But they might come across a terrorist cell buried in a safe house in one of their communities, making this manual relevant to them as well.

After 9/11, terrorist cells were uncovered in small, out-of-the-way towns, and gradually theory gave way to a practical, new reality: Terrorists—including suicide bombers—seemed to be out there, planning, waiting, and preparing for the next attack. How could all these officers in law enforcement get ready to defend their communities against these real possibilities? To answer this question, the authors offer much advice throughout the manual.

WHY A SUICIDE BOMBING IS SO TERRIFYING

To start to deal with defending against suicide bombing, we have to understand what makes the phenomenon so frightening. The answer is its callously brutal force, stunning mercilessness, and frightening randomness—employed against unarmed civilians to disrupt their normal routines as much as possible.

Those disruptions induce a feeling of vulnerability that, however briefly, leads millions to become numb, paralyzed, and unable to function normally. A feeling of helplessness sets in. Above all, it is the cruel nature of the suicide bomber—his abnormal indifference to his victims, his willingness to kill women and children without regret—that makes him so petrifying.

A female suicide bomber enters a restaurant, sits down, eats a meal, and then pays the bill, finally blowing herself up, killing and wounding scores of fellow diners. Western societies value life above all other things.

8

And those societies create rules to protect lives. Suicide bombers indiscriminately break those rules and snuff out life as easily as they would kill a tiny ant.

Prime Minister Ariel Sharon visits site of suicide bombing on bus at Patt Junction in Jerusalem on June 18, 2002, in which 19 were killed. (*Credit*: **Israel Government Press Office**)

THE RANDOMNESS OF THE BOMBING

It is the very randomness of suicide bombing, heightening the sense of fear among potential victims, that arouses victims—direct and indirect—to switch over to new behavior, encouraging the terrorists to believe that they have gained some success. The lesson for victims is not to let the randomness of the act induce fear and helplessness. Statistics show that, in Israel, someone is far more likely to be injured or killed in a car accident than in a suicide bombing—a good reason to continue to ride buses even at the height of a suicide bombing wave.

It is only natural to be scared of the randomness and ruthlessness of the suicide bomber. What is so terrifying is the suicide bomber's ability to succeed in the mission, no matter what. With other forms of violent crime, a police officer has some chance of keeping a perpetrator from carrying out the nefarious deed. He might catch a robber inside a store or might come upon a murderer soon after someone has been killed.

But the suicide bomber can kill himself and others simply by activating a toggle switch, making him nearly impossible to apprehend. Indeed, the mere fact that a police officer approaches a suspected suicide bomber will probably induce the bomber to blow himself up, however prematurely, killing the policeman and perhaps others. To be sure, all terror is frightening, random, and lethal—and can happen anywhere. But because the perpetrator is prepared to die as part of the terror attack, the suicide bombing seems even more menacing.

TACTICAL AND STRATEGIC GOALS

It is crucial that we know when a suicide bombing has occurred—and when it has not. If political leaders want to demonstrate their citizens' resolve in fighting suicide bombers, it is vital to know whether a suicide bombing has taken place. There is no point in encouraging civilians to return to their normal routines to thwart the will of terrorists if the "bomb" was the backfire of a bus. That is one reason why first responders, upon hearing of an incident, give priority to figuring out whether a suicide bombing has occurred. What, then, is a suicide bombing?

Suicide bombing is a violent attack designed to inflict mass casualties against unarmed civilians in which the attacker knows in advance that he will die as part of the action. There is an important distinction between suicide bombing as a strategic weapon and as a terror tactic. Given that this distinction exists, a suicide bombing can still have both tactical and strategic aims.

Let's look at the distinction between suicide bombing as a tactic and as a strategy. Suicide bombing is a tactical weapon when the goal is simply to kill as many people as possible. However, when a suicide bomber kills people to achieve a larger "big picture" goal—terrorizing a population, creating a sense of fear and instability within the civilian population, changing a government, or ending a military occupation—this is considered to be a strategic use of suicide bombing.

Some suicide bombing attacks, like 9/11 and the Park Hotel assault in Israel, employ suicide bombing both tactically and strategically. The 19 9/11 hijackers wanted to kill as many people as possible—using suicide bombing as a tactic—but they also wanted to put pressure on the United States to removes its "occupying" troops from Saudi Arabia, thereby using suicide bombing as a strategy.

The killing of soldiers is also both a tactic and a strategy. Suicide bombers seek to kill soldiers when possible (it is not always possible or even desirable) because they want to send a message to their enemy that even soldiers are not invulnerable—a strategic aim. When suicide bombers kill civilians, they do not care which ones they kill, which is a tactical move; but they do want to use the attack to instill fear in the wide civilian community, which is very much a strategic goal.

Both Hezbollah and Hamas, two of the most powerful terror groups in the Middle East, at times used suicide bombing as both a tactical and strategic weapon. Hezbollah launched a massive attack against the U.S. Marine barracks in 1983 that aimed at killing as many American soldiers as possible (a tactical aim) and at expelling American troops from Lebanon (a strategic goal). Hamas carried out a series of suicide bombings against Israel in the early 2000s, seeking to kill as many civilians as possible—its tactical objective. However, those same suicide bombings were strategic as well, in that Hamas hoped to replace the State of Israel with an Islamic state.

Both terror groups employed suicide bombings as a tactical and strategic weapon on other occasions, hoping to take as many victims as possible while frightening the wider civilian population and foster instability. The fact that Hamas deploys suicide bombing as a strategic weapon is the reason why this book devotes so much attention to the history and the aims of this terror group. If we assume that terrorists employ suicide bombings simply as a tactical weapon—to kill as many as possible—we miss the point. We need to take into account that terror groups can have "big picture" strategic objectives, and we all have to be cognizant of those aims.

IS SUICIDE BOMBING A SIN?

Those who justify suicide bombers, for instance Islamic extremists, describe the act of suicide bombing as an *isshtahad*, meaning a martyrdom operation, which is not a sin at all. The suicide bomber is lauded as a *shahid*, meaning literally a "witness" or "martyr." The word *witness* implies someone who dies in order to testify to his faith in God (Allah). In contrast, those who label these acts as evil prefer to call them "homicide bombings," insisting that the bombers are not martyrs or heroes, but common murderers.

Christianity, Judaism, and Islam condemn the act of suicide. Nevertheless, suicide is rather common and is widely considered to be the act of someone desperate, perhaps even crazy, with no hope of a better future. The act of suicide is generally thought to be sinful.

In the Jewish tradition, the most famous incident of suicide has surprisingly been treated as heroic, not sinful. It happened at Masada, the mountain southeast of Jerusalem near the Dead Sea, when on April 16, 83 CE, the Roman army discovered that the 960 Jewish inhabitants on top of the mountain had committed suicide. The Masada incident stands out as uncommon in Jewish history, inasmuch as Jews do not often commit suicide en masse rather than wait to be killed.

Ironically, some regard the Jews of Masada as heroes because they chose death over Roman captivity; others, appalled by the mass Jewish suicide, feel that enough Masadas have occurred. It is more heroic to fight than to commit suicide.

Radical Islamists justify suicide bombings by citing the Koran, Sura 17:33: "You shall not kill any person—for GOD has made life sacred—except in the course of justice" [5]. These radical Islamists are, however, quite willing to ignore another Koranic admonition (4:29–31): "O ye who believe!... (Do not) ... kill or destroy yourselves, for God has been most merciful to you. If any do that in rancor and injustice, soon shall we cast them into the fire, and that is easy for God" [6]. The Hadith contains many references to Mohammed condemning suicide, noting that the person committing suicide will burn in hell and will forever die from the same instrument that he used to take his life.

GOALS OF THIS MANUAL

The primary goal is to provide an in-depth understanding of suicide bombings in a Western urban environment and to examine key factors that will contribute to their prevention or, failing that, to reduce casualties during such attacks. One can, by following the advice presented in this book, limit the destruction—human and material—caused by suicide bombings. But, just as one can reduce the murder rate in a Western city, but not wipe out murder, suicide bombings can be contained but not eliminated completely as a terrorist tactic.

Though President Barack Obama expressed the view that terror, including suicide bombings, can in time be completely eradicated, we argue that the phenomenon will never entirely disappear [7]. Once the genie is out of the bottle, once the technique of suicide bombing is shown to be effective, one can make the genie smaller but not make it disappear entirely. Accordingly, we do not provide instructions on how to eliminate suicide bombing entirely. Western armies have invaded countries with that hope in mind without eradicating the phenomenon of suicide bombing. The only relevant issue—and the one that is at the heart of this manual—is what steps to take to prevent suicide bombings and to reduce casualties that arise from a suicide bombing.

Until now, conventional wisdom decreed that reducing casualties in a suicide bombing attack was all but impossible. So pitiless and random were suicide bombers, so great was their stealth, that finding and capturing them seemed out of the question. Willing to die, they were free to kill and injure as many victims as they could get near.

Having monitored the building of defenses against suicide bombings on a continuing basis, largely in Israel, we believe that reducing casualties in a suicide bombing is possible. Paying with blood for the knowledge they acquired, due to the two waves of suicide bombings in the late 1990s and early 2000s, Israeli first responders gained valuable insights about the tactics employed by suicide bombers. Those insights led law enforcement officers to establish best practices for recognizing bombers, foiling possible attacks, and reducing casualties during an attack.

Other Western countries, lacking the Israelis' hands-on experience, have had the luxury of learning valuable lessons from the Israelis without having to endure the pressure of day-to-day suicide bombings. This begs the question: Will Western law enforcement officers exploit the peace and quiet in the West to learn from the sad experiences of others? We urge all Western security professionals to adopt the best practices that we spell out in this manual as soon as possible. The threat of suicide bombings is very real.

We offer best-practice counterterror measures obtained from our experiences with the Israel National Police, some of which have already been integrated into the routine operations of the New York City Police Department and have filtered to the police forces of other American cities. In offering these best practices, we also explain which of these could be applied to American law enforcement agencies—and which could not. Our hope is that in learning these best practices, readers will give a new sense of priority toward identifying would-be suicide bombers and reducing the bloody effects of the bombers' missions.

Our aim is to empower law enforcement personnel to broaden the scope of their responsibilities to include an awareness of lurking suicide bombers. We argue that these officers must be as much on the alert

13

for potential suicide bombings as they are for the array of "traditional" crimes. Toward that end, we provide tools for first responders—from the patrolman to the most senior law enforcement officer—to detect a potential suicide bomber and perhaps even to foil a suicide bombing. Given that foiling a suicide bombing is difficult, we focus much of our attention on ways to reduce casualties should a bombing occur.

We offer operational strategies and tactics for policing in an environment where a suicide bombing might occur. We provide instruction on how to fortify likely targets against suicide bombers, suggesting measures that will reduce casualties significantly.

MYTHS REGARDING SUICIDE BOMBERS

The myths are powerful and remain a part of routine thinking about suicide bombers. But they are myths. Among them are:

- All suicide bombers look the same; in effect, they come out of "central casting": male religious fanatics with scruffy dark beards, swarthy features, and kaffiyehs wrapped around their heads.
- A suicide bomber is part of a small group of disgruntled victims forced by poverty to agree to these missions.
- A suicide bomber is most likely to strike at symbols of power, whether it is the New York Stock Exchange, the Statue of Liberty, or the White House.

These myths are shattered on these pages to prepare security professionals for the realities of the suicide bombing phenomenon and to help them place a new focus on counterterror tactics.

Myths about suicide bombers:

> All suicide bombers look the same.
> A suicide bomber is one of a few disgruntled, impoverished victims.
> A suicide bomber is most likely to strike at symbols of power.

ADJUST LESSONS LEARNED TO LOCAL CONDITIONS

It is our firm belief that if and when a wave of suicide bombings occurs in American cities, the awful negative effects of that wave can be mitigated. It will require vigilance, but most important, it will require figuring out how to "translate" and integrate the best practices from other places into the realities found in a police force's local community.

We do not pretend to provide all the answers for dealing with suicide bombers. Still, we remind everyone that first responders must solve some of the problems in their local communities on their own, using their eyes, ears, instincts, intuition, and knowledge of those communities, to take those last-minute steps that will mitigate the effects of suicide bombing attacks.

As we pass along lessons learned and best practices, we are fully conscious that security professionals must not simply adopt our suggestions but modify them to fit local conditions and limitations. We ask readers to think creatively. As instructors in the Israel National Police like to say, "We are giving you the tool box. You have to build the shed."

Given that suicide bombing is dynamic and each suicide bomber tailors his technique to the environment he works in, the person who knows that environment better than anybody else is the local first responder. Our manual draws heavily from our experience with Palestinian suicide bombers, but American security professionals might face all sorts of domestic groups with local grievances, and the person who knows the most about those groups is the local law enforcement officer.

That officer will know far better than we will what vulnerabilities exist with regard to local private security arrangements: What's in place, what's not in place. Most important, the local officer will know what potential conveyors of violence lurk out there. He will know which local high school and college football games attract a certain size crowd. The local security professional will know that the vast majority of those attending these games care more about tailgating parties, eating hamburgers, and drinking beer than watching for suspicious people or packages.

FOCUS ON ISRAEL AND AMERICA

It is no coincidence that this book devotes so much attention to suicide bombings in Israel. No Western country has suffered more from suicide bombings than the State of Israel, and no Western country has confronted an enemy using suicide bombing as its core military strategy rather than as a mere sideline.

This manual also focuses on the United States, although much of the information can be applied to other Western countries. A clear connection exists between Israel's experience with suicide bombings and what America may face one day if suicide bombers launch a campaign on American soil. Both Israel and America face the same enemy—radical

Islam. Indeed the entire Western world is facing this enemy, but Israel shares a special bond with America. So the two countries need to cooperate as closely as they can to learn from one another, and to protect each other.

In the days and months after 9/11, many Americans were convinced that more suicide bombings would soon arrive at their doorstep. Yet, as America's enemies largely avoided engaging in terror on American soil, the fear of terror, including suicide bombings, subsided. But, as the 39 planned terror attacks against the United States (from 9/11 to May 20, 2011) have shown, the threat of suicide bombings against key targets in major American cities remains very much alive [8].

SCOPE OF THE MANUAL

This manual looks at case studies of suicide bombings and the threat of future ones in urban environments (especially in the Middle East, Europe, and Russia), where police departments have responsibility for and are the primary responders to these bombings. The book does not touch on suicide bombings in nonurban military zones in Iraq, Afghanistan, and Pakistan, inasmuch as the military—and not the police—is responsible for public security in these places. The focus of this book is on urban policing, not military tactics in war zones. Within these war zones, combatants use high-powered military weapons, whether tanks, rocket-propelled grenades (RPGs), or hand grenades. For them, suicide bombing is a "sideline," not the primary military tactic.

In Afghanistan, Pakistan, and Iraq, insurgents use suicide bombers as part of an overall deployment of guerilla tactics. In some ways, suicide bombers in these war zones operate very much as their counterparts do in Western urban environments: They choose a target to achieve mass casualties and then blow themselves up. But in those war zones, suicide car bombers targeting American military forces conduct guerilla warfare, not urban terror.

We do not foresee that America will face guerilla warfare on the streets of New York or elsewhere on its soil. Suicide bombers will act alone and may well be few and far between. American cities will also not face continuing bedlam, a civil war—insurgents against law enforcement officers—with armed groups in Virginia attacking police in Kentucky. Furthermore, we do not write about these insurgents because our expertise falls within a very specific geographical space: urban environments in the West where civilians are the main targets. As Western police officers, we are looking for a solution to suicide bombings—or at least as good a solution as is possible—but we are not looking for a solution to wipe out insurgency groups employing suicide bombing tactics in war zones.

The next chapter delves into how a suicide bomber operates and the techniques used to plan and carry out an attack: in short, what a suicide bombing looks like.

NOTES

1. We include as Western the following countries: United States, Western Europe, Russia, Canada, Australia, and New Zealand. We distinguish these countries from Asian or Middle Eastern ones, such as Afghanistan, Pakistan, and Iraq, which we think of as non-Western.
2. For the figures on 9/11, see http://www.guardian.co.uk/world/2002/aug/18/usa.terrorism.
3. www.mfa.gov.il. Go to: terrorism; terrorism since 2000; suicide and other bombing attacks in Israel since the Declaration of Principles (September 1993). All other statistics in this book related to Palestinian suicide bombings against Israel are derived from the same Web site.
4. Ruth Eglash, "On the Eve of 2011, Israel's Population Reaches 7.7 Million," December 29, 2010, http://www.jpost.com/NationalNews/Article.aspx?id=201430.
5. The Authorized English Translation of the Quran, Sura-17, http://www.submission.org/suras/sura17.htm.
6. The American Muslim (TAM), http://www.theamericanmuslim.org/tam.php/features/articles/quranic_verses_against_extremism/.
7. President Barack Obama, news conference at the White House, September 11, 2010, http://blogs.wsj.com/washwire/2010/09/10/transcript-of-obamas-news-c.
8. Jena Baker McNeill, James Jay Carafano, Ph.D., and Jessica Zuckerman, The Heritage Foundation, May 20, 2011, Background #2556. "39 Terror Plots Foiled Since 9/11: Examining Counterterrorism's Success Stories."

2

The Act

How Does a Suicide Bomber Operate?

Israelis have learned all too well what a suicide bombing looks like because of the frequency of such bombings in their midst. However, the average Israeli has not been able to listen in on the suicide bomber's sponsors guiding the bomber through his mission; nor has the average Israeli been able to watch the bomber as he stealthfully, carefully approaches his target.

Still, Israelis know from watching the aftermath of a suicide bombing on television what these highly chaotic but grisly scenes look like. The only experience Americans have had of watching a suicide bombing on their turf was the 9/11 suicide bombings, and even then, what Americans saw was a sanitized version because the media's access was severely curtailed.

In the foreword, we offered a composite portrait of a suicide bomber in his final hours before setting out on the mission. Here we pick up the narrative as the suicide bomber moves toward the target. Through this portrait, we try to illustrate what the mission looks like from the bomber's perspective. What goes through the suicide bomber's mind in the last minutes before he blows himself up? As with the portrait in the foreword, this one is drawn from conversations that Dzikansky and Kleiman have had with Israeli intelligence officers, investigators, and bomb technicians as well as from media interviews with Palestinian suicide bombers caught before they could blow themselves up.

19

A SUICIDE BOMBING IN PROGRESS

Meeting his sponsors at a designated safe house, the young suicide bomber feels the high of the moment. What had seemed years off just a few weeks ago was now about to happen. The two sponsors make no attempt to lighten the mood. Time matters now. Placing the lethal explosives on the bomber is the first step of the dangerous, delicate preparations. As one sponsor lifts the suicide belt off a bed, the soon-to-be suicide bomber feels his first chill of the day. It is happening now; it is real; "I am about to die"—still, the bomber does not panic. He will not allow himself to shudder at what he is about to do.

Having learned from operatives that there will be no checkpoints between the safe house and the target, the sponsor feels it is safe to put the suicide bomb belt on the would-be bomber at this point. For the first time, the bomber feels the weight of the belt: It is heavy, but he is sure he can move around with it without tiring or give the impression that he is carrying an extra-heavy load, perhaps drawing suspicion. Had the sponsors received reports of the existence of enemy checkpoints, they would have waited until after the bomber passed through the checkpoints before helping him put on the suicide belt.

Three-Hundred Yards Away

As much as he tries to listen to each instruction, knowing how crucial each detail is, the bomber cannot keep his mind from drifting off to the event itself, maybe a half hour away. He will be dropped off 300 yards or so from a bus traveling its usual route along an Israeli street. His sponsors place the bomb belt around his waist and on his shoulders (the belt is held up by straps on the shoulders). The detonator switch, an on-off toggle switch attached to plus and minus wires that are attached to the belt, lies in his left-hand pocket. One sponsor says it is time to go.

The other sponsor drives him from the safe house to a spot near the targeted crowd. As the planning dictates, during the short 10-minute drive, the sponsor and the bomber say nothing to one another. When the sponsor stops the car, the bomber exits. The driver remains silent; there is no wish of "good luck," no last-minute review of instructions, not even a final shout of *Allah akbar* (God is great). He puts his two hands on the shoulders of the young man, as if to say, "This is it. The moment is here. You can do this." Proud to be carrying out the mission, the young man nods his head, hoping to display confidence, signaling that he is ready.

Heading for the Crowd

Adopting a trancelike stare, the bomber heads for the crowd at a pace that is neither too fast nor too slow. He does not want to draw attention. His finger on the detonator switch, he suddenly fears that, out of nervousness, he might push the switch prematurely. He dreads disappointing his sponsors as he takes each fatal step. He does not think of his imminent death or the equally imminent death of nearby victims. He thinks only of his two facilitators: A number of times he says to himself, "I want them to be pleased with me."

Seconds later, he spots the bus stop where 15 people are waiting to board a bus that should arrive in the next minute or two. His target is the people in that oncoming bus. It does not matter how many are waiting; even if no one is, his orders are to board. Other passengers will be on the bus, having boarded at previous stops, and they are worthy targets.

Instructed to avoid standing off to the side, perhaps arousing suspicion, he approaches the group, telling himself to remain calm. He breathes normally, not deeply. He keeps his eyes focused straight ahead, not allowing them to dart from one person to another. He makes a special point of not fidgeting.

The Critical Moment

This, he knows, is the critical moment of his mission. So much time and effort has been expended on the next few seconds. Pride runs through him. He feels special, someone who has been chosen to do something very important for his cause. He tells himself to be particularly careful from now on. Anything, anything at all, that draws attention to him will probably doom the mission.

Remembering his sponsor's instructions, he does not rush to board the bus, allowing the bus driver an unobstructed view of him. It is crucial that other passengers climb the steps first, concealing him for as long as possible from the bus driver along with his explosives, wiring, and detonator switch.

Letting five others board before him, the bomber, as per his instructions, holds exact change in one hand, so that he spends as little time in full view of the bus driver as possible. As the bomber hands over the change, the bus driver hardly looks at him. Instead, the driver seems intent on gazing past him to find out how many more passengers are boarding.

The young man remembers being instructed to get to the center of the bus and not to sit down—his standing will cause the greatest possible harm. The bomber stares straight into the crowd on the bus. It is filled with 40 or 50 people, some talking, some reading, and some gazing out the window. He inches toward his destination.

Arriving at the Center of the Bus

Reaching the center of the bus, his finger on the detonator switch, the would-be suicide bomber keeps his finger in that position so that if he is tackled or otherwise identified, he can blow himself up right away.

The bomber knows that he has at most five seconds before pressing the switch. If he takes more than five seconds, he might have second thoughts, or a fellow passenger might spot him. Thus, in these last seconds of his life, he must not dwell on what awaits him in heaven or the cause he will soon die for, or whether he will feel pain when the bomb explodes. He focuses only on what he must do.

Pressing the Switch

The time has come. He utters a silent prayer—to Allah—and then he presses the switch. For bus passengers, in the next millisecond, an unfathomable noise and a blinding light occur together, a horrific sound and light show that offers no time for anyone to comprehend that a catastrophe is occurring. Billowing smoke engulfs the vehicle. Bodies are hurled from their seats as if shot out of a cannon, literally blown out of their shoes. For passengers caught in the full throes of the explosion, death is almost instantaneous; they feel nothing.

For passengers seated and standing farther from the suicide bomber, the sound and the light are more frightening than for the dead. They do not die at once: Some will die in a day or a month; some will survive; many will be maimed for life. So all their minds and senses are working overtime: "A bomb has exploded. I must get off the bus. But I can't move. It hurts too much. I feel something sticky—blood. How badly am I hurt? Maybe another bomb will go off. How can I get to a safe spot?"

After what seems an eternity, but is actually only a few seconds, Good Samaritans rush to the bus, eager to save as many lives as possible. One reaches for a cell phone, inhaling smoke, ignoring the screams and moans. He dials 100, the Israeli equivalent of 911. A woman answers. She is trained to be calm and to get as much information as possible.

THERE'S BEEN A BOMB

"There's been a bomb," the Samaritan screams into the phone. "A suicide bomber, a suicide bomber. Some are dead. Some are badly wounded. The bus blew up."

"Where are you?" the woman asks. The Samaritan replies with an approximate location.

"We are on the way," promises the woman in a composed voice, a voice that belies the drama that is unfolding.

First to arrive at the scene are medical personnel, some in ambulances, some on motorcycles. EMS personnel take only a minute or two to reach the scene. Next to arrive are four ambulances and several policemen. EMS paramedics race to grab stretchers and medical equipment. Then come the bomb technicians, followed by forensics officers. After barreling down the streets, firefighters arrive in five fire trucks, sirens whining. EMS personnel need to prioritize. They need to begin triage. The dead are everywhere, some still in their seats, some lying outside the bus. Pools of blood ooze from them. They do not move nor do they scream, evidence that they are dead.

The paramedics move past the dead. The dead are beyond help. Soon, an emergency response team (in Israel, the organization is called ZAKA) will tend to the dead and gather body parts. Focusing on the wounded, the paramedics try to determine how many are injured. Which are in the worst shape? How many more doctors and paramedics will be needed? How many more ambulances? How many emergency rooms need to be activated?

Within minutes of the attack, all first responders are at the site doing their jobs: evacuating the wounded, searching for secondary bombs, cordoning off the crime scene. Also at the site are intelligence agents from the Shabak—the Israel Intelligence Agency, the Israeli equivalent of the FBI—receiving pertinent intelligence from first responders. Within 15 minutes of the bombing, ambulances have removed all of the wounded, taking them to hospitals.

IDENTIFYING THE SUICIDE BOMBER

Thinking of how to prevent the next suicide bombing, bomb squad technicians scramble to identify the kind of explosives used on the bus. Meanwhile, investigative officers, intelligence agents, and bomb squad technicians make it a priority to identify the suicide bomber. Identifying

23

the bomber may help first responders identify the terrorist organization that sent him and the bomber's sponsors who have fled the scene. There will be an immediate search for the sponsors.

On the surface, identifying the bomber would appear to be a low priority. After all, the bomber has not escaped. He cannot escape. He does not need to be caught. Unlike a murderer who kills victims and then departs the scene, the suicide bomber requires no roadblocks, no all-points bulletins, no assignment of law enforcement personnel to monitor bus, railroad, and airport terminals.

Had this been a homicide after which the murderer escaped, 90 percent of police work would focus on catching the killer, but not in this case, where the killer is dead. First responders need to devote most of their work to catching the planners behind this bombing, and so they occupy themselves with that crucial task. Roadblocks are set up, and witnesses who might have seen a fleeing car are interviewed.

The suicide bomber will be identified, perhaps within hours, though he may have simply evaporated from the blast. If his body is still intact, his head is likely to be detached and his torso severed from his legs. His sponsors may deliver a video to the media minutes after the attack, showing the bomber a few days earlier, a suicide belt around his body, a rifle in his hand, giving his name and his village and boasting of his deed.

The suicide bomber will be identified, perhaps within hours, though he may have simply evaporated from the blast. If his body is still intact, his head is likely to be detached and his torso severed from his legs.

The scene is chaotic, but the chaos is controlled. Israeli first responders work efficiently but speedily. They want to return the suicide bombing site back to normal as quickly as possible. They want to send a message to the terrorists: You have killed and wounded some of us today, but you have not defeated us.

Now that we have an idea of how a suicide bomber operates as he carries out his deadly mission, let's look in the next chapter at the history of suicide bombings.

3

The Past
A Brief History of Suicide Bombing

Though we focus in this manual on the modern era of suicide bombing, we take note that the phenomenon of suicide killings dates back to the 11th and 12th centuries. Then the Assassins, disciples of the Persian master Alamut, carried out suicide raids in ancient Iran against enemy leaders in nearby fortresses.

Some argue that European anarchists from the early 20th century were the first to use suicide attacks as the tool of stateless terrorists. Suicide bombing as a political tool first occurred in the modern era with the assassination of Czar Alexander II of Russia in 1881, when a Polish suicide bomber attacked the czar. As the czar drove on a main street of St. Petersburg near the Winter Palace, the suicide bomber threw handmade grenades at him, killing himself and mortally wounding the czar, who died a few hours later.

The Polish bomber differed from later suicide bombers in that he did not try to induce chaos, panic, or fear in the wider community. Nor was he aiming for mass casualties. He was trying to change the political regime and, in that sense, employed his suicide attack strategically, as later suicide bombers would do. He needed a way to get close to the czar, even at the cost of his life. Poisoning the czar was complicated. Finding a nearby place where he could administer the poison would not be easy. Had he tried to shoot the czar, he might have been caught before pulling the trigger. A hand grenade did the trick.

Toward the end of World War II, in 1944, Japanese kamikaze bombers employed self-sacrifice missions during combat, turning their planes into flying bombs. Growing Japanese losses and the declining quality of Japanese pilots led to these desperate kamikaze raids, flying straight into American ships. The raids were very successful: Carrying out 2,800 kamikaze attacks, 34 American ships were sunk, another 368 were damaged, and 4,900 American naval personnel were killed [1].

The Japanese kamikazes used suicide bombing as a tactical weapon, hoping to take out as many American personnel and equipment as possible. They did not use suicide bombing strategically, as modern-era suicide bombers would, hoping to alter a political regime or end a military occupation.

The phenomenon of suicide bombing disappeared for nearly four decades after the kamikaze assaults. In one instance in 1963, 1,000 Buddhist monks protested the oppression of Buddhism in Vietnam by setting themselves on fire. But their acts did not constitute suicide bombings, as they did not seek to kill others in taking their own lives. During those nearly four decades, nation states had ample amounts of force at their disposal without having to enlist individuals to blow themselves up in order to kill many others.

FIRST MODERN SUICIDE BOMBING

The first modern suicide bombing took place in Iran in 1980 when a 13-year-old boy blew himself up while running up to an Iraqi tank early in the Iran–Iraq War. The boy's mission was tactical: the boy's object was to blow up the Iraqi tank as an act of defiance, and the only way he could get close to it was by sacrificing his own life. He had no wider, strategic goal.

In the modern era, suicide bombing has morphed from sporadic, individual acts into systematized terror campaigns. The phenomenon hardly existed in the 1970s. Even during the 1980s, when suicide bombings emerged as an ongoing terror tactic, there was an average of fewer than five suicide attacks per year; but the number grew to 180 per year between 2000 and 2005, with 460 attacks in 2005 [2].

THE BOMBING OF THE MARINE BARRACKS

Time magazine cover photograph of 1983 marine barracks suicide bombing. (*Credit*: *Time* magazine, October 31, 1983)

It was during the early 1980s that suicide bombings were used methodically for the first time, not one mega event that had been planned for years, but a series of smaller-sized tactical bombings designed to inject fear and instability into the wider population.

Radical elements of the Shiite resistance in southern Lebanon in 1982 had formed a Lebanese terrorist-based political party called Hezbollah that had its own paramilitary wing and that received support from Iran and Syria. On November 11, 1982, Hezbollah launched its first suicide attack, killing 76 Israeli security personnel stationed in a building in the Lebanese coastal town of Tyre. (Over the next 16 years, Hezbollah would carry out 37 suicide bombings [3].) With its success at Tyre, Hezbollah next flexed its muscles by staging the worst terrorist attack against Americans to that date.

Suicide bombing gained worldwide attention when Hezbollah bombed the American embassy in Beirut on April 18, 1983, and assaulted the American marine and French barracks, also in Beirut, the following

27

October 23. These bombings are widely recognized as the start of modern-day suicide bombings. Hezbollah still exists as of March 2011 as an active terror organization in Lebanon, slowly gaining political traction, eventually becoming part of the Lebanese government.

The bombing of the U.S. embassy killed 63 and wounded 120. An organization calling itself Islamic Jihad claimed responsibility for the attack, but some insisted that Islamic Jihad was another name used by Hezbollah. The bombing of the U.S. marine and French barracks, for which Hezbollah took credit, killed 299: 241 U.S. servicemen and 58 French paratroops in simultaneous operations. These Hezbollah suicide bombings resulted in the eventual departure of American and French troops from Lebanon. In this case, the bombings were strategic, meant to alter the broad political picture in Lebanon. The bombings achieved that aim.

Advocates of suicide bombings pointed to those departures as proof that suicide bombing paid dividends. Responding to the message, the Tamil Tigers of Sri Lanka and Islamic groups, especially Hamas, turned to suicide bombings. Emerging from a resistance movement in Sri Lanka that hoped for autonomy and independence, the Tamil Tigers started using suicide bombing in 1987. Since then, the group has conducted 200 suicide attacks. The FBI has noted that the Tigers invented the suicide belt and pioneered the use of women in suicide bombing. The Tigers wear cyanide capsules around their necks so they can commit suicide if captured [4].

As these suicide bombings were not aimed at the West, they received scant attention in the Western media. While the Tamil Tigers are considered the first modern group to perfect suicide bombing, it was only in the 1990s that suicide bombing began in earnest, its geographical center in the Middle East: in Lebanon, in the Israeli-occupied territories, in Israel proper, and in Iraq. These attacks were routinely aimed against the West.

One expert on terrorism, Ehud Sprinzak, noted that the tactic of dying in order to carry out the mission stunned security experts.

Two centuries of experience suggested that terrorists, though ready to risk their lives, wished to live life after the terrorist act in order to benefit from its accomplishments. But this new terrorism defied that belief. It seemed qualitatively different, appearing almost supernatural, extremely lethal and impossible to stop. Within six months French and U.S. Presidents Francois Mitterrand and Ronald Reagan pulled their troops out of Lebanon—a tacit admission that the new terrorism rendered all known counterterrorist measures useless. [5]

28

A CORE ISLAMIST TERROR TACTIC

No other country has faced suicide bombings as continuously as the State of Israel. Starting in the mid-1990s, suicide bombing became a core Islamist terror tactic employed largely against Israeli civilians, carried out by various Palestinian resistance groups: Hamas, Palestinian Islamic Jihad, Fatah, Popular Front for the Liberation of Palestine (PFLP), Tanzim, and the Al-Aqsa Martyrs Brigade.

List of Palestinian terror organizations that used suicide bombing

Hamas
Palestinian Islamic Jihad
Al-Aqsa Martyrs Brigade
Fatah
Popular Front for the Liberation
    of Palestine (PFLP)
Tanzim

Some Palestinian militant groups were secular (Fatah, Tanzim, and the PFLP); some were religious (Hamas and Islamic Jihad). Suicide bombings became a secular tool of war for the first time as Palestinian secular groups took on a larger and larger role in the bombings.

The Palestinian suicide bombings against Israeli targets from 1993 to 1999 left 164 Israelis dead, well below the number of those who died (543) during the early 2000s. Between the first wave of Palestinian suicide bombings in the 1990s and the second wave in the early 2000s, the Palestinians made vast improvements in their suicide bombing program, accounting for the higher Israeli casualties.

By the mid-1990s, a militant Islamist group, called al-Qaeda, began planning mega terror against the United States on American soil; until then, U.S. soil had been untargeted by global terrorists. In the worst suicide bombing in history, 19 suicide bombers attacked the United States on September 11, 2001, when four American civilian jetliners were hijacked and then crashed into the World Trade Center and Pentagon, killing 3,214 people.

A number of suicide attacks occurred in Russia due to the Chechen conflict, ranging from the 2002 Moscow theater hostage crisis to the 2004 Beslan school hostage crisis. Suicide bombings have occurred in Iraq since the American-led invasion in March 2003 and in Pakistan and Afghanistan since 2005. On July 7, 2005, a suicide attack against the London public transport system killed 52 and wounded 700.

GROWING PALESTINIAN MILITANCY

Starting with their defeat in the 1948 Israel War of Independence, Palestinian Arabs have continuously engaged in violence against Israel in

29

the hope that the State of Israel would fall. Because of the military superiority of the Israel Defense Forces (IDF), with tanks and fighter planes, the Palestinians engaged in terror, believing that this was the best way to bring harm to the Israelis.

When the Palestinians conducted cross-border raids from Egypt into Israel in the early 1950s, Israel retaliated in the 1956 Suez War, wiping out Egyptian bases that supported Palestinian Arab operations against the Israelis. Though Egypt, Syria, and Jordan suffered huge defeats at the hands of the IDF a decade later in the 1967 Six-Day War, those military routes set in motion the emergence of a fully-blown Palestinian resistance. Founded by Yasser Arafat in 1957, the terrorist Fatah group, after the Six-Day War, seemed to be the only significant military force in the Arab world.

THE PLO AND HAMAS

In 1968, Arafat's Fatah amalgamated with the Palestine Liberation Organization (PLO), and for the next 18 years the PLO was the most important political and military factor for the Palestinian Arabs. The PLO wanted to drive Israel into the sea; Israel had no interest in negotiating with terrorists, its description of PLO members.

By the late 1980s, the glow that had kept the PLO preeminent among Palestinians had worn off. Hamas, a new radical Islamist force, was starting to gain traction. To Hamas, the PLO looked tame. The Israeli occupation of the West Bank and the Gaza Strip remained, and the PLO appeared to be doing little to change that status quo.

THE INTIFADA

A seemingly minor traffic incident on December 8, 1987, sparked the first Palestinian uprising against Israel's occupation of the West Bank and Gaza Strip. It became known as the Intifada (Arabic for "shaking off"). An Israeli army tank transporter had crashed into some Palestinians from the Jabalya refugee camp in the Gaza Strip, killing four and wounding seven. Was it a simple car accident or a deliberate act of revenge on the part of the Israelis? Palestinians claimed that the traffic "accident" had been in revenge for the stabbing death of an Israeli salesman in the Gaza Strip two days earlier.

Still, when the incident occurred, both the Israelis and PLO dismissed it as a fleeting example of Palestinian frustration. However, inspired by Hamas, the Intifada—a determined attempt at revolution on the West Bank and in the Gaza Strip—swept through the Palestinian population.

When Hamas broke on the scene in the Gaza Strip, its leaders insisted they were nothing more than social reformers, hoping to steal the thunder from Arafat's PLO. Ironically, the IDF found common cause with Hamas at the time—both wanted to stamp out the PLO—and tours were organized to the Gaza Strip for foreign journalists to gain an appreciation of the new social reformists.

In fact, Hamas differentiated itself from the more docile PLO, not by advocating the liberation of Palestine from Israeli occupiers—that theme was shared by all militant Palestinian groups—but by its willingness to become militant in pursuit of creating an Islamic state on the West Bank, in the Gaza Strip, and in Israel. But in the early days of the Intifada, lacking an aggressive military wing, Hamas had to rely on youngsters throwing Molotov cocktails and rocks at Israeli military vehicles as its most daring form of attacks.

As Hamas was searching for a more powerful form of violence to inflict on the Israelis, a member of the Palestinian Islamic Jihad, a Hamas forerunner, carried out the first suicide attack against Israelis on July 6, 1989. The attacker, 25-year-old Abd al-Hadi Ghanayem, did not wear a suicide belt with explosives, as in later suicide bombing attacks, and he survived. While the Tel Aviv–Jerusalem bus 405 was heading for Jerusalem, Ghanayem seized the steering wheel from the driver and pulled the bus over a steep precipice into a ravine near Qiryat Ye'arim. Sixteen civilians were killed and 30 others were wounded.

Even though the terrorist lived and went on to serve life sentences in an Israeli jail, the attack was considered the first Palestinian suicide attack. The reason: the terrorist planned to die as part of his mission. Israeli security officials later noted that both the attacker and the 19 hijackers of 9/11 did not use explosives but still managed to carry out what amounted to suicide attacks.

Undoubtedly, Hamas learned a valuable lesson from the bus attack: Israelis were vulnerable in all sorts of ways, and it no longer had to rely on rocks and Molotov cocktails. Eventually, by adopting suicide bombing as its main terror tactic and launching one successful suicide attack after another against Israel, Hamas acknowledged that its social reformist bent was a fig leaf for its terrorism. Through the terror it launched against Israel, Hamas captured the hearts and minds of the majority of Palestinians on both the West Bank and in the Gaza Strip.

Some argue that the Palestinians adopted suicide bombing following October 8, 1990, when hundreds of Palestinian worshippers walked out of the al-Aqsa mosque in Jerusalem's Old City. Throwing stones at Israeli police officers as well as at Jewish worshipers praying at the nearby Western Wall, holiest site to Jews, the Palestinians were met with a barrage of gunfire from the police. Eighteen Palestinians were killed, and Hamas called for jihad (holy war). But there was no real response other than from a man named Omar Abu Sirah, who ran through a Jerusalem neighborhood, killing three Israelis with his butcher's knife. In time, such lone attackers left their butchers' knives behind and became suicide bombers.

In 1991, Hamas created a military wing known as Izz al-Din al-Qassam. It began by executing Palestinian collaborators in the Gaza Strip; a year later it began killing Israeli settlers living on what the Palestinians considered occupied Palestinian land by using car bombs.

HAMAS TURNS TO SYSTEMATIC TERROR

Stepping up its terror campaign between October and December 1992, a series of Hamas-organized terrorist attacks led to the decision taken by Israel's Prime Minister Yitzhak Rabin on December 16, 1992, to deport 415 Islamic Palestinian activists, most of whom belonged to Hamas; another 50 belonged to the Palestinian Islamic Jihad group.

The deportations backfired on the Israelis: rather than achieve its aim of isolating Hamas, they turned the deportees into heroes worthy of sympathy and support and the vital core of a revitalized Hamas militarism. By developing close relations with Hezbollah, pioneers of suicide bombing in the Middle East, the deportees obtained valuable instruction on how to conduct the next phase of its fight against Israel.

Frustrated by their inability to reach a political agreement with the Palestinians, and stung by the continuing suicide bombings against their civilians, the Israelis discovered to their shock that a new political overture they had made toward the Palestinians at the end of 1992 seemed to be moving forward. Starting in December 1992, Dr. Joseph "Yossi" Beillin, the Israeli deputy foreign minister, and Terje Rod-Larsen, a Norwegian researcher, organized a series of secret meetings in Oslo between PLO representative Ahmed Qurei, Israeli history professor Yair Hirschfeld, and Ron Pundak, an Israeli historian and journalist.

Qurei, Hirschfeld, and Pundak, got along well enough to hold 13 more secret sessions in Oslo. The ease with which both sides got along was reflected in their staying in the same residence, and eating breakfast, lunch, and dinner at the same table. In time, Beillin convinced Israel's Foreign Minister Shimon Peres to join in the negotiations.

White House signing ceremony of Oslo accords on September 13, 2003: Prime Minister Yitzhak Rabin (second from left), American president Bill Clinton standing just behind a seated Foreign Minister Shimon Peres, and PLO chairman Yasser Arafat (with kaffiyeh headdress). (*Credit*: Israel Government Press Office)

As a reminder of how distant peace was, Palestinian militants undertook the first suicide bombing against an Israeli target—at the Israeli-occupied town of Mehola on the West Bank—on April 16, 1993. The blast killed the suicide bomber, Saher Tamam al-Nabulsi, but no one else. He chose to blow himself up between two buses, which absorbed the worst effects of the bomb. Eight others were injured.

That event and other violence brought Prime Minister Yitzhak Rabin into the negotiations for Israel. As violence continued against Israel, Rabin had to choose continuously between breaking off and carrying on with negotiations with the Palestinians. He chose to continue to talk secretly with the PLO. In August 1993, both sides reached an agreement, which led to a White House signing ceremony on September 13, 1993.

It was at the White House ceremony that Rabin and Arafat shook hands for the first time, a dramatic and once almost unthinkable event that, despite the awkwardness of the two men in each other's presence, offered optimism. The Oslo accords were the first agreement between Israel and Arafat's PLO—a dramatic policy change for both sides: putting an end to Israel's long-standing refusal to recognize or negotiate with the PLO and to the PLO's long-time determination to destroy the State of Israel. Providing for the establishment of a Palestinian National Authority (PNA), the agreement decreed that the Palestinian Authority would be responsible for the administration of the territory under its control. The accords further called for the withdrawal of the IDF from parts of the Gaza Strip and the West Bank.

The accords were an interim arrangement that was to last five years, during which time negotiations would proceed toward a final peace agreement. Left for the later stages of those negotiations would be such sensitive issues as the status of Jerusalem, the Palestinian refugees, Israeli settlements on the West Bank, Israeli security, and the final borders between Israel and a new Palestinian state. Meanwhile, Israel agreed to grant interim Palestinian self-government in stages.

Though they represented a breakthrough in the Palestinian–Israeli conflict, the accords did not result in curbing Palestinian terror. Refusing to sign the agreement, terrorists continued their violence against Israeli targets, dooming future peace talks almost from the start. Much in the accords was anathema to Hamas, as they called for de facto Palestinian recognition of Israel, a stop to the fighting, and the eventual recognition of Israel's right to exist. Hamas took up its armed struggle against Israel more intensely, killing 26 Israelis within a month of the White House ceremony.

Along with the 1995 Madrid Conference that followed, the Oslo accords led to no further agreement between Israel and the Palestinians—only to more and more violence. Though Hamas was largely responsible for the failure of Oslo to lead to a more concrete agreement, the terror organization felt it still represented no more than a mere nuisance to Israel. It searched for a more dramatic way to achieve its goals.

It found a solution in suicide bombing. On April 6, 1994, Hamas organized the first suicide bombing against Israeli civilians in Israel proper in the northern Israeli city of Afula, resulting in eight dead and 34 wounded. Ten more suicide bombings followed between April 1994 and June 1996. Based on the results of the Israeli election that June, these suicide bombings appeared to push Israelis farther to the political right, as signified by Binyamin Netanyahu's victory as prime minister.

In Hamas's view, electing a decidedly right-wing prime minister was a positive development: It meant that Israelis were saying no to the PLO as peace partners, and no to the peace process in general. From 1996 to the summer of 2000, at which time U.S. president Bill Clinton sought to reinvigorate the Israeli–Palestinian peace prospects by holding the abortive Camp David II conference, Hamas laid low. Israel had caught many of its terrorist leaders, leading Hamas to wait and see what might come out of the peace talks.

Reflecting a certain distancing from suicide bombing, a senior Hamas leader in Gaza, Mahmud Al-Zahar, noted:

> We must calculate the benefits and cost of continued armed operations. If we can fulfill our goals without violence, we will do so.
>
> Violence is a means, not a goal. Hamas's decision to adopt self-restraint does not contradict our aims, including the establishment of an Islamic state instead of Israel. We will never recognize Israel, but it is possible that a truce…could prevail between us for days, months, or years. [6]

After the failure of Camp David II in July 2000 and Likud Opposition leader Ariel Sharon's controversial visit to the Temple Mount on September 28, 2000, a new Palestinian uprising known as the Second Intifada began. Israel pointed to Arafat's walkout on the Camp David negotiations as the cause for the new uprising; Palestinians blamed the uprising on Sharon's "provocative" visit to the Temple Mount. Whatever the actual cause, the self-described Hamas restraint came to an end on October 30, 2000, when a suicide bomber killed 15 people in Jerusalem. The attack was supposedly in response to Sharon's visit.

In this chapter we have offered a detailed history of suicide bombings. In the next chapter we start to dig into the inner workings of a modern-age suicide bomber. We ask: Who would possibly want to become a suicide bomber? We look at the various motives that compel a suicide bomber to sign up for a mission.

NOTES

1. http://aboutfacts.net/Weapons51.htm
2. Scott Atran, "The Moral Logic and Growth of Suicide Terrorism," Figs. 1 and 2, 128–129, http://www.sitemaker.umich.edu/satran/files/twq06spring_atran.pdf.

3. Pape, Robert, *Dying to Win: The Strategic Logic of Suicide Terrorism*. New York: Random House. 2005. "Suicide Terrorist Campaigns, 1980–2003," Appendix 1.
4. Bhattacharji, Preeti (21 July 2008, updated). "Liberation Tigers of Tamil Eelam (Sri Lanka, separatists)." *Council on Foreign Relations*.
5. Ehud Sprinzak, "Rational Fanatics," *Foreign Policy*, September 1, 2000.
6. Mahmud Al-Zahar, *Al Quds*, October 12, 1995, in *The Palestinian Hamas*, trans. Shaul Mishal and Avraham Sela (New York: Columbia University Press, 2000), p. 71.

Section II

A Suicide Bomber's Motives

4

Motives I
Why Someone Becomes a Suicide Bomber

What could possibly turn someone into a suicide bomber? What motive could be strong enough to persuade someone to give up his or her life? These questions have aroused great interest among American and Israeli scholars. None that we have come across believes in the one-dimensional attitude that all suicide bombers are crazy. We do not subscribe to that view either.

To their credit, scholars devote huge amounts of time and energy to searching for "rational" explanations for what seems on the surface to be a wholly irrational act. And so they ask what motivates suicide bombers: religion, politics, or personal experiences? Is one of these three motives primary? Are all three motives at play in some cases? From their research, most scholars conclude that there is one primary motive that drives these bombers.

The researchers' goal is not to stop suicide bombers from carrying out their deeds. That is the job of intelligence and law enforcement officers. Their more limited goal is to understand the psyche of the suicide bomber and, in doing so, to aid those in power to make more-informed decisions in fighting terror.

For scholars to make judgments on what motivates a potential suicide bomber is not easy. Their only means of doing hands-on research is to interview failed suicide bombers. The fact that these are would-be suicide bombers who failed, or those with second thoughts on the way to committing the act, limits the ability of scholars and journalists to determine what truly motivates the bombers. The pool of possible interview subjects is substantially reduced by the fact that successful suicide bombers are dead.

Moreover, security officers, for their own reasons and motives, allow only a handful of those in custody to be interviewed. Once given access to failed suicide bombers serving jail sentences, scholars and journalists have no guarantee that they will receive truthful, complete answers to their questions. Having failed in their mission, suicide bombers may look upon the interview as an opportunity to issue slogans designed to please their terror organization and the wider community. Still, these interviews are the only interaction scholars and journalists have with anyone who has trained to become a suicide bomber, and for that reason alone, those interviews take on significance for the researchers beyond what they should.

Though the Israelis cannot be 100 percent certain what the failed bombers will say to a journalist, they hope that the callousness and evil of the prisoner comes through. Israeli security officials' worst fear is that the interviewee will come off as a freedom fighter with a just cause. But they have already spent time with the bomber and are confident that he will come off either as apologetic and remorseful, or so extreme that his evil will shine through.

Failed suicide bombers in Pakistan, Afghanistan, and Iraq, however, are hardly ever interviewed.

ON DETECTING A SUICIDE BOMBER'S MOTIVES

We agree with the scholars who assert that suicide bombers have one primary motive in deciding to undertake their horrific missions. And this of course begs the question: What is that primary motive? Because the authors of this book, Mordecai Dzikansky and Gil Kleiman, come from different backgrounds, they differ on what that primary motive is. Dzikansky, though he has lived in Israel since 2003, still thinks himself first and foremost as an American with a law enforcement background. Kleiman, though he was born and grew up in the United States, regards himself as an Israeli and part of the security establishment.

To Dzikansky and his fellow American law enforcement officers, the one event that best illustrates the brutality of the suicide bomber is 9/11. Unable to interview the dead suicide bombers, these officials concluded from other evidence that the event was conceived and carried out by Islamic fundamentalists, whose religious zealotry motivated them to find and destroy "infidels" in keeping with the Koran's scriptures. It was not a political act per se. While the bombers' organization, al-Qaeda, often talks in political terms, saying that its hope is to replace existing regimes with

40

Islamic states, the bombers' true drive is pleasing Allah, not figuring out how to topple governments.

For Gil Kleiman and his colleagues in the Israeli security establishment, the central organizing factor in their interactions with terror was not 9/11, but the continuing tale of Palestinian suicide bombing. To them, Palestinian suicide bombers and their facilitators harbor political, not religious, motives for carrying out their lethal missions. The bombers want to destroy the state of Israel and replace it with an Islamic regime. Many bombers speak at length of performing their actions to honor Allah and to become martyrs, but these are simply political objectives wrapped in the guise of religion.

American and Israeli security analysts cling to their views on the motives of suicide bombers with great passion and conviction. After lengthy discussions between themselves, Dzikansky and Kleiman realized that they held conflicting views over the primary motive of suicide bombers. They decided that the best way to present their views in this manual was to spell them out in full, explaining what each felt and why.

A good place to start is to point out what they agree on. Let's take the issue of whether suicide bombers are insane. Some believe they are. If a rational human being would not commit suicide, soon-to-be suicide bombers had to be irrational. Both Dzikansky and Kleiman believe that suicide bombers on the whole are sane, rational actors—not at all crazy.

Agreeing with them, scholars and other commentators discounted this theory that suicide bombers were insane, for it ignored the "rational" way that would-be suicide bombers behaved: They gave much thought to becoming suicide bombers; they went through extensive training to learn the "craft." Their sponsors put them through a series of tests to determine if they were serious about volunteering for the deed.

One scholar who believes that suicide bombers are not crazy, impoverished, or undereducated, as the popular view had it for some time, is Robert Pape, professor of political science at the University of Chicago and founder of the Chicago Project on Security and Terrorism:

> In general, suicide attackers are rarely socially isolated, clinically insane, or economically destitute individuals, but are most often educated, socially integrated, and highly capable people who could be expected to have a good future.
>
> There is no documented mental illness in any case of suicide terrorism.... Arab suicide terrorists are in general better educated than average

and are from the working or middle classes.... [T]hey resemble the kind of politically conscious individuals who might join a grassroots movement more than they do wayward adolescents or religious fanatics. [1]

Dzikansky and Kleiman agree with Pape's analysis. From their witnessing of would-be suicide bombers caught just before carrying out an attack, they have certainly come across young men, a glazed, vacant look in their eyes, who appear mentally challenged. But most of the wannabe suicide bombers whom they have watched are cool, deliberate in their thinking, stoic—hardly material for mental hospitals. In their view, it is far too simplistic to place all potential suicide bombers into a single "they're all crazy" basket.

Now we turn to Dzikansky and Kleiman's conflicting views on the motives of suicide bombers. We start with Mordecai Dzikansky:

For American first responders and security establishment, our point of reference in counter terror is not the occupation of Palestine, as it is with our Israeli colleagues. We do not confront clever political operatives whose main aim is to overthrow the United States. America was targeted on 9/11 because, to al-Qaeda, we are the "infidels," and in their twisted minds, we deserve to be punished for our so-called lack of faith.

When we look at the 19 suicide bombers who carried out 9/11, we see a bunch of religious fanatics who thought of obeying Allah by killing 'infidels' and nothing more. To argue that their motives were political is to treat them with more respect than they deserve.

When I hear Israelis argue that al-Qaeda's religious zealotry is just mumbo-jumbo and what al-Qaeda really wants are political gains, I believe those Israelis are latched on to a mind-set that has as its main reference point the Israeli–Palestinian conflict.

Agreeing with Mordecai Dzikansky, Marc Sageman, author of *Understanding Terror Networks*, debunks the notion that al-Qaeda is solely motivated by political objectives: "This is not about occupation; it's about [al-Qaeda] establishing an Islamic state in a core Arab region." Sageman further noted that the lead hijacker on 9/11, Mohamed Atta, was Egyptian—and "to my knowledge, I don't think we are occupying Egypt" [2].

Committing suicide on behalf of religion has quite an appeal for suicide bombers, including the Palestinian ones. They do not know very much about politics, nor do they care about it. But they can be seduced into committing suicide by the lure of religious martyrdom, a blissful "life" in heaven, those 72 virgins, and the blessings that accrue from doing God's will. They believe that it is nobler to die for a set of religious principles than for little-understood or highly controversial and complicated political objectives. As a *New York Times* journalist perceptively noted:

> Their stunted horizons create a volatile mix of hopelessness and anger. The humiliations of Israeli-controlled checkpoints, work permits and curfews give focus to their frustration. Then politicized Islamic militants step in and offer an out: die for the cause and enter the fast lane to paradise. In the process you get revenge, you get glory and your family gets a stipend. [3]

That is why mosques have been such breeding grounds for suicide bomber recruits. The recruiting process often starts with members of the military cells of Hamas and the Islamic Resistance Movement who circulate among the organizations' schools and mosques during religious instruction. The recruiter drops the idea of dying for God into the conversation and gauges the students' reactions. The trainers zoom in on those who discuss the idea seriously. "Islam is an appealing new identity because Arab nationalism has been defeated," says Dr. Eyad Sarraj, program director for Gaza's community mental health program. "Islam gives you a sense of hope and moral victory, especially when you come from an environment of despair and defeat" [4].

In such an environment, religion looks pretty good. The potential bombers practice the religion and abstain from drink; the men grow beards. They wish to become martyrs and to serve Allah. They are even willing to die for religion. Sometimes the recruits leave for their suicide bombing missions directly from the mosques.

Hewing to an Israeli perspective, Gil Kleiman believes that religion is not the real motive of suicide bombers; politics is.

> I know that lots of suicide bombers and their terrorist leaders spout religious justifications for their evil deeds but that doesn't mean that religious is their main motive for their actions.
>
> What really drives them is a wish to take part in a cultural and political war, a war that sometimes uses religion to spur on suicide bombers and sometimes does not.
>
> Let's keep in mind that there have been secular groups sponsoring suicide bombings that have had a distinctly anti-religious agenda; and not all of the 19 suicide bombers that carried out 9/11 were religious. Let us also keep in mind that targets in Israel and the United States are never

symbols of religion whether churches, synagogues, religious figures. It is just the opposite.

The targets of 9/11 were the World Trade Center, the Pentagon, and perhaps the White House or the U.S. Capitol, the epitome of secular Western capitalistic culture—as far away from religion as can be. Similarly in Israel, no synagogues or religious leaders were attacked because they were religious per se. When religious people or schools were attacked it was because they were Israelis. The suicide bombing campaign has been against the Israelis, because they are Western and a cultural threat to the Moslem world.

Religion, argues Kleiman, while an important element in the suicide bombing program for recruitment and indoctrination purposes, is merely the tool that terror leaders and facilitators use to entice candidates into the program, and to attain political ends. Politics, therefore, is the ultimate objective of suicide bombers. Believing that religion is the motivator actually gives the terrorist much more credit than he deserves. His motives are about politics and culture, the control of resources, and the ultimate evil—money. Religion is only a tool to encourage and incite suicide bombers.

Those who share Gil Kleiman's convictions point out that personal motives sometimes arise in the bomber's mind: He may be desperate because he sees no way out of his miserable poverty; a female suicide bomber may feel tarnished by her adultery, fearing her family's scorn and abandonment; other suicide bombers may feel vengeful after a close relative is killed by the enemy's forces. Religion is not uppermost in the minds of these troubled people.

Those who debunk religion as a motive argue that facilitators of suicide bombers deviously use religion as a lure into the world of suicide bombing, with their promise of 72 virgins, a direct route to Allah's heaven, and all that. The facilitators are too clever to overtly employ a political agenda as a lure to the potential suicide bomber even though they want to use new recruits to carry out political objectives: to end an occupation, to bring down a tyrannical regime, and the like.

It was once widely believed among scholars that desperation was the suicide bomber's primary motive for volunteering to launch an attack. Learning of the potential bomber's desperation, a terrorist leader lures him into becoming a suicide bomber with the promise of becoming an instant hero at home and an eternal martyr in heaven. To be sure, a few suicide bombers have been desperate for one reason or another, but for the theory to be true, all suicide bombers would have to display desperation, and most do not. Besides, for the theory to be true, all desperate people in the world should show an interest in becoming a suicide bomber, and most do not.

We do not believe that desperation is the prime motive of potential suicide bombers. Too many suicide bombers in the West come from middle-class backgrounds, are educated, and have a good life awaiting them. Nor do we believe that some failed Palestinian suicide bombers act only out of personal revenge, though some failed bombers argue that they do.

Among the many examples that Palestinians mention: A young Palestinian man has lost a brother, killed by the Israeli occupiers. Israeli soldiers at checkpoints speak unkindly to a young Palestinian woman seeking medical treatment in an Israeli hospital. Both the young man and woman volunteer to become suicide bombers

Agreeing with Gil Kleiman, scholar Robert Pape believes that politics is the underlying motive of suicide bombers. He chose to study suicide attacks and suicide bombers by building his own database of 315 suicide terrorism campaigns around the world from 1980 to 2003 and 462 individual suicide terrorists, among whom were 71 from al-Qaeda, who have operated during that same period. Studying their lives, he read documents that terror groups published and then did statistical analysis, which led to conclusions that surprised him. Rather than point to the conclusion, as he thought it would, that suicide terrorism was largely a function of Islamic fundamentalism, he argued that it was not. "In fact...right after 9/11, I went and grabbed the Koran because I wanted to know what's wrong with Islam that this is driving people to do suicide terrorism" [5]. But he concluded that what "over 95 percent of all suicide attacks around the world since 1980 until today (2005) have in common is not religion, but a clear, strategic objective: to compel a modern democracy to withdraw military forces from the territory that the terrorists view as their homeland." In other words, politics is the prime motivator of suicide bombers.

As a corollary, Pape [5] concluded that occupation politics, not religion, had motivated the 19 suicide hijackers, 15 of whom came from Saudi Arabia, where nearly 5,000 U.S. combat troops had been stationed at the time. When Pape looked at the beliefs of 384 of the 462 suicide attackers, he found that 43 percent were religious, but 57 percent were secular. Also, 301 of the 315 suicide terrorist attacks perpetrated between 1980 and 2003 were part of what Pape called strategic campaigns designed "for specific political, mainly secular goals."

45

Buttressing his argument that occupation politics, not religion, drove suicide bombers, Pape studied the nationalities of 67 of the 71 al-Qaeda suicide bombers and discovered that two-thirds of the 71 al-Qaeda terrorists came from countries (Saudi Arabia, Turkey, Afghanistan, and the United Arab Emirates) that had a U.S. combat presence prior to the attackers becoming suicide terrorists. The other third came from countries with governments that were heavily supported by the United States (Egypt, Pakistan, Indonesia, and Morocco).

Al-Qaeda expert Peter Bergen, author of *Holy War Inc.*, backing Pape's analysis, said: "It's comforting to think that a bunch of Islamic nut cases fresh out of madrassas are attacking us, but it turns out that a group of rational political actors who are as well educated as most Americans are attacking us" [6].

A POLITICAL MOTIVE I: THE SPONSORS

Jerusalem Post reporter Erik Schechter interviewed dispatchers—Mahmoud Sarahneh and Bilal Othman Barghouti—while they were serving life sentences in an Israeli prison [7]. Sarahneh, 27, had been a Fatah member since his mid-teens and had personally dispatched four suicide bombers, including one who killed 11 people in Jerusalem's Beit Yisrael neighborhood in March 2002. Expressing no regret, he scornfully claimed that the Israelis were to blame: "They are the ones who caused me to do what I did."

In contrast, Bilal Othman Barghouti, a heavy-set, balding 27-year-old, projecting a friendly tone, openly admitted to recruiting suicide bombers for Hamas at Birzeit University in the West Bank town of Ramallah. Schechter asked a tough question: Would he recruit his own parents to be suicide bombers? Barghouti dealt with the question objectively: Becoming a *shahid* (martyr) is an "individual decision," implying that, if they so desired, he would send his own mother and father to die.

Barghouti was an explosives expert and the man behind the Sbarro Restaurant bombing in Jerusalem in August 2001 that left 15 dead, including 7 children. Barghouti's motive in sending suicide bombers on their missions was political. He blamed his actions on the Israelis. Asked to look at photos of the dead children, he quickly suggested: "I do not accept responsibility for their deaths. I feel pain, of course. They are little children. But the government of Israel is solely responsible."

46

Aerial shot of scene after suicide bombing at Sbarro Restaurant in downtown Jerusalem on August 9, 2001. (*Credit*: Israel Government Press Office)

Sarahneh insisted that suicide bombing had nothing to do with religion; it was simply a tactic of war. Suicide bombing, in Barghouti's view, was "a new method to fight the occupation. We had weapons, but the idea was not around before 1993." Sarahneh defined the motives of suicide bombers as purely political: "It does not make a difference: Fatah, Hamas, we all want to liberate Palestine. I am now sitting in Palestine." Added Barghouti: "So long as there is an occupation, there will be ways to fight it."

A POLITICAL MOTIVE II: FIGHTING FOR DIGNITY

We offer the tale of 23-year-old Arin Ahmed Shaebat, who wanted to become a suicide bomber for political reasons, but was seduced into a suicide mission by her facilitators by their use of religious rhetoric [8].

She looked around at the life that she, her relatives and friends had been leading. She felt that she lacked dignity; she felt embarrassed, humiliated. To her, the occupying Israelis were to blame. All that she felt, all that motivated her, was political.

47

She had grown up in the West Bank town of Bet Sahur under the care of aunts and uncles after her father died when she was a baby. When she was 10 years old, her mother remarried and abandoned her to live in Jordan. Four years later, her grandfather, with whom she had been living, died.

Fluent in English, knowing some Hebrew, articulate, and bright, Arin had studied communications and computer programming at Bethlehem University. On March 8, 2002, her boyfriend of 18 months, Jad Salem, a member of Tanzim, a Palestinian secular terrorist group, was killed. Founded in 1995 to counter Palestinian Islamist fundamentalism, the Tanzim is an offshoot of Fatah. Its leader is Marwan Barghouti, who in 2010 was serving consecutive life sentences for murder in an Israeli prison. Tanzim has also recruited female suicide bombers, one of whom was Andaleeb Takatka, a 20-year-old Bethlehem woman who blew herself up at a Jerusalem bus stop at the entrance to an open-air market in April 12, 2002, killing six Israeli civilians, and wounding 104.

Hoping to avenge Jad Salem's death, Arin gave almost no thought to how she would do that. One evening, she and friends were talking about how they wanted to organize a reprisal action against all the Israeli military actions in the last months. Arin thought of Jad.

"And all of a sudden, I said to them, 'You know what? I'm going to do a suicide bombing.' That was it. A moment earlier, I hadn't thought of anything like that." Why the change in her? "You see your people suffering humiliations and struggling to survive. I was thinking that I wanted to change the circumstances and that I had a message. We have to fight in order to live our lives in a dignified way."

This was on a Friday. Afterward, she went home. She soon spoke with someone in the Tanzim and told him that she wanted to become a suicide bomber. She assumed that training and instruction about weapons would take a few months. But just four days later, some Tanzim militants told her in person: "Congratulations. You're going to do a suicide bombing." She went into shock, unable to believe that she was to carry out the mission so soon.

In addition to training, she was promised that great things awaited her after she blew herself up. "You'll gain a very special status among the women suicide bombers. You'll be a real heroine. It's for Jad's memory. You'll be reunited with him in heaven. You'll be with him in paradise." While Arin certainly had a political motive, her sponsors sought to lure her into suicide bombing by playing the religious card—and it worked. None of the promises were directly political. Her sponsors knew better than to argue that she was giving up her life for a political cause about which she may not have felt as deeply as they did. And so they provided a religious motive for her to think about: joining her boyfriend in paradise.

When they felt that Arin was indeed prepared to undertake the mission, the Tanzim terrorists trained her for a suicide bombing in Rishon LeZion, south of Tel Aviv. On May 22, 2002, the day of the planned attack, Arin wore tight pants and a tiny top, leaving her bellybutton exposed to disguise herself as a young Israeli woman. She met 16-year-old Issam Badir for the first time that day. He was from the West Bank town of Beit Jala and had been told he would carry out a joint attack with Arin. He had dyed his hair blond to conceal that he was an Arab.

Packed into black knapsacks, the bombs they would both carry contained explosives and nails, and weighed 60 pounds. A switch that protruded from the rear of the knapsacks was linked to wires that would activate the bombs. She and Issam Badir were driven to a spot near the target. They were to receive instructions soon via cell phone on where to stand to maximize casualties.

Arin and Issam got out of the car and, with their heavy knapsacks, walked to opposite sides of the street in an open plaza. Arin immediately spotted many people, mothers with children, teenage boys and girls. The scene got to her and made her think of an Israeli woman her age with whom she had once been friendly. Standing at her designated spot for 10 minutes, Arin watched Issam, as he was about to blow himself up. He was having second thoughts, but his sponsors, talking to him over the cell phone, convinced him to go ahead with the action. Seconds later, he blew himself up, killing a teenage boy and an elderly man.

Was it the sight of Issam carrying out his mission, or of the unarmed Israeli civilians she had gazed at that gave her pause? Whatever the main reason, she asked herself: "How can I do such a thing? I can't do the same thing that the Israeli soldiers do and that we hate them for. I can't take other people's lives" [9]. Arin left suddenly, reached the parked car where her sponsors sat, and, even with the suicide bomb belt still strapped to her body, told them that she no longer wanted to blow herself up.

Furious with her, her sponsors sought to change her mind. They reminded her that she would achieve great status, and that much honor awaited her in paradise. Their pleas did not move her. They returned her to Bethlehem, yelling at her the entire trip back. They tried to convince her to carry out another attack in Jerusalem, but she was no longer interested in being a suicide bomber.

Acting on information received from Palestinian sources, Israeli Defense Forces (IDF) soldiers arrested Arin at her home a week later.

She spent seven years in jail for planning an attack and was released in February 2009. She became a business administration student at Bethlehem University with hopes of working at a small company or founding her own business.

A PERSONAL MOTIVE: I AM UGLY AND SCORNED

As we noted, Gil Kleiman and the Israeli security establishment are convinced that even when a suicide bomber decides to take on a mission for the most personal or religious of reasons, the bomber acts primarily for political goals. The motives or reasons in this case are personal. We offer the case study of Wafa al-Biri, who had seemingly deeply personal reasons for becoming a suicide bomber, yet her primary motive, as Gil Kleiman would argue, was politics: She wanted to help expel the Israelis from Palestinian occupied land.

For Wafa al-Biri, a 21-year-old Palestinian woman from the Jabalya refugee camp in the Gaza Strip, the decision to become a suicide bomber seemed deeply personal, hardly tinged with religious or political motives [10]. One day in the spring of 2005, a gas cooker in her Gaza home exploded while she was preparing dinner. She suffered burns on nearly half her body. Only her face was untouched. Before the accident, she seemed happy; a friend described her as "a very funny girl, very active, laughing a lot." To get the kind of medical help required, she decided to cross over into Israel to get treatment at Soroka Hospital in the Israeli city of Beersheba.

Given 12 blood transfusions that saved her life, she was not charged for the medical care. Her family in Gaza was so grateful to the Israeli doctors that members wrote a note thanking doctors and nurses for their "great efforts and wonderful, warm attitude" in aiding Wafa to survive her burns. Still, Wafa grew tired and depressed. Looking into a mirror, she thought her scarred body ugly. Reinforcing her plunge into depression, her fiancé had left her, her brothers were shamed, and her parents were frightened how others would express their shame at the family's "dishonor." When hospital staff gave her the good news that she was being released from Soroka, she begged to remain hospitalized; but she was returned to the Gaza Strip on a stretcher. Back in Jabalya, she was shunned by friends and felt lonely. Again, she said she wanted to commit suicide. "If there is anyone who will give me a bomb to blow myself up, I will do it." Her mother screamed at her: "Shut up—don't say that. We don't need more problems." Her family proposed that she see a psychiatrist.

Opposing such a step, her brother thought that others would think her crazy, thus damaging the family's reputation.

Learning of her suicidal state and that she had Israeli approval to visit Soroka Hospital, members of the al-Aqsa Martyrs' Brigade persuaded her that, as she had become disfigured, she would never find a husband; she was better off becoming a religious martyr.

They gave her a bomb, drove her to the Erez checkpoint, and ordered her to target the hospital. Her sponsors doubted that anyone would check the underwear of a sick young woman going to a hospital for medical treatment. (Similarly, the "underwear bomber," Umar Farouk Abdulmutallab, was able to enter a commercial airliner on Christmas Day, December 25, 2009, but he was caught before blowing himself up.)

Due for a follow-up appointment at the hospital on June 20 at 8 a.m., Wafa al-Biri carried with her the letter from the Israelis giving her permission to cross into Israel—for humanitarian reasons—and confirming the appointment. In her underwear, she also carried a 20-pound bomb that she planned to detonate while at the Soroka outpatient clinic in the midst of 100 outpatients and the very doctor who had saved her life.

The Shabak, the Israel Intelligence Agency, provided a tip to soldiers at the Erez checkpoint that a female suicide bomber was on her way to an Israeli target. Soldiers were ready for her when Wafa showed up at the checkpoint. She found herself locked into an area from which she could not go forward or back. A soldier shouted orders through a loudspeaker to drop her pants and the bomb.

Frustrated at realizing that she would now not reach Soroka, she sought to end her life anyway, using her deformed right hand to pull the detonator switch from her right pocket. But the string to the detonator switch was all that she could grab, and it was obviously no longer attached to the explosive charge. Over and over she tried to get the detonator switch in her pocket to work, but it would not. Eventually she began crying, realizing that she was going to live.

Her facilitators insisted that Wafa's motives were political. But, soon after her capture, she noted to an Israel Television reporter from Channel 10 that from the time she was a child, she had a dream—and still had—of being a shahid (martyr) and dying for the sake of Allah [11]. When she put the bomb into her underwear, however, her plan was to kill as many people as possible—to go out in the most dramatic way possible—to die for her people in aid of their political causes: the war against Israel, not the war against the Jewish religion. In other words, her primary driver was a political motive.

A RELIGIOUS MOTIVE: DEVOTED TO THE KORAN

Majdi Abu Warda reflects the kind of suicide bomber that Mordecai Dzikansky is talking about when he says that religion is what ultimately drives the bomber. Majdi showed that it was easy for facilitators to convince him that it was worth dying for Allah. It was a Friday, February 23, 1996. Majdi Abu Warda spent an hour quietly arguing with his mother about going on a family picnic. He was one of 11 children. Mother and son also disputed whether Majdi should get a job first or complete his studies first. His mother insisted that he finish school before seeking work. Seemingly disturbed at her marching orders, Majdi skipped the Friday picnic.

Two days later, February 25, the 18-year-old Majdi boarded the Number 18 Jerusalem bus traveling down Jaffa Road near the Jerusalem Central Bus Station; he ignited a satchel packed with TNT, blowing himself up, killing 26 passengers, and wounding 48 others [12].

The entire Abu Warda family read the Koran with devotion, and after the attack, relatives said Majdi was pious, but hardly a zealot. He would sometimes skip the first prayer of the day, which requires rising before dawn. But he focused mostly on religion, going to bed by 8:00 every night and never watching television. If he was interested in politics, family members said, he kept it to himself.

In lengthy study sessions with Majdi, bomber recruits focused on all the verses referring to the glory of dying for God in the Koran and the Hadith, the sayings of the Prophet Mohammed that form the basis of Islamic law. They especially focused on the Koranic verse that was: "Think not of those who are slain in God's way as dead. Nay, they are living, finding their sustenance in the presence of their Lord" [13]. The religion emphasized that life on earth was a transition; that the next life was the real one. Scriptures and sermons described the afterlife in glowing terms, a place with wonderful palaces, food, and accommodating women.

To Gil Kleiman, such attitudes are old-fashioned. Even if the terrorist group behind Majdi's suicide bombing had a religious bent, its target was a very secular Israeli target: a bus. There is, Kleiman emphasizes, no religious war against Israel.

Counterintuitive as it is that modern-day women would turn to suicide bombing, the fact is that more and more women are engaging in such action, making it more difficult to defend against suicide bombing in general. We now turn to a subject that has baffled and intrigued scholars studying terror and suicide bombings: women suicide bombers.

NOTES

1. Robert Pape, *Dying to Win: The Strategic Logic of Suicide Terrorism* (New York: Random House, 2005), 210–211.
2. Marc Sageman, *Understanding Terror Networks* (Philadelphia: University of Pennsylvania Press, 2004).
3. "Portrait of a Suicide Bomber: Devout, Apolitical and Angry," *New York Times*, March 18, 1996.
4. Ibid.
5. "A Scholarly Look at Terror Sees Bootprints in the Sand," *Washington Post*. July 10, 2005.
6. Ibid.
7. Erik Schechter, "My Interview with a Would-Be Martyr: Where Have All the Bombers Gone?" *Jerusalem Post*, August 9, 2004. All quotes from Sarahneh and Barghouti are from the Schechter piece.
8. Vered Levy Barzilai, "An Experience of Near-Death," *Ha'aretz*, June 2002.
9. Ibid.
10. Martin Fletcher, "Descent from patient to suicide bomber," NBC News, June 23, 2005, http://www.msnbc.msn.com/id/8330374/ns/world_news-mideast/n_africa/.
11. Center for Special Studies (CSS), Intelligence and Terrorism Information Center, Israel Television, Channel 10, June 20, 2005, http://www.terrorism-info.org.il/malam_multimedia/html/final/eng/sib/6_05/count_t.htm.
12. Ibid.
13. Koran 3:169.

5

Motives II
Why Do Women Become Suicide Bombers?
Leaving the Women at Home

In most premodern societies, the men would fight while the women would stay home. Men, when necessary, would attack or defend. Considered the weaker of the two sexes, women would raise children and run the home. It was as unimaginable that men would cook meals and keep the home clean as it was that women would hunt for food and defend the family in battle.

Male religious leaders argued that women could not engage in battle. The leaders hoped in that way to keep women pure. If men and women trained and fought together, they were likely to touch one another, an impure act that had to be avoided. A man might have to touch a woman while preparing her for battle. Or failed Palestinian female suicide bombers could wind up in Israeli jails, where they were likely to come in contact with men, making it impossible to maintain the women's high standards of modesty. Hence, the traditional ban on women acting as warriors.

And yet female combatants appear from time to time in Western history. Among the martyred female saints in the Catholic Church is Joan of Arc. Women terrorists were part of the Red Brigades in Italy, the Baader-Meinhof gang in Germany, and the Weathermen in the United States. Even within the Israeli–Arab conflict, Palestinian women were not unique to the battle: The Israel Defense Forces (IDF) has long had females in its ranks and recently as female fighter pilots. But none of these women engaged in suicide bombing.

CHANGING THE RULES OF THE GAME

Suicide bombing changed the traditional rules of war; female suicide bombers changed those rules even more. No longer is there a distinction between combatants (traditionally male) and noncombatants (traditionally women and children). No longer is there a distinction between terrorists (traditionally male) and innocent civilians (traditionally, men, women, and children).

For Israel, indeed for all Western urban environments, the revised rules that women were being employed as suicide bombers meant that bombers were even harder to identify. Any Palestinian, male or female, might become a potential terrorist. If, by dispelling the notion that all suicide bombers came out of "central casting," the terrorists could confuse Israelis, all the better. In their confusion, the Israelis might grow militarily weaker—a major terrorist goal.

One female suicide bomber after another took on the Israelis. On January 27, 2002, Yasser Arafat called on Palestinian women to join in the struggle against Israeli occupation. On the day that he issued the statement, a 28-year-old woman named Wafa Idris became the first female Palestinian suicide bomber.

A divorced paramedic, she lived in the Am'ari Refugee Camp in the West Bank town of Ramallah. Arriving outside a shoe store on Jerusalem's Jaffa Road, she detonated a 22-pound bomb that killed her and an 81-year-old Israeli man and wounded more than 100 others. Rather than strap the bomb to her body, she carried it in a backpack. Until the attack, Palestinian women had helped plant bombs but had not blown themselves up. Accordingly, the first reaction was that she could not have intended to conduct a suicide bombing: The explosion must have been accidental.

But upon investigation, it was decided that she was indeed a suicide bomber. She had been angry at Israeli violence, but was not active in any of the Palestinian political, religious, or militant groups. Her motivation seemed more personal than political. Forced into marriage at a young age, she was unable to bear children and thus was considered worthless in her society. Her husband had left her for another woman with whom he had children. Worried that she might scar her family's reputation, Wafa Idris chose suicide bombing to achieve some degree of honor.

2002–2007: Eighty-eight Palestinian women attempt suicide bombings; eight are successful.

From 2002 to 2007, 88 Palestinian women attempted suicide bombings: Eight were successful. Of the six Palestinian suicide bombings in 2006, women carried out two of them [1].

56

Debate ensued over the question: Does the growing number of female suicide bombers reflect a rising status of women in Arab culture? Some commentators said yes. Others, however, dismissed such talk, arguing that women suicide bombers were low-level pawns, hardly evidence of their improved status.

THE ADVANTAGES OF A FEMALE SUICIDE BOMBER

In the modern era, terrorist organizations decided that women could be used to carry out acts of terror, especially suicide bombings. One practical reason was that women tended to be more successful than their male counterparts. Because they did not arouse suspicion as a male suicide bomber might, they could meld into crowds and blow themselves up with relative ease. Women were less likely to be searched. If searched, women would win wide support from friends and relatives who would be angry at the enemy for scrutinizing women so carefully. It was also easier to recruit a woman for suicide bombing than a man, if she learned that the enemy had killed a close relative or boyfriend,

Female suicide bombers had another advantage over their male counterparts: They were more likely to attract widespread media coverage. With terrorist organizations competing for media attention, a female suicide bomber offered a terror group sponsoring her an opportunity to increase its media profile. While all suicide bombers proved shocking, the traditional view that women gave life and did not destroy it made female suicide bombers a media draw.

WHO IS THE TYPICAL FEMALE SUICIDE BOMBER?

It is not at all clear that there is a typical female suicide bomber. One study showed the following: Between January 2002, when the first female suicide bomber (Wafa Idris) blew herself up, until May 2006, 67 Palestinian women planned to carry out suicide bombings. Eight blew themselves up; of these, Fatah sent five; Islamic Jihad in Palestine sent two; and Hamas sent one. A majority of the 67 women (58 percent) were unmarried; 39 percent were 18 to 25 years old; 16 percent were 26 to 35 years old; 11 percent were under 18. Nearly half were educated, with 22 percent having more than a high school education; 26 percent had a high school education and were qualified for nonskilled labor jobs. Some were very young women with no high school education or professions [2].

WHAT MOTIVATES A FEMALE SUICIDE BOMBER?

At first, scholars believed that what motivated women to become suicide bombers were factors related to their gender: They resented being religiously subordinated to men; they were frustrated with their sexual inequality; they remained unmarried into a late age, not succeeding in having children; they engaged in premarital sex or extramarital sex. Over time, however, other scholars determined that the same religious motivations that drove men to suicide bombing prompted a woman bomber as well.

Potential male suicide bombers are promised, for carrying out their suicide missions, a reward of 72 virgins waiting for them in heaven. But what are women suicide bombers offered? Very little is said on the subject. But a ninth-century scholar named Al-Tabarani noted that women would be reunited with their husbands upon arriving in heaven; those who had several husbands could choose the best one to be their eternal spouses. Other commentators decided that a woman who never married could marry any man in heaven [3]. Back in the ninth century, of course, no one was talking of women suicide bombers.

In the modern era, some women wanted to fight side by side with men. They sought ways to take part in the battles that men had traditionally fought on their own. But obstacles existed. Women who were part of ultraconservative patriarchic societies found it impossible to receive adequate personal training to take part in military battles involving only men. In such societies, it was taboo for a man to teach a woman military skills. The fundamentalist Islamic terror organizations, including Hamas, at first shunned female suicide bombers; but in time, Hamas came around and used women for suicide missions.

Suicide bombing was the one path open to women who wanted to take part

Palestinian female suicide bombers (2001–2004):

Wafa Idris, 28, January 27, 2002; one dead, 100 wounded

Dareen Abu Aisha, 21, February 27, 2002; four wounded

Ayet Al-Akhras, 18, March 29, 2002; two dead

Andalib Suleiman Takatka, 20, April 12, 2002; six dead

Hiba Daraghmeh, 19, May 19, 2003; three dead

Hanadi Jaradat, 29, October 4, 2003; 21 dead

Reem al-Riyashi, 22, January 14, 2004; four dead

Zaynab Abu Salem, 28, September 22, 2004; two dead

in fighting the enemy. Terrorist leaders had no trouble substituting female suicide bombers for males, as the men were freed for other, more complicated military tasks. Many female suicide bombers have some unfortunate personal event looming in their future, which they want to avoid: an arranged marriage, a father who refuses to let his daughter marry a boyfriend, the need to restore the family's honor. All of these events give the sponsors leverage to entice women.

Head of female suicide bomber, Zaynab Abu Salem, still wearing Arab headdress after she blew herself up in Jerusalem on September 22, 2004. (*Credit*: Gil Kleiman photo collection)

MALE VERSUS FEMALE SUICIDE BOMBERS

As the number of women volunteers for suicide missions grew, their sponsors were reluctant to have large numbers of them participate in suicide missions. The facilitators worried that their own patriarchic status could be threatened if too many women were let into the fold; the sponsors were also concerned that the use of women as suicide bombers would convey weakness on their part to other terrorist groups: that their men were not "man enough" to engage in suicide bombings.

THE STORY OF AYET AL-AKHRAS:
SHAME ON THE ARAB ARMIES

Suicide bomber Ayat Al-Akhras's detached torso after suicide bombing on Jerusalem supermarket on March 29, 2002. Shown are EMS technician, bomb tech, and two forensics officers. (*Credit*: Gil Kleiman photo collection)

Ayet Al-Akhras was an 18-year-old Palestinian woman, with dark eyes and long black hair. On a Friday, March 29, 2002, the day that Israel launched its military offensive, Operation Defensive Shield, against Palestinian suicide bombers and their sponsors, the young woman crossed over from the West Bank into Israel. It was easier for Ayet Al-Akhras to make the journey to Israel than it was for her male counterparts that day. The IDF typically limited the access of West Bank Palestinian males under age 40 to Jerusalem on Fridays, and especially enforced the rule on that day because it was the first day of the Israeli offensive.

60

On that Friday, Ayet Al-Akhras stood at the entrance to a Jerusalem supermarket and blew herself up, killing two and wounding 28. In a video she made that was released

"Shame on the Arab armies who are sitting and watching the girls of Palestine fight while they are asleep."

after the attack, she assailed Arab Muslim governments: "I say to the Arab leaders, stop sleeping. Stop failing to fulfill your duty. Shame on the Arab armies who are sitting and watching the girls of Palestine fight while they are asleep."

She was determined to carry out the mission, even when offered a last-minute chance to abort the action. With the bomb in a bag on the car floor at her feet, she listened as her driver suggested that she simply throw the bomb away, and dash for home. She demurred; "I'm not afraid. I want to kill people" [4].

One of the two people she killed was a 17-year-old Israeli woman named Rachel Levy. Her death prompted U.S. President George W. Bush to say: "When an 18-year-old Palestinian girl is induced to blow herself up and in the process kills a 17-year-old Israeli girl, the future itself is dying; the future of the Palestinian people and the future of the Israeli people" [5].

The true hero of the action was the Israeli security guard, Haim Smadar, who grew suspicious of Akhras after she warned two Arab women selling vegetables outside the supermarket entrance to leave. His suspicion led him to prevent Akhras from entering the supermarket, saving numerous lives. Smadar, however, was the second fatality.

Apparently what had motivated Akhras was an incident three weeks earlier when a stray IDF bullet hit her. That triggered her efforts to join a Palestinian terror organization. At first, Hamas spurned her, claiming it did not use women suicide bombers. However, the al-Aqsa Martyrs' Brigades, a group linked to the armed wing of Fatah, agreed to deploy her.

Ayet Al-Akhras was the third Palestinian woman to carry out a suicide bombing, even though she fit none of the usual stereotypes of a "typical" suicide bomber. She was not a man, not religious. Her family had not been estranged from her, nor had she joined any terror group.

She seemed to have everything to live for: She had emerged from the Deheishe Refugee Camp in Bethlehem, where she had grown up, with much hope on the horizon. Young, a straight-A student, engaged to be married the following July, she talked of becoming a news reporter. Underlying what motivated her, however, was her pregnancy at the time that she blew herself up; she may have carried out the mission to avoid tainting the reputation of her family.

61

THE STORY OF REEM RIYASHI: MOMMY, WHAT ARE YOU CARRYING IN YOUR ARMS?

Reem Riyashi was a mother of two, 22 years old on January 14, 2004, the day she blew herself up in a suicide bombing against Israeli soldiers at the Erez border crossing between Israel and the Gaza Strip.

Upon reaching the metal detector at the terminal, pretending to be crippled, she claimed to have metal plates in her leg, which would sound the alarm. Asking for a body search instead, she was taken to an area where soldiers and policemen were checking bags. She was told to wait for a woman who would search her in a cubicle. It was then that she detonated the explosive device, killing two Israeli soldiers, a policeman, and a civilian security worker. Seven other Israelis and four Palestinians were injured.

Two months later, a program, on the Hamas television channel, aimed at Palestinian children, portrayed four-year-old Duha (meant to be one of Riyashi's children) seated on a bed, watching her mother get dressed before leaving home. Her daughter sings, "Mommy, what are you carrying in your arms instead of me?" The program shows the evening news the next day with an answer for Duha: Her mother, carrying explosives in her arms, blew herself up, killing four Israelis.

In the final scene on the TV program, Duha searches through her mother's bedside table and finds a hidden dynamite stick. She picks it up with the not-so-subtle message that she will one day follow in her martyred mother's footsteps. The two-minute sketch was a reenactment of the life of Reem Riyashi.

Palestinians on the West Bank and in the Gaza Strip treated her as a heroine. But her motives were not political. Her husband had found out that she was having an affair with a senior Hamas commander, a crime punishable by death among conservative Palestinians. She was given the option of becoming a martyr.

A few hours before carrying out the suicide bombing, Riyashi, in a military-like uniform and holding an automatic rifle with a rocket-propelled grenade in the foreground, spoke into a video camera, noting that since the age of 13: "I have always wished to knock at the door of heaven after turning my body into deadly shrapnel against the Zionists" [1].

Now she sounded as if her motive was not personal at all, but politics. She looked upset, suggesting ambivalence about blowing herself up. Unlike other suicide bombers, Riyashi came from a family of wealth. The eighth Palestinian female suicide bomber, she was the second to have left behind children and the first female suicide bomber sent by Hamas after its spiritual leader, Sheikh Ahmed Yassin, had reversed himself and allowed women to engage in suicide bombings.

"I have always wished to knock at the door of heaven after turning my body into deadly shrapnel against the Zionists."

Hamas endured unprecedented, scathing criticism in the Palestinian media for turning a young mother into a suicide bomber and for publishing photographs of Riyashi posing with her children and weapons. One photo showed Riyashi's son clutching what appeared to be a mortar shell, wearing a Hamas headband; a second photo had Riyashi gazing at her children. Defending the decision to publish the photos, Hamas argued that the photos demonstrated the despair that Palestinian women felt and their wish to defeat the Israeli occupation.

THE STORY OF HANADI JARADAT:
A MOTIVE OF REVENGE

Maxim Restaurant (Haifa) suicide bomber Hanadi Jaradat prior to October 4, 2003, bombing. (*Credit*: From the video Jaradat made prior to the attack)

63

No one appeared less like a suicide bomber than Hanadi Jaradat. She was 29 years old, an attorney, and attractive. She did not seem desperate; she had not dishonored her family; she was an up-and-coming Palestinian woman with a great future in store for herself.

On October 4, 2003, she coolly walked into a restaurant in Haifa called Maxim's with 80 diners and blew herself up, killing 21 Israelis and wounding 60 others. It was one of the bloodiest of all Palestinian suicide bombings. Among the victims were two entire families, including four children, one a two-month-old baby. The bombing was one of the most shocking to Israelis: The target had been a popular hangout for Jewish and Arab Israelis. What made this incident unique was that, for the first time, a Palestinian suicide bomber had been a professional woman, not an average, uneducated woman.

At a certain point, Gil Kleiman took Mordecai Dzikansky, both of whom had raced to the scene, into the bombed-out restaurant to show him the bomber post-attack. The front portion of her head had been separated from her torso. The upper portion of her body was shattered and her legs were cut off below the pelvis.

Remains of Hanadi Jaradat moments after she blew herself up at the Maxim Restaurant. (*Credit*: Mordecai Dzikansky photo collection)

The Palestinian Islamic Jihad terrorist group claimed responsibility for the attack. The group aimed to destroy the State of Israel and replace it with a Palestinian Islamic state. Hanadi Jaradat had been only the sixth female suicide bomber in Palestinian history. Her motive was personal: revenge. In June 2003 the Israeli army had killed her younger brother and cousin, members of the Palestinian Islamic Jihad. Initially planning to attack Rambam hospital in Haifa, Jaradat discovered that security at the hospital entrance was too tight, so, sensing that security at the restaurant was weak, she changed her target to Maxim's.

Hanadi Jaradat's family had been supportive of her when she took a job at a law firm in Jenin after receiving her law degree from Jareesh University in Jordan. After her action at Maxim's, Palestinians, including her father, commended her for her "martyrdom" and portrayed her as a heroine.

It had been Jaradat's luck that Maxim's, a restaurant co-owned by Jewish and Arab Israelis, had a complete security breakdown that afternoon. The so-called security guard, who in fact had doubled as a waiter, was also responsible for the restaurant's security. He was not at the front entrance when Jaradat arrived. Thus, no one detected that she was carrying an explosive on her. If the waiter/"guard" had done his job properly, the bomber would have blown herself up outside; but even if he had been at the front entrance, it was unlikely that he would have thought an attractive, young Arab woman was suspicious.

Therefore she was able to enter the restaurant, eat an entire meal, visit the restroom, pay the bill, return to the table, and while still standing, blow herself up. Standing, rather than sitting, was important to suicide bombers; the metal fragments in her bomb were more likely to hit customers in their heads.

65

TECHNICAL ANALYSIS OF MAXIM
RESTAURANT SUICIDE BOMBING

Mordecai Dzikansky
NYPD

Date: October 4, 2003

Time: 14:15 hours

Location: Maxim Restaurant, Haifa. Approximately 80 people in the restaurant at the time of the explosion

Victims: 21 killed, 60 injured

Bomber's position at detonation: Bomber was standing toward the center of the restaurant facing front.

Camouflage: Vest, with explosive arranged around the bomber's waist area (covered by clothing)

Explosive material: High improvised explosive (urea nitrate); 13.2 pounds of explosives with various types of fragmentation that were arranged on the explosive sheet as a directional fragmentation charge

Explosive effect: Bomber's body—upper body shattered; legs severed below pelvis; front of severed head found intact

The fact that the bomber was standing while the majority of victims were sitting increased the impact of the fragmentation, causing many head wounds; in addition, the closed environment (windows and doors of the restaurant were closed at time of blast) caused further damage by the explosive material.

Over 100 fragmentation marks found throughout the restaurant and majority of windows shattered.

If Hanadi Jaradat caught the world's attention for a few days during October 2003, that attention was fleeting compared to the world's reaction to an event that had happened two years earlier, an event that we focus on in the next two chapters. It was that event that changed the way the world looked at suicide bombers.

NOTES

1. Tim McGirk, "Palestinian Moms Becoming Martyrs," *Time*, May 3, 2007, http://www.time.com/time/magazine/article/0,9171,1617542,00.html.
2. Yoram Schweitzer, "Palestinian Female Suicide Bombers: Reality vs. Myth," in *Female Suicide Bombers: Dying for Equality*, ed. Yoram Schweitzer (Tel Aviv, Israel: JCSS, Tel Aviv University), 25–42, http://www.gees.org/documentos/Documen-01398.pdf.
3. Michelle Tsai, "Honey, I'm dead!" *Slate Magazine*, March 29, 2010, http://www.slate.com/id/2249122/.
4. James Bennet, "Mideast Turmoil: Violence; In Suicide Bombings, the Taxi Man Got Away," *New York Times*, June 13, 2002, http://www.nytimes.com/2002/06/13/world/mideast-turmoil-violence-in-suicide-bombings-the-taxi-man-got-away.html?src=pm.
5. "How Two Lives Met in Death," *Newsweek*, April 15, 2002, http://www.newsweek.com/2002/04/14/how-two-lives-met-in-death.html.

Section III

Evaluating Suicide Bombing

6

9/11 1

The Worst Suicide Bombing Ever

It happened on one of those beautiful late-summer days in 2001: temperatures in the 70s, blue skies, humidity lower than usual, a Tuesday almost midway through September when New Yorkers were adjusting to being back to work after recent summer vacations. In many ways it seemed like a fairly routine day. But nothing that was about to happen was routine.

Until that day, Americans—New Yorkers included—had put suicide bombing and other forms of terror on the back burner, even after the mega bombing of the Alfred P. Murrah Federal Building in downtown Oklahoma City nearly six and a half years earlier on April 19, 1995. Then, Timothy McVeigh, a sympathizer of American militia movements, detonated a bomb-filled truck parked in front of the Murrah Building. McVeigh's partner was Terry Nichols, who assisted in the preparation of the bomb.

Because there was no global radical Islamist component, Americans considered this attack an isolated event that would not spread to other major American cities. The Oklahoma City attack, which killed 168, including 19 children under age 6, and wounded another 680, was the worst terror act on American soil until this balmy September morning.

71

TERROR IN AMERICA UNIMAGINABLE

New York City had suffered terrorism in the 1990s that had an international flavor, but law enforcement treated these as isolated, nonrepeating events. And certainly few members of American intelligence believed that terrorists could pull off a mega event despite the fact that Oklahoma City showed it could be done.

For most American intelligence and law enforcement officials, Islam-centered terrorism was something that happened far away and was of no concern to the United States. According to Lawrence Wright, in his Pulitzer Prize–winning book, *The Looming Tower*, only one FBI man, John P. O'Neill, recognized that the nature of terrorism was changing, that it had gone international and turned to murder [1].

Terror in the United State had been largely domestic: Its main instigators were the Ku Klux Klan, the Black Panthers, and the Jewish Defense League. During the 1970s and early 1980s, one group, the Fuerzaz Armadas de Liberacion Nacional (FALN), supporting Puerto Rican independence, had carried out 150 terror acts, but it had not committed deliberate murder. Radical Islamists had an agenda that included large-scale murder. Only O'Neill understood the size of their operation and that they already had placed activists inside the United States. And he was the first to recognize Osama bin Laden as the leader of a global terror network and his dream of destroying the United States and the West.

Still skeptical that radical Islamists could hurt Americans on their own soil, most American government and military leaders were shocked on that infamous morning of September 11, 2001, when the worst suicide bombing in human history occurred, an event of such magnitude and significance that it turned long-entrenched American political and military perceptions on their heads. Stunning America and the world because of its wicked brutality, the attacks against high-profile American targets—the World Trade Center; the Pentagon, and apparently either the Capitol or the White House—found the United States largely unprepared for this new kind of warfare.

It was impossible to sense at the time of 9/11, but that single event, among the many other things that it changed, had a significant impact upon the phenomenon of suicide bombing for the next decade. Inspired by the unimaginable results of 9/11, terrorists in various parts of Western Europe and the Middle East turned to suicide bombing with a new enthusiasm as their weapon of choice.

Public facilities in European cities, North Africa, and Russia became targets of terror, including suicide bombings: Madrid, London (twice),

Casablanca, Istanbul, and Moscow (three times). From what we have learned of the planning behind these incidents, none thought of duplicating 9/11; none sought to undertake a mega suicide bombing that came close to killing the same number (3,214) as those cut down on 9/11.

Until 9/11, the United States and other Western nations had taken for granted that their enemies would be nation states and that wars would be fought using infantry, tanks, missiles, and fighter planes. It was assumed as well that enemies would be easily identifiable and located. The events of September 11, 2001, challenged those assumptions.

The purpose of this chapter is to focus not only on 9/11, but to explain as well how that single event set America on a new path in a war against terror. With 9/11, the United States confronted as its enemy an extremist Islamist terrorist organization named al-Qaeda (Arabic for "the base"), a faceless, stateless, amorphous assemblage that emulated the suicide bombing tactics of Hezbollah, a Lebanese-based terrorist group, and was emulated by Palestinian terror groups such as the Palestinian Hamas organization. In American intelligence circles, little was known of al-Qaeda. Indeed, when presidential candidates George W. Bush and Al Gore held their debates in the fall of 2000, the names Osama bin Laden and al-Qaeda were not mentioned.

World Trade Center in New York City prior to suicide bomber attacks on September 11, 2001. (*Credit*: Israel Government Press Office)

For America on that September morning, there was the initial numbing shock, then the fear that the attacks would produce a far higher death toll than that other mass murder on American soil: the December 7, 1941, Japanese assault on the U.S. naval base at Pearl Harbor that killed 2,402 Americans. Until 2001, the attack on Pearl Harbor had been the worst foreign assault on American soil; it brought the United States into World War Two.

Americans did not imagine that terrorists in 2001 would deploy commercial airliners as weapons of mass destruction. Until then, terrorists had hijacked commercial airplanes in order to bargain for the release of imprisoned colleagues; but they had shown no desire to die by crashing a plane into a high-profile American target.

CHAIN OF EVENTS

The horrific chain of events began at 6:00 a.m., when Mohamed Atta, the ringleader of the 19 hijackers, and a second hijacker, Abdulaziz al-Omari, boarded a Colgan Air flight from Portland International Jetport in Portland, Maine, to Logan International Airport in Boston.

Early in September, Atta had gone to Boston, where he had picked up al-Omari, an airport security guard and imam, who joined the hijacking plot. Al-Omari was one of the five hijackers who would board American Airlines flight 11 in a few hours. Atta and al-Omari drove a rented car from Boston to the Comfort Inn in Portland, Maine, spending the night there. They made two ATM withdrawals and shopped at Wal-Mart.

Atta and al-Omari arrived at the Portland International Jetport at 5:43 a.m. on September 11. Later, after the September 11 attacks, a journalist viewed the surveillance camera photos of Atta moving swiftly through security at the Portland Airport; the journalist suggested that the Pulitzer Prize for news photography go to the hidden camera. The photos were "riveting for their grainy banality, and for what they say about the duality in all of us. Here were ordinary-looking people engaged in ordinary-looking activities, indistinguishable from any of us, with dreadful secrets in their heads" [2].

"Here were ordinary-looking people engaged in ordinary-looking activities, indistinguishable from any of us, with dreadful secrets in their heads."

Atta and al-Omari's Portland plane arrived at Boston at 6:45 a.m. Seven minutes later, Marwan al-Shehhi, another hijacker, phoned Atta from another terminal at Logan to confirm that the attacks were about to start. Atta answered in the affirmative.

Checking in for Flight 11, Atta went through security again and, at 7:35 a.m., took a business-class seat on the flight, a Boeing 767 with 81 passengers plus 11 crewmembers headed for Los Angeles International Airport. Five minutes later, three other hijackers boarded the plane. It departed Logan at 7:59 a.m. Because Atta's flight from Portland to Boston had been delayed, his luggage did not get on Flight 11.

Fourteen minutes later (8:13 a.m.), Flight 11 had its final routine communication with the air traffic control center of the Federal Aviation Authority (FAA) in Boston. The plane failed to heed the air traffic controller's instruction to climb to 35,000 feet. A minute later, at 8:14 a.m., United Airlines Flight 175, a Boeing 767 with 56 passengers, including five hijackers and nine crewmembers aboard, departed from Boston's Logan International Airport, also bound for Los Angeles International Airport.

While beverages were being served aboard Flight 11 at 8:14 a.m., Atta and his fellow hijackers went into action. Ground controllers lost voice contact with the pilot, and thus could not tell that the plane had been rerouted and was heading for New York City.

At 8:19 a.m., a flight attendant aboard Flight 11 named Betty Ong, using an air phone, alerted American Airlines to alarming news: "The cockpit is not answering. Somebody's been stabbed in business class—and I think there's Mace—that we can't breathe—I don't know, I think we're getting hijacked." She then reported on two flight attendants being stabbed. Hearing the news, FAA Boston Center flight controllers concluded that Flight 11 had probably been hijacked.

> "The cockpit is not answering, somebody's been stabbed in business class—and I think there's Mace—that we can't breathe—I don't know, I think we're getting hijacked."

One minute later, at 8:20 a.m., American Airlines Flight 77, a Boeing 757 with 58 passengers, including five hijackers and six crewmembers, departed Washington Dulles International Airport, also bound for Los Angeles International Airport.

A minute later, at 8:21 a.m., Flight 11's transponder signal was turned off. Still the plane remained on radar screens as a blip, with no one in authority receiving further additional information. Three minutes later, at 8:24 a.m., the plane made a 100-degree turn to the south, heading toward New York City. A radio transmission came from Flight 11: "We have some planes. Just stay quiet, and you'll be okay. We are returning to the airport." A few seconds later, Atta was heard to say: "Nobody move. Everything will be OK. If you try to make any moves, you'll endanger yourself and the airplane. Just

> "Just stay quiet, and you'll be okay. We are returning to the airport."

stay quiet. We are going back to the airport. Don't try to make any stupid moves" [3].

At 8:40 a.m., the FAA notified the Northeast Air Defense Sector of the North American Aerospace Defense Command (NORAD) of the suspected hijacking of American Airlines Flight 11. Two minutes later, at 8:42 a.m., United Airlines Flight 93, a Boeing 757 with 37 passengers, including four hijackers and seven crewmembers, departed from Newark International Airport bound for San Francisco International Airport.

A minute later, at 8:43 a.m., the FAA notified NORAD's Northeast Air Defense Sector of another suspected hijacking, this one of United Airlines Flight 175 headed for Los Angeles.

One minute later, at 8:44 a.m., flight attendant Amy Sweeney, aboard Flight 11, reported to American Airlines in Boston: "Something is wrong. We are in a rapid descent...we are all over the place" [4]. A minute later, asked to describe what she saw outside the window, she replied: "I see the water. I see the buildings. I see buildings." After a short pause, she reported, "We are flying low. We are flying very, very low. We are flying way too low." Seconds later she said, "Oh my God, we are way too low." The call ended with a burst of very loud, sustained static.

At the same time, at 8:45 a.m., American Airlines Flight 11, traveling at 490 miles an hour, crashed into the North Tower of New York City's World Trade Center between the 93rd and 99th floors. People below the floors where the plane impacted began to evacuate; no one above the impact zone could do the same. Smoke was too dense for an airborne evacuation. An estimated 100 to 250 people, trapped by fire and smoke on the upper floors, leapt or were sucked out of the building.

For those who witnessed the plane plowing into the 110-story North Tower, and for those who soon heard about the plane, the first thought was: This must be a terrible accident. Many undoubtedly recalled a seemingly similar event on July 28, 1945, when a B-25 bomber, flying in thick fog, crashed into New York City's Empire State Building between the 79th and 80th floors, killing 14 people.

Yet, on this day, the weather was clear and it was unimaginable that a seasoned pilot flying a Boeing 767 commercial airliner would even accidentally fly a plane into a New York skyscraper. Even the president of the United States, George W. Bush, and his immediate staff assumed, upon hearing the news, that this was some kind of horrible accident. Thus it was that the day began in confusion and bewilderment for just about every American.

Two minutes after the crash, at 8:48 a.m., WNYW, a local New York television station, broke into a trailer for the movie *Zoolander* with the first live TV pictures of black smoke emerging from the North Tower, relayed to the station by a WNYW cameraman on the street to cover New York's mayoral primary election. A minute later, at 8:49 a.m., CNN informed the world of the "World Trade Center disaster."

THE PRESIDENT'S INITIAL RESPONSES

Nothing illustrated the confusion and bewilderment that Americans felt that September morning more than the way that President Bush faced the day in those early morning hours. Browsing the newspapers over a light breakfast in his suite at the Colony Beach and Tennis Resort near Sarasota, Florida, Bush recalled later that one headline was about the New York mayoral primary; another was about a suspected case of mad cow disease in Japan.

At 8 a.m. he received the daily presidential intelligence briefing that focused on the Palestinian uprising on the West Bank, Russia, and China—in other words, nothing earthshaking. He then left for a visit to an elementary school where he would watch children do reading drills—as relaxing a morning as he could imagine.

As the president walked from his car to the classroom, his chief policy adviser, Karl Rove, told the president that an airplane had crashed into the World Trade Center. Bush responded passively: "Get more details." The president found the news strange but hardly shocking; he assumed that a small propeller plane had gotten terribly lost.

Once inside the school, the president heard on a secure phone from his national security adviser, Condoleezza Rice, that the plane that had crashed into the building had been a commercial airliner. The president asked himself how a trained pilot could fly into a skyscraper on a clear day. Perhaps he had suffered a mid-air heart attack. Bush told Dan Bartlett, his communications director, to draft a statement promising the full support of federal emergency management services.

Unbeknownst to Bush and most others, a second plane had been hijacked, at 8:52 a.m., United Flight 175; its passengers, including Peter Hanson, were frantically trying to understand what was happening. Hanson phoned his father Lee: "I think they've taken over the cockpit— an attendant has been stabbed—and someone else up front may have been killed. The plane is making strange moves" [5].

In a second phone call to his father, Hanson noted that "it's getting bad, Dad. They seem to have knives and Mace. They said they have a bomb. Passengers are throwing up and getting sick. The plane is making jerky movements. I think we are going down. I think they intend to go to Chicago or someplace and fly into a building. Don't worry, Dad. If it happens, it'll be very fast. My God, my God." With a woman screaming in the background, the call ended abruptly. A few minutes later, at 9:03 a.m., Flight 175, traveling at 590 miles an hour, crashed into the South Tower of the World Trade Center between the 77th and 85th floors.

"A second plane hit the second tower. America is under attack."

With the news still vague, the president sat down in a room full of second-graders, who proceeded with a reading drill. Approaching the president, Andrew Card, his chief of staff, whispered in his ear: "A second plane hit the second tower. America is under attack."

CBS News reported at 9:17 a.m., for the first time, that the American intelligence community had named al-Qaeda leader Osama bin Laden as a probable suspect in the day's dreadful events.

Six minutes later, Flight 93 received a warning message text from a United Airlines flight dispatcher: "Beware any cockpit intrusion—two a/c [aircraft] hit World Trade Center." Just five minutes later, at 9:28 a.m., the four hijackers aboard that flight commandeered the plane, hoping to crash it into the Capitol or perhaps the White House.

Enraged by the attacks, Bush vowed to himself that the perpetrators would pay. But he realized that he could not just bolt the classroom in panic, hardly the message he wanted journalists in the back of the classroom to communicate to the world. He continued to listen to the reading lesson. His mind began racing with questions that he would have to ask—and answer—urgently: Who did this? How bad were the casualties? What should his government do?

Bush's press secretary, Ari Fleischer, shrewdly placing himself between the journalists and Bush, held up a sign for the president to see: "Don't say anything yet." Agreeing, the president decided that he would leave the classroom calmly without saying a word to the reporters. Reaching a nearby room with his staff, Bush watched the replayed slow-motion television footage of the second plane hitting the South Tower. "We're at war," Bush said calmly. "Get me the director of the FBI and the vice president." He then read a statement to reporters: "Ladies and gentlemen, this is a difficult moment for America.... Two airplanes have crashed into the World Trade Center in an apparent terrorist attack on our country. Terrorism against our nation will not stand."

Leaving the school at 9:35 a.m., Bush did not know that two minutes later, American Airlines Flight 77 had crashed into the western side of the Pentagon, starting an immense fire, striking a section that consisted mostly of newly renovated, unoccupied offices. All 64 people on board the plane were killed along with 125 Pentagon personnel; another 106 were wounded. It was the first time since the War of 1812 that an enemy had struck at the American capitol.

On CNN at 9:30 a.m., an announcer was speculating that pilot error was unlikely and that a high probability existed that the crashing planes had been terror attacks. Meanwhile, thick black and gray smoke enveloped the Towers. At 9:45 a.m., Secretary of Transportation Norman Mineta ordered all civilian aircraft out of the sky at once.

While driving back to *Air Force One*, Bush listened over a secure phone as Rice told him that a third plane had crashed into the Pentagon. Bush wrote in his memoirs, *Decision Points*: "The first plane could have been an accident. The second was definitely an attack. The third was a declaration of war" [6]. He did not reveal his innermost thoughts at that moment, but years later he wrote: "My blood was boiling. We were going to find out who did this, and kick their ass."

> "The first plane could have been an accident. The second was definitely an attack. The third was a declaration of war."

While the president was heading to *Air Force One*, two events occurred at 9:45 a.m.: An operator received a cell phone call from a United Airlines Flight 93 passenger who reported that the flight had been hijacked and that the passengers were going to fight back. In a radio transmission from the plane overheard by Cleveland flight controllers, someone said: "Keep remaining sitting. We have a bomb on board."

The FAA ordered all airborne aircraft over 4,500 feet in the air to land at the nearest airport. Three minutes later, at 9:48 a.m., the White House's West Wing and the U.S. Capitol were evacuated. At 9:55 a.m., the first scrambled jet fighters reached the Washington, D.C., area.

Arriving at *Air Force One*, Bush noticed that his Secret Service agents had already assumed a wartime stance, brandishing assault rifles while surrounding the plane. He hugged two flight attendants and assured them everything would be all right. Everyone was told to board immediately and did so in a record 10 minutes. Upon boarding, the president declared, "Gentlemen, we're at war." (Later, Bush would tell Karl Rove that he knew instinctively that the attacks were a defining moment in American history. "I didn't need any legal briefs. I didn't need any consultations. I knew we were at war" [7].

Fear permeated everyone charged with protecting the president. At 9:57 a.m., under Secret Service instructions, the pilot rolled down the runway faster than usual and ascended as fast as possible to get out of range. At first the president's plane flew aimlessly, but at 10:15 a.m. it headed for a secret destination with fighter escorts visible outside. That destination, it was revealed later, was Barksdale Air Force base near Shreveport, Louisiana. The plane eventually reached 45,000 feet, far higher than on a routine flight. The Secret Service feared that terrorists might use shoulder-launched ground-to-air missiles to bring *Air Force One* down.

"I didn't need any legal briefs. I didn't need any consultations. I knew we were at war."

Meanwhile, the president gave his first order that day to Vice President Dick Cheney, who had been whisked to the underground Presidential Emergency Operations Center after the Secret Service feared that a plane might be heading for the White House.

The president's order was that all pilots in the newly dispatched combat air patrols were to contact any suspicious planes around New York and Washington, D.C., and try to get them to land peacefully. If the planes remained airborne, Bush told the vice president to instruct the military to shoot them down.

THE TOWERS COLLAPSE

Meanwhile, two minutes after *Air Force One* had taken off, at 9:59 a.m., the South Tower of the World Trade Center collapsed, destroying any hope that trapped people on the upper floors might have been saved.

At 10:07 a.m., United Airlines Flight 93 crashed to the ground in Pennsylvania. One hijacker, Ziad Jarrah, a trained pilot, had taken control of the aircraft and diverted it toward Washington, D.C. Using their cell phones, a few passengers and crewmembers learned about the planes that had crashed into the World Trade Center and the Pentagon. Fearing their plane too would soon crash, passengers mounted an assault against the hijackers, but a few minutes later the plane crashed in a field near Shanksville, Pennsylvania, 80 miles southeast of Pittsburgh and 150 miles northwest of Washington, D.C., killing all passengers, including the four hijackers.

The news grew grimmer. At 10:28 a.m., the North Tower of the Word Trade Center collapsed, carried live on television. Bush wanted to return to Washington, D.C., to reassure the nation that he was indeed leading the response to the attacks and to demonstrate that he was not going to let the terrorists frighten him; but Andy Card and the Secret Service insisted that the nation's capitol was still too vulnerable to attack. Though Bush ranted at Card, "I am the president," Card and the Secret Service felt palpable concern that the attacks that morning were a prelude to a full-scale attack on American government leaders, especially the president of the United States. They tried to delay the president's return to Washington, D.C., for as long as possible.

Their concern intensified when it was reported (erroneously) that another three hijacked planes were in the air besides the four that had already crashed. Reports came in—all of which eventually proved false— that *Air Force One* was under threat, as was the president's ranch in Crawford, Texas; and that a hijacked Korean airliner was bound for the United States.

It seemed remarkable that in 2001 the security services of the mightiest nation in the world could not guarantee getting the president of the United States from somewhere in the United States to the White House safely. But that was precisely what Andrew Card was telling the president, and Bush decided to relent—for a while.

THE PERPETRATORS: OSAMA BIN LADEN AND AL-QAEDA

It would take a few hours for people to fathom the audacity of the attack, the scope of the tragedy, and the implications of this day for America. That first plane (American Airlines 11) crashing into the North Tower was no accident; it was the start of a series of coordinated attacks upon the United States planned and carried out by al-Qaeda terrorists.

Early estimates of fatalities at the towers put the number disturbingly at 50,000, because that was the number of people who worked in the towers on a typical day; but, since the attacks came early in the morning, those inside the buildings numbered "only" 14,000. New Yorkers were in a state of panic. Even those who were near the targeted area could not tell what was happening. Not only was there concern over who had died and been injured, but fear of more attacks coursed through every New Yorker's mind that morning.

It seemed a mundane point at the time, but at 10:30 a.m., New York's primary elections were postponed. Paradoxically, at 10:56 a.m., Palestinian leader Yasser Arafat, a notorious organizer of terrorist activity, offered the United States his condolences for the day's events. Four minutes later, at 11 a.m., New York mayor Rudy Giuliani ordered the evacuation of lower Manhattan south of Canal Street. At 11:04 a.m. the United Nations was evacuated.

The 57-year-old mayor of New York City had been in office since 1994 and was due to leave office in a few months. He provided such a visibly calming role on radio and television during that day that he stood out from other leaders who failed to step forward to reassure the nation. Giuliani provided the one consoling voice. "Tomorrow New York is going to be here," he said, "and we're going to rebuild, and we're going to be stronger than we were before.… I want the people of New York to be an example to the rest of the country, and the rest of the world, that terrorism can't stop us" [8].

At 11: 44 a.m., *Air Force One* approached Barksdale Air Force Base in Louisiana. Meanwhile, a Shreveport, Louisiana, television station showed the plane in the air preparing to land with fighter escorts surrounding it. The Secret Service became even more concerned, but, as Karl Rove noted later, it seemed unlikely that a terrorist cell in northwest Louisiana was about to launch surface-to-air missiles at the plane.

Once at Barksdale, the president phoned Defense Secretary Donald Rumsfeld to say that he approved of his decision to raise the military readiness level to DefCon Three—the first time that had been done since the 1973 October War between Israel and the Arabs. All American military bases around the world increased security preparations. Bush also gave Rumsfeld an order to start preparing for a military response, though at that moment it was still not clear against whom the United States would respond.

Meanwhile, Los Angeles International Airport, destination of three of the hijacked planes, was shut down and evacuated, as was San Francisco International Airport, destination of United Airlines Flight 93. By 12:30 p.m., only 50 flights remained airborne over American skies.

Again, the president felt a need to speak to the American people. By now he knew how confused the media, air traffic controllers, and the general public had become. News organizations broadcast unconfirmed and often contradictory reports. One of the most widely spread reports was that a car bomb had been detonated at the State Department. Soon after reporting on the Pentagon crash, some news media also briefly reported that a fire had broken out on the National Mall. Yet another erroneous report, from the Associated Press, had it that a Delta Air Lines airliner—Flight 189—had been hijacked.

ATTACKED BY A FACELESS COWARD

The president wanted to calm everyone's frayed nerves, so in his message he declared that the government was responding and that the nation would meet the challenge:

> Freedom itself was attacked this morning by a faceless coward. And freedom will be defended. I want to reassure the American people that the full resources of the federal government are working to assist local authorities to save lives and to help the victims of these attacks. Make no mistake, the United States will hunt down and punish those responsible for these cowardly acts. We have taken all appropriate security precautions to protect the American people. The resolve of our great nation is being tested, but make no mistake. We will show the world that we will pass this test. [9]

Albeit on a much smaller scale, the uncertainty and confusion that occurred in the immediate aftermath of 9/11 occurs at every suicide bombing. Even though the attacks occurred in New York City, Washington, D.C., and Pennsylvania, Americans in California, Nebraska, and everywhere else in the United States felt threatened.

In the next chapter we continue our description of the worst suicide bombing ever.

NOTES

1. Lawrence Wright, *The Looming Tower: Al-Qaeda and the Road to 9/11* (New York: Alfred A. Knopf, 2007), 208.
2. Gene Weingarten, "Fear Itself: Learning to Live in the Age of Terrorism," *Washington Post*, August 22, 2004, W18.
3. National Commission on Terrorist Attacks upon the United States, "We Have Some Planes" in *9/11 Commission Report* (New York: W.W. Norton, 2004), 6, http://www.9-11commission.gov/report/911Report_Ch1.pdf.
4. BBC News, "Extract: 'We have some planes,'" July 23, 2004, http://news.bbc.co.uk/2/hi/americas/3919613.stm.
5. National Commission on Terrorist Attacks upon the United States, "We Have Some Planes" in *9/11 Commission Report* (New York: W.W. Norton, 2004), 7–8, http://www.9-11commission.gov/report/911Report_Ch1.pdf.
6. George Bush, *Decision Points* (New York: Crown, 2010), 128.
7. *Sixty Minutes*, September 10, 2009. "The President's Story." http://www.cbsnews.com/stories/2002/09/11/60II/main521718.shtml.
8. Eric Pooley, "Mayor of the World," *Time*, December 31, 2001, http://www.time.com/time/poy2001/poyprofile.html.
9. http://www.youtube.com/watch?v=TVM=6Z8113U.

7

9/11 II
More than We Can Bear

The president yearned to return to Washington, D.C., but his aides thought he would be better off going to the strategic command at Offutt Air Force Base in Nebraska, which could house him and his staff safely and where the communications would be better than what existed on *Air Force One*. With the fear of an attack on the presidential plane still very much alive, extra food and water were taken on board.

At 2:39 p.m., New York City's mayor Rudy Giuliani was asked to estimate the number of casualties at the World Trade Center. "More than any of us can bear," was his reply.

Asked to estimate the number of casualties, Mayor Rudy Giuliani said: "More than any of us can bear."

No sooner had Bush arrived at Offutt at 3:07 p.m. than he received word from a high-ranking military official that an unresponsive plane was coming in from Madrid. Would the military shoot down the plane? "When is this going to end?" the president asked himself. Once it was certain that the plane had not been hijacked, the president was determined to leave Offutt for Washington, D.C. He wanted to speak to the nation again, but not from an underground bunker in Nebraska.

Bush returned to Washington at 6:35 p.m. While the president and his staff prepared additional remarks for an evening message to the nation, Karl Rove sought out information on how many had died in the attacks. Thousands, he was told by a New York City official, not tens of thousands as had been originally feared. Bush entered the phrase "thousands of lives" into the president's remarks at the last minute.

For Mordecai Dzikansky, at that time a New York Police Department homicide detective whose area of responsibility was Manhattan South—the heart of Ground Zero—that Tuesday morning started off as just another routine day. But there was nothing routine about the panicked voice message that his wife Meryl, phoning from near the World Trade Center, left on their home answering machine at 9 a.m. assuring her husband that she was okay; she was traumatized but physically unharmed; she had just witnessed—from the tenth floor of the World Financial Center, where she worked as a Lehman Brothers vice president—a large plane smashing into the North Tower near the top floors. Had this been pilot error or a terror attack? Neither she nor anyone else could know for sure at that moment.

By midday, Mordecai Dzikansky had reached New York City from his Long Island home, had joined other police officers near the scene, and had observed the aftermath of the morning's disaster up close:

> I looked down toward where the World Trade Center had stood only a few hours earlier. Clouds of smoke and confetti-like paper swirled around the skies, giving the appearance of snow. But snow falls downward; this "confetti" was circulating through the air. It was an eerie, almost supernatural site. I was staring into a complete haze. [1]

At first, Dzikansky was asked to follow up on incoming tips from citizens that might lead to information related to those responsible for 9/11. Later that day he was assigned to Ground Zero. It was only after 10 p.m. that same day that Dzikansky, along with four other homicide detectives, arrived at the site to check a few things out at their commander's request. This is what he saw:

> The air was filled with grayish smoke, water had accumulated on parts of the street, whether from fire hoses or from the towers themselves. The scene could have come out of a horror film. As we got closer, we stared in utter disbelief: before us was overwhelming devastation. We saw crushed fire trucks and police cars that looked like Tonka toys. The ground was covered in soot and ash. The Towers had been reduced to jagged steel girders. First responders, covered with white soot, searched and dug for survivors. The only lighting was from emergency generators, which contributed to the otherworldly nature of the scene. None of us could speak. It was all so hard to digest. An eerie calm prevailed.

"We saw crushed fire trucks and police cars that looked like Tonka toys. The ground was covered in soot and ash. The Towers had been reduced to jagged steel girders."

86

Some of Dzikansky's police colleagues had been at the World Trade Center attack seven and a half years earlier on February 26, 1993, when a truck bomb exploded below the North Tower of the World Trade Center. The terrorists' goal was to knock the North Tower into the South Tower, causing them both to fall. They hoped to kill 250,000 people. The attack, however, killed six people and wounded another 1,042. The number of dead was small, but the number of wounded was the largest number of hospitalized casualties in the United States since the Civil War.

In that 1993 attack, terrorist bomb maker Ramzi Yousef had entered the World Trade Center's huge basement parking garage in a rented Ford Econoline van. It was unclear if Osama bin Laden had sent him, but Yousef had trained at an al-Qaeda camp in Afghanistan, where he had learned bomb making. Yousef's improvised explosive device (IED), complete with four 20-foot-long fuses, was the largest IED the FBI had ever come upon. To increase casualties, Yousef added sodium cyanide to ammonium nitrate and fuel oil (ANFO). After lighting the fuses, Yousef escaped to a spot north of Canal Street to watch the Twin Towers fall. But the Towers did not fall.

Yousef's mother was Palestinian; his father Pakistani. Yousef had grown up in Kuwait City, and then studied electrical engineering in Wales. For him, the Palestinian cause meant more than religion. Ramzi Yousef was the first Islamist terrorist to attack American soil.

To Mordecai Dzikansky's colleagues who remembered that 1993 event, the September 11th attack was déjà vu, a nightmare magnified a thousand times beyond that previous event because of its likely death toll. A young policeman took Dzikansky and the other detectives to a spot where a plane engine lay on the ground, then to another location where a torso lay on the same ground, someone's upper body with the head nowhere in sight. The torso had breasts. Dzikansky and his colleagues thought the woman might have been on one of the two planes that had left Boston that morning and crashed into one of the Towers, because she had a label from a Boston store on her sweater.

Unlike a normal crime scene, limited in scope and relatively easy to control, in the wreckage of the Twin Towers, Dzikansky understood that New Yorkers were confronting the most appalling crime scene in American history, worse even than most battlefields. Indeed, the place resembled a battlefield more than a crime scene.

It would take months to go through the rubble at what would soon be termed Ground Zero, the site of the World Trade Center. At 2 a.m., ready to leave the site and head home, Dzikansky wondered how police business would change. For one thing, he understood now what the term "crime against humanity" meant. The suicide bombers who carried out 9/11 were ruthless killers whose radical Islamic ideology inspired them to believe that nonbelievers such as Jews and Christians, because they were "infidels," did not deserve to live. Dzikansky sensed that all Americans, New Yorkers included, would have to give suicide bombing and terror in general a new priority.

FINDING THE 9/11 PERPETRATORS

As the rescue and recovery missions continued over the next few days, American intelligence agencies began the urgent task of discovering who had been behind the attacks. For a number of reasons, they focused on radical Islamists: the scale of the attack, the attempt to kill as many Americans as possible, and the high-profile targets selected.

Assigning a record 7,000 agents to the case, the FBI came up with the names of the 19 suspected hijackers. The more intelligence agents probed, the more they realized that their stereotypical images of would-be suicide bombings were outdated: young men in their 20s, hardly educated, poverty-stricken, and fanatical. Yes, the 19 suicide bombers were fanatical, but the other stereotypes did not hold true: Some hijackers had been in their thirties, were quite educated (seven were pilots), and some had come from middle-class backgrounds. The ringleader of the 19 suicide bombers was Egyptian-born Mohamed Atta, one of the pilots. He died in the attack aboard American Airlines Flight 11, the first plane to crash into the World Trade Center's North Tower.

THE MASTERMIND

It took only until midday September 11 for the U.S. National Security Agency to intercept communications that suggested strongly that Osama bin Laden, the 44-year-old member of a prominent Saudi Arabian family and founder of al-Qaeda, had masterminded the attacks.

Al-Qaeda's beginnings went back to 1979, when the Soviet Union attacked Afghanistan. Soon thereafter, bin Laden helped to organize resistance to the Soviets, receiving American and Saudi financial support.

After the Soviets withdrew from Afghanistan in 1989, bin Laden became more radical. He objected strongly to American support for Israel and America's continued military presence in Saudi Arabia. Bin Laden's name had arisen in intelligence circles for the first time in 1993; he was described then as a Saudi prince who supported radical Islamists who planned to blow up New York City landmarks. No one within the U.S. intelligence community thought he constituted a serious threat to America.

While American intelligence clung to that view, bin Laden was busy gaining followers from various countries with his vague message that the "infidels" should be destroyed. Al-Qaeda seemed to have little desire to capture territory or replace governments. It exploited regional conflicts to recruit local volunteers, convincing those volunteers that their struggle was not only local; it was global as well—and that they should help al-Qaeda in its struggle against the "infidels."

Bin Laden had been thrown out of Saudi Arabia after he had opposed the Saudi decision taken during the 1991 Gulf War to permit American troops to be stationed on Saudi soil. He relocated to Pakistan.

In the early 1990s bin Laden possessed more ideology than expertise in carrying out actionable plans. He wanted to attack an American Embassy but needed expert advice on how to do it. Thinking back to Hezbollah's mega terror attack against the U.S. Marine barracks in 1983, he contacted Hezbollah leaders despite their religious differences with al-Qaeda (Hezbollah was Shiite while al-Qaeda was Sunni). Hezbollah representatives took the al-Qaeda operatives step by step through planning and implementing suicide bombing attacks against embassies and other targets.

In 1996, the man who came up with the idea of 9/11 approached Osama bin Laden with a plan to hijack planes and crash them into American landmarks. His name is Khalid Sheikh Mohammed. At the time, the 32 year-old Mohammed led al-Qaeda's propaganda department. The uncle of Ramzi Yousef, Mohammed had little in common with Osama bin Laden other than a hatred for America. As one al-Qaeda historian put it:

> Mohammed was short and squat; pious but poorly trained in religion; an actor and a cutup; a drinker and a womanizer. Whereas bin Laden was provincial and hated travel, especially in the West. Mohammed was a globe-trotter fluent in several languages, including English, which he perfected while studying mechanical engineering at North Carolina Agricultural and Technical State University, a mostly black school in Greensboro. [2]

In 1994, while together in the Philippines, Mohammed and Yousef began planning to bomb 12 American jumbo jets over the Pacific. Yousef believed he had come up with the perfect bomb: a small nitroglycerine device that airport security would not detect. Meanwhile, bin Laden had other targets in mind: He asked Yousef to assassinate Bill Clinton in November 1994 when the President would be in Manila, but Yousef thought the security was too tight and convinced bin Laden to scrub the idea. When it was announced that Pope John Paul II would visit Manila the next month, Yousef thought of killing him, but that plan never got off the ground. With his other grandiose schemes shelved, Khalid Sheikh Mohammed brought plans up to bin Laden for future assaults on the United States, including a scheme that required training pilots to crash airplanes into buildings.

In August 1996, bin Laden declared war on the United States. No one took him seriously. From a cave in Afghanistan, he issued a fatwa (an Islamic scholar's religious opinion dealing with Islamic law):

> Terrorizing you, while you are carrying arms on our land, is a legitimate and morally demanded duty. It is a legitimate right well known to all humans and other creatures. Your example and our example is [sic] like a snake, which entered into a house of a man and got killed by him. The coward is the one who lets you walk, while carrying arms, freely on his land and provides you with peace and security. [3]

In November 1996, the FBI heard of al-Qaeda—all 93 members—for the first time. A Sudanese informer, who said he had worked for bin Laden in Khartoum, mentioned the name of the fledgling terrorist group. The informant talked of sleeper cells and training camps. But, believing that the United States no longer faced serious adversaries, the FBI regarded terrorism as a nuisance, not an actual threat. Accordingly, it gave al-Qaeda no priority, pursuing more pressing investigations.

"Terrorizing you, while you are carrying arms on our land, is a legitimate and morally demanded duty."

As Lawrence Wright wrote:

> The most frightening aspect of this new threat, was the fact that almost no one took it seriously. It was too bizarre, too primitive and exotic. Up against the confidence that Americans placed in modernity and technology and their own ideals to protect them from the savage pageant of history, the defiant gestures of bin Laden and his followers seemed absurd and even pathetic. [4]

Al-Qaeda had a fondness for high-profile terrorist attacks. In 1998, simultaneous bombings had occurred against two American embassies in East Africa, killing 223 and wounding more than 5,000. In October 2000, al-Qaeda terrorists had also killed 17 American sailors off the coast of Yemen in an attack on the USS *Cole*.

Prior to 9/11, American intelligence personnel were not entirely in the dark over al-Qaeda's plans for some kind of mega terror attack on American soil. The CIA, for instance, reported to President Bill Clinton in December 1998 that al-Qaeda was planning attacks in America and was training people to hijack aircraft. But the intelligence was far too vague to be useful [5].

The *Washington Post* revealed that on July 10, 2001, the CIA director George J. Tenet had been so impressed with the latest intelligence that showed the increasing likelihood that al-Qaeda would soon attack the United States that he urgently went to see the national security adviser, Condoleezza Rice [6].

In the past, Defense Secretary Donald Rumsfeld had questioned whether similar intelligence might be a deception, perhaps a test of America's reactions and defense capabilities. Tenet urged Rice to spread the word that the United States must take some kind of action against bin Laden to thwart his plans, but Tenet's words fell on deaf ears. American plans existed to take out bin Laden, but they would take time to implement, and President George W. Bush seemed hesitant to take preemptive action against the al-Qaeda leader.

Tenet later regarded the July 10th meeting with Rice as a significant, lost opportunity to prevent 9/11. The Tenet warning was but one of many such warnings that were given to the Bush administration.

Concerned that al-Qaeda would most likely strike overseas, the CIA could find few willing to take the intelligence seriously. Throughout the spring and early summer of 2001, American embassies were fortified; cooperation between American and foreign intelligence services was enhanced; and the FAA issued warnings of possible hijackings on international flights. In early August 2001, responding to a presidential request for the latest intelligence on a possible al-Qaeda attack on the United States, the CIA suggested to the president that bin Laden had a long-standing desire to strike America; but the agency had not learned of any specific plans and could not confirm reports that bin Laden wanted to hijack American aircraft.

Three years before—in late 1998 or early 1999—bin Laden approved Khalid Sheikh Mohammed's plan to stage a mega terror event. Mohammed studied target choices and aided in making travel arrangements for the hijackers. When Mohammed suggested attacking the U.S. Bank Tower in Los Angeles, bin Laden turned him down on grounds that it would take too long to prepare for an operation of that magnitude.

Providing the financial backing for the Mohammed plot that became 9/11, bin Laden also secured four possible participants in late 1999: Mohammed Atta, Marwan al-Shehhi, Ziad Jarrah, and Ramzi Binalshibh. They lived in the West, spoke English, and were educated. A fifth person joined in: Hani Hanjour, who possessed a commercial pilot's license, and was thus considered a big asset.

Four of the five men, including Atta, arrived in the United States between December 2000 and the end of June 2001. Atta arrived on June 3, 2000. Binalshibh had to drop out, unable to get the requisite visa. Other hijackers arrived that spring. It turned out that of the 19 hijackers, 15 were from Saudi Arabia, 2 from the United Arab Emirates, 1 from Egypt (Atta), and 1 from Lebanon.

MOHAMED ATTA: RINGLEADER

Mohamed Atta was 33 years old on 9/11. Ringleader of the 19 hijackers, he had been born in 1968 in a small town in Egypt's Nile Delta. Moving with his family to the Abdeen section of Cairo at age 10, Atta studied architecture at Cairo University and graduated in 1990. He continued his studies in Hamburg, Germany, at the Technical University of Hamburg. At a local mosque he met future hijackers Marwan al-Shehhi and Ziad Jarrah, and together they formed a Hamburg terrorist cell.

In late 1999 and early 2000, Atta visited Afghanistan, where he met bin Laden and other senior al-Qaeda leaders. It was then that bin Laden and Khalid Sheikh Mohammed recruited Atta and the Hamburg cell for the "planes operation" in America. In February 2000, Atta was back in Hamburg inquiring about flight training the United States.

He became more religious, attended a mosque often. Friends deemed him intelligent and angry at America over its policy toward the Middle East. Planning for the "planes" plot moved ahead when, on March 22, 2000, in Germany, Atta e-mailed a flight school in Lakeland, Florida, asking about getting instruction in flight training:

> Dear Sir, we are a small group of young men from different Arab countries. Now we are living in Germany since a while for study purposes.

We would like to start training for the career of airline professional pilots. In this field we haven't yet any knowledge but we are ready to undergo an intensive training program [7].

Atta sent 50 or so similar e-mails to other flight training schools in the United States.

"Dear Sir, we are a small group of young men from different Arab countries.... We would like to start training for the career of airline professional pilots."

Applying for an American visa on May 17, 2000, Atta was given a five-year B-1/B-2 (tourist/business) visa the following day from the U.S. Embassy in Berlin. No one scrutinized him carefully. He was a good student, and nothing indicated he might be a threat to the United States. At the time, if an Arab applied for flight training school in America, it raised no warning signs.

Sometime in May or June 2000, Atta talked for several hours to Johnelle Bryant, a loan officer at the U.S. Department of Agriculture in South Florida, asking to finance a twin-engine, six-passenger aircraft that he could use for charter flights and crop-dusting. When Bryant wrote his name in her notes as A-T-T-A-H, he corrected her and said it was A-T-T-A, as in "'atta boy!" He told her that he was from Egypt, but had moved from Afghanistan to the United States, and had an engineering degree from Germany. He had sold all of his belongings and had come to the United States to fulfill a dream, he said, of attending flight school, getting his pilot's license, and working as a charter pilot and crop duster.

He sought a $650,000 loan, but misread a pamphlet on U.S. government loans that he thought allowed him to simply show up at Bryant's office and walk out with the money in cash. When she explained to him that there was an applications process that would take some time, he grew agitated, asking her (rhetorically, he assured her) what would prevent him from going behind her desk and cutting her throat, and making off with a million dollars of cash? He noted that there seemed to be no security surrounding the safe. Chuckling, she told him that, for one thing, there was no cash in the safe.

Atta entered an accelerated pilot program in south Florida at Huffman Aviation, obtaining instrument ratings in November 2000. He kept training on simulators, and the following July 2001 he worked on the final target selection. Bin Laden signaled to the would-be hijackers that he was eager for the attack to happen as quickly as possible. In August, Atta traveled on surveillance flights to decide how to carry out the attacks.

Meanwhile, Palestinian Arabs were employing suicide bombings against Israelis: 21 attacks from 1993 to 1999 that had killed 164 Israelis.

A second wave had begun in September 2000 with the outbreak of the Second Intifada. It was not that Americans were indifferent to the suffering that Palestinians were inflicting on Israelis; but they viewed suicide bombings in Israel as events that occurred thousands of miles from American shores, that were localized and thus nonthreatening to the United States. And so Americans were unbending in their conviction that the phenomenon of suicide bombing would not metastasize to the United States.

An event that occurred a month before 9/11 illustrated the small impact that Palestinian suicide bombings against Israel were having in the United States. It happened on August 12, 2001, when a Palestinian suicide bomber attacked the Wall Street Café in Kiriat Motzkin, a suburb of Haifa. A 28 year-old man, Muhammad Mahmoud Nasser, entered the café with explosives strapped to his body, approached a waitress, lifted his T-shirt, and asked her if she knew what "that" was, pointing to the suicide belt. Realizing what he planned to do, people in the coffeehouse started to scream and threw chairs in his way, and then rushed outside. He blew himself up: His head landed on a table, and his torso was split in two. Twenty-one people were injured, but no Israeli was killed. The event received little coverage in the American media. Suicide bombing was still not a frightening, dramatic, or headline-making event in the United States. That the Palestinian-Israeli conflict was a proxy war for the possible larger confrontation between Islam and the West fell on deaf ears in Washington, D.C.

Mohamed Atta's luggage, left behind at Boston's Logan Airport, was discovered in the afternoon of September 11. It contained a treasure trove of information concerning the identification of the 19 hijackers as well as other clues about their background, plans, and motives. Inside the luggage were airline uniforms; flight manuals; a copy of Atta's will that he had composed in 1996, written in Arabic; and a list of instructions, also in Arabic: "Make an oath to die and renew your intentions"; "you should feel complete tranquility, because the time between you and your marriage in heaven is very short. You must make your knife sharp and you must not discomfort your animal during the slaughter" [8].

The picture that emerged of the 19 suicide hijackers was widely divergent from the accepted profile of Middle Eastern terrorists. Intelligence agencies did a good job in piecing together the movements of the hijackers in the months and years leading up to the attack. But they had more difficulty figuring out how only 19 men, assumed to be religious fanatics of one sort or another, could engineer such a mega event.

The hijackers turned out to have led normal lives all the while they were planning the September 11 attacks. While living in Germany for years, they were recalled as introverted and antisocial, but friendly and warm as well. They were religious, but they enjoyed a drink now and then; they danced and even flirted. The Lebanese hijacker, Ziad Jarrah, phoned his girlfriend on the morning of September 11 to say farewell. Once, in a motel room in Florida, noticing pictures of semi-naked women hanging on the wall, the hijackers draped hand towels over the pictures. At the same time, they also watched a pay-per-view pornographic movie on television.

Mohamed Atta had an especially peculiar attitude toward women, but no one would have guessed. It was only when his will was found that the public learned of his idiosyncrasies: He decreed in the will that no woman should be permitted to visit his grave; that his corpse had to be prepared only by women wearing gloves; and that no one be allowed to touch his genitals, male or female. It is unlikely then that, as with later suicide bombers, he was looking forward to heaven and getting pleasure from the 72 virgins. None of the hijackers' behavior, however, even remotely called attention to what they were planning.

Ironically, the 9/11 terrorists inspired future suicide bombers *not* to try for another mega event. The terrorists of the early 2000s thought more in terms of lower-level suicide bombings, resulting in far fewer casualties. We dwell on these latter types of suicide bombers throughout this manual for several reasons:

1. They have become the stereotypical suicide bombers in the Palestinian-Israeli conflict, the "laboratory" that provided us with our experience and expertise.
2. The greatest threat that Americans face is not from more 9/11s, but from suicide bombers who plan to blow themselves up inside New York City's Grand Central Station; in a Washington, D.C., Metro commuter train; or at some other landmark that has a lower profile than the World Trade Center or the Pentagon.

With that in mind, we take a close look in the next chapter at the advantages and disadvantages of suicide bombings carried out on the ground in crowds.

NOTES

1. Mordecai Dzikansky, recollections of his visit to the World Trade Center site on September 11, 2001, November 21, 2010.
2. Lawrence Wright, *The Looming Tower: Al-Qaeda and the Road to 9/11* (New York: Alfred A. Knopf, 2007), 235.
3. PBS Newshour, August 1996, http://www.pbs.org/newshour/terrorism/international/fatwa_1996.html. Osama bin Laden fatwa entitled "Declaration of War against the Americans Occupying the Land of the Two Holy Places" was first published in *Al Quds Al Arabi*, a London-based newspaper, in August 1996.
4. Lawrence Wright, *Looming Tower* (see note 2), 6.
5. Director Central Intelligence (DCI), "Bin Laden Preparing to Hijack U.S. Aircraft and Other Attacks," declassified memorandum from DCI Counterterrorism Center, December 4, 1998, http://www.foia.cia.gov/docs/DOC_0001110635/0001110635_0001.gif.
6. "Two Months before 9/11, an Urgent Warning to Rice," *Washington Post*, October 1, 2006, http://www.washingtonpost.com/wp-dyn/content/article/2006/09/30/AR2006093000282.html.
7. *Zacarias Moussauoi v. the United States* (trial testimony), United States District Court, Eastern District of Virginia, Alexandria Division, March 7, 2006, http://cryptome.org/usa-v-zm-030706-02.htm.
8. Michael Dorman, "Unraveling 9-11 Was in the Bags," *Newsday*, April 17, 2006.

8

Plusses and Minuses
Advantages and Constraints
for Suicide Bombers

A suicide bombing seems random, and only one individual appears to be involved. However, the act in most cases is far more organized, systematic, planned, and thought out than seems the case. The terrorists do not simply build a bomb, find someone bent on committing suicide, and send him or her off to find a target where the "enemy" gathers. To pit that single individual against a formidable enemy (as in the case of Palestinian suicide bombers against Israel) requires a whole set of tactical moves. To assure that the would-be bomber kills and wounds as many as possible, the bomber's facilitators need to decide on the tactics related to the mission in advance and revamp them as conditions change.

In this chapter, we discuss the tactics that suicide bombers employ. We also note the advantages and disadvantages that a suicide bomber has over other forms of terror. What constitutes a successful suicide bombing? The bomber and his or her sponsors measure success by the number of casualties or the killing of high-ranking officials.

SUICIDE BOMBING AS A TACTIC

The goal of suicide bombers is to instill a sense of fear and create a pervasive sense of instability among the civilian population in order to gain a psychological and military advantage over the enemy. To achieve that that goal, the bomber's sponsors could have chosen other terror tactics: a car bomb, an improvised explosive device, an unattended explosive package, stabbings, or sniping. Instead they chose a far more dramatic tactic: suicide bombing.

The suicide bomber is not determined in the short run to get rid of the enemy completely; to accomplish that strategic goal would require many soldiers, tanks, artillery, and jet fighter planes. But the bomber and the sponsors do want to inflict a "defeat" on the enemy to demonstrate how vulnerable the enemy's society is and to weaken that society. For the time being, these terrorists are content to inflict as much damage as possible.

The terrorist can choose what tactics to employ within his very severe limitations and which tactics not to deploy based on common sense and his own limited capabilities. He examines his tactics at all times with one criterion: Will it further his goal of striking fear and creating instability in the wider community?

What makes the suicide bomber's mission simpler to execute than missions of other "soldiers" is that the bomber needs no preplanned escape route. He will only need an escape route if he recants on his way to carrying out the bombing or if the device malfunctions. A traditional murderer or burglar has a far more complicated task: In addition to committing the murder or carrying out the robbery, he must devote ample time and effort to arrange an escape route and to avoid leaving evidence that could aid law enforcement in his capture. In contrast, a suicide bomber has no concern about being caught. If all goes as planned, the bomber will be dead.

CONSTRAINTS OF A SUICIDE BOMBER

That the person carrying out the suicide bombing gives up his life to assure the mission's success does impose important restraints on the bomber and on his sponsors.

First, facilitators cannot afford to volunteer for a mission. As organizers, they are too critical to suicide bombing operations to be allowed to go on a mission themselves. Second, because the organizers can only use available explosive materials that are powerful but small in size (in order to conceal them), these facilitators are left with less powerful and less focused blasts than those that emanate from traditional military weapons. With less-than-desirable weaponry, terrorists frequently cannot inflict severe or extensive damage on armored or significantly fortified targets.

One way for the terrorists to overcome this constraint is to add more explosives, but such mass is likely to be heavier than the would-be suicide bomber can carry to his target. Deploying a large volume of explosives also would make it that much harder for the suicide bomber to blend into large crowds, as the bulkiness of the explosives will make it difficult for him to walk normally; not walking normally might arouse suspicion.

Due to this constraint, the suicide bomber is limited to "soft targets," civilian targets such as recreational or commercial locations on crowded streets as opposed to high-profile ones. A suicide bomber, with a suicide bomb strapped to his body, would not be used to bring down the Hoover Dam, the World Trade Center, or to sink a ship.

Of course, one way for terrorists to avoid these issues would be to replace suicide bombing with suicide car bombing: One can place a much larger amount of explosives inside a vehicle than a suicide bomber can carry. But Palestinian terrorists face obstacles with regard to car bombs: Israel does not permit Palestinians to drive their cars from the West Bank and Gaza Strip into Israel; for a Palestinian car to slip by an Israeli checkpoint would be very difficult.

The most significant constraint for the suicide bomber is that the operation requires him to blow himself up. To be sure, throughout history, soldiers have been willing—however reluctantly—to take on near "suicide missions" if the situation required it, such as attempting to rescue a wounded soldier in the middle of a battlefield. The soldier risks his life and sometimes pays with his life. But the heroic soldier does not wake up intent to die in battle in order to kill as many of the enemy as possible.

> The most significant constraint for the suicide bomber is that the operation requires him to blow himself up.

Underwear bomber at Erez crossing between Gaza Strip and Israel, August 31, 2004, 3:14 a.m. (*Credit*: IDF spokesman's office)

The constraint on sponsors of a suicide bombing mission is self-evident: In order to recruit someone into a suicide bombing mission, sponsors must make clear that the person will be expected to blow himself up as part of the mission. That is a major constraint, since the second that a candidate hears that he is being asked to carry out a suicide bombing, he may immediately bow out. As a result, the search for candidates and their psychological conditioning can be long and complicated.

A traditional military commander knows full well that one or more of his soldiers might die on any mission, but the commander has no reason to inform his soldiers that some will definitely die. They may live—and, as part of their training, they learn how to protect themselves from danger. Further, the military commander does not need every one of his soldiers to be suicidal for the mission to succeed. The commander's battle cry is just the opposite; we will smite the enemy and live to tell of it. George S. Patton said it best: "No bastard ever won a war by dying for his country.

He won it by making the other poor dumb bastard die for his country" [1].

"No bastard ever won a war by dying for his country. He won it by making the other poor dumb bastard die for his country."

A further constraint on the suicide bomber is that, because he will die, he will carry out only one mission. He can blow himself up only once! This means that his sponsors have no chance of creating leaders—i.e., other terror leaders—from within the ranks of suicide bombers, leaders who could have learned from their experiences and, as a result, improved tactics here and there. While a private in an army can become a general, no suicide bomber graduates to the rank of leader.

Lacking the chance to replenish their ranks, those facilitators of suicide bombers become that much more valuable to the overall suicide bombing campaign. The terrorists, especially the bomb makers, become key targets for the enemy. Eliminating one or more of them is likely to reduce the number of suicide bombings. Through so-called targeted assassinations, the Israelis sought to diminish the ranks of terror leaders, facilitators, and bomb makers.

Israeli security officials noticed after several targeted assassinations that the replacements for the eliminated bomb makers and planners were younger and less experienced. The terrorist organizations, however, did not give up. But when they sought out replacements for the dead terrorists, they had only a limited number from whom to choose.

KEY DECISIONS FOR SUICIDE BOMBING ORGANIZERS

Suicide bombing organizers face a set of decisions on tactics that have to do with the timing and the size of future suicide bombings:

1. *Timing*: Should suicide bombings be carried out once every few months, once a week, or once a day? That decision has to be made by terrorist and political leaders (sometimes one and the same), for this is a fundamental issue affecting the overall suicide bombing campaign. Various factors are at play:

   Do suicide bomber organizers want to provoke the other side into a major confrontation? If they do, the more suicide bombings there are, the more likely a confrontation. In 2002, nearly midway through the 2000–2006 Second Intifada, Palestinians sanctioned more and more suicide bombings that produced more and more casualties. By doing that, Palestinian leaders provoked Israel into launching a major military attack against Palestinian terror cells, including bomb makers, on the West Bank.

The effect of almost daily suicide bombings against Israel was to goad Israel into launching Operation Defensive Shield at the end of March. After the Defensive Shield operation, suicide bombers were forced to launch fewer attacks, weekly rather than almost daily as in the past.

On the other hand, if political leaders simply wish to remind the enemy that they can, from time to time, unleash an attack that will prove excruciatingly painful, daily suicide missions are not necessary; suicide bombings every four to six weeks will suffice.

In the end, the timing of suicide bombings—shorter or longer durations—depends on a whole array of factors: Have other tactics arisen that may be more effective than suicide bombings? Has the enemy taken new security measures to defend itself better against those bombings? Such measures include strengthening checkpoints, increasing intelligence efforts, and making mass arrests of terror leaders and sponsors. But ultimately the terror leaders decide how many bombers to send out in a given time in order to be effective.

2. *Size of the attack*: Another major tactic suicide bomb facilitators might employ is to launch a single mega suicide bombing that is so effective and so devastating that, while not landing an outright knockout blow to the enemy, precludes the need for any further suicide bombings for a long time.

The 9/11 mega attack illustrates the advantages of launching just one big operation and then "laying low." Had there had been 10 suicide bombings against American targets over the few months after 9/11, those subsequent events would have diminished the uniqueness of 9/11, although it would have added to the general public's fear.

That seems to have been al-Qaeda's post-9/11 thinking. To unleash further mega terror attacks again and again against American targets just might, they seem to have concluded, take some of the spotlight off of 9/11. After all, as one of the major American military defeats in its history, 9/11 required—so this corollary went—no quick repetition, especially on a smaller scale, to amplify its astonishing results.

There is another point. Launching an event on the scale of 9/11 required a set of complicated measures made even more complicated by the fact that al-Qaeda had no base of operations within the United States.

The states of Maine and Florida were not the West Bank, where the Palestinians enjoyed relative freedom of movement; nor did those American states offer the secret lairs that Afghanistan did. The hijacker/ suicide bombers had to live in obscure motels, keep on the move, study airline schedules, keep the other perpetrators informed—all in secret, all away from their home base. In short, given the way the suicide bombers of 9/11 had to operate, it was easier for them to plan and execute a mega terror event than to conduct a series of suicide bombings, as the Palestinians did.

We cannot confirm that al-Qaeda's leaders made a decision to avoid further mega terror events on American soil, but law enforcement authorities since 9/11 to May 20, 2011, have uncovered a relatively small number of terror plots (39) against targets on American soil, none of them on the scale of 9/11. Since 9/11 to July 1, 2011, terrorists have not launched a single successful mission against targets in the United States, large or small.

Since 9/11, terrorists have not launched a single successful mission against targets in the United States, large or small.

By the standard of 9/11—or even smaller suicide bombing attacks in London (56 killed on July 7, 2005) and Moscow (40 killed on March 29, 2010)—Palestinian Arabs have not carried out mega suicide bombings. The single worst Palestinian suicide bombing in terms of casualties was the Park Hotel attack (30 killed and 140 wounded), where large numbers had gathered.

With Israeli security generally on high alert, it became extremely difficult for terrorists to carry out a mega suicide bombing event during the Second Intifada. Instead, once the Second Intifada began, Palestinians adopted a serial approach, carrying out as many suicide bombings as they could from 2000 to 2002. In 2002 alone, there were 55 suicide bombing attacks killing 220 Israelis—an average of one successful suicide bombing a week, every week for an entire year.

The continuous suicide bombings had a deep psychological impact upon Israeli society. While Israelis made a special point of trying to return to their normal lives after each suicide bombing as quickly as possible, the scars remained. Many were traumatized. Cars become more popular than buses. Restaurants and malls had fewer visitors. Any loud noise startled usually calm people. Israelis ordered take-out food in unprecedented quantities as citizens stayed home rather than go to restaurants.

Downtown Jerusalem, the locale of numerous suicide bombings, became a ghost town. Sitting down to a night of TV watching, once a calming experience for Israeli families, became a fidgety, nerve-wracking one, as each time a suicide bombing occurred, TV anchors suddenly interrupted the regular programming, breathlessly announcing the event and providing continuing updated details along with live, unedited footage from the scene.

During breaks in the coverage, funereal music played in the background on television, as Israel Television played during all-out wars, depressing the public even more. Until Israelis were able to get themselves back to normal—and it took time—it was safe to say that the suicide bombing campaign was highly effective.

ADVANTAGES OF SUICIDE BOMBING

Advantages do exist for suicide bombers as they carry out their lethal missions. While law enforcement authorities have to be successful in preventing suicide bombers 100 percent of the time, the bomber has to be successful only once.

Hard to identify as he carries out his suicide bombing mission, the bomber is difficult to foil. Willing to die as part of the mission, in no need of an escape route, he can easily arrive at and mix in large crowds. The suicide bomber also benefits from being mobile: He can maneuver from one possible target to another at the last minute to achieve maximum casualties. In contrast, bombs left in an unattended package on a street or in a parked car cannot be maneuvered at all.

No Worry about Being Gunned Down

Suicide bombers have the advantage of not worrying about being gunned down. Because they are willing to die as part of the attack, they confront their mission without worry of being killed by the enemy. People who are willing to die for their cause are almost impossible to stop. Threats do not work. To shout out: "Don't set off that bomb, or I'm going to kill you!" is meaningless.

On July 30, 2002, a would-be suicide bomber was walking on Prophets Street in downtown Jerusalem when a female civilian became suspicious of him; she quickly notified two nearby Israel police officers who decided to approach the suspicious person. Police cannot just shoot anyone who is suspicious, giving a suicide bomber an automatic advantage. When the bomber realized police officers were nearing him, he blew himself up, injuring the two officers.

For the suicide bomber, getting close to a target is easy. In standard military engagements, no single soldier would act so foolishly as to try to take on the enemy at close range, relying upon his automatic rifle, hoping that firing off 20 or 30 shots would allow him to kill 20 or 30 of the enemy—and escape. The suicide bomber, on the other hand, without having to worry about making an escape, can place himself in the midst of the "enemy," giving the bomber the advantage of easy access to his target.

The suicide bomber could be spotted in advance of carrying out his mission. To avoid being identified, he has the advantage of wearing a disguise. Still, the disguise can only help him so far. The disguise must not hinder his carrying a bomb that is well hidden yet easy to activate. The explosive charge, its wires, the battery, and the detonator switch must all fit comfortably on his body without arousing suspicion or be carried in a bag that fits the surroundings.

Hard to Subdue near Target

Another big advantage is that suicide bombers are hard to subdue near the target. Because it is difficult to identify suicide bombers in a crowd of civilians, it is tough to prevent them from executing their mission. While burglars need much time to carry out their crimes, increasing the possibility that they will get caught, suicide bombers need only a matter of minutes to place themselves in a crowd and push the detonator switch.

An important advantage that suicide bombers have is their ability to switch targets at the last minute.

Switching Targets at Last Minute

An important advantage that suicide bombers have is their ability to switch targets at the last minute. Being able to adjust their movements enables suicide bombers to adapt to last-minute circumstances in ways that other weapons cannot. Unlike a timed explosive, for instance, a suicide bomber can evaluate how tight security is—where, precisely, guards are stationed—and then modify his target, seeking alternative crowds with less security.

Here are two examples from the Israeli experience where a suicide bomber showed flexibility, either changing his target or aborting a pending attack due to unexpected circumstances at the initial site.

105

Park Hotel, Netanya, March 27, 2002

Initially, the bomber planned to launch his assault against a restaurant or club in Tel Aviv, but he realized at a certain point that Jews had gathered for a seder (the traditional Passover meal) at home or in hotels to celebrate the Passover holiday. Accordingly, the suicide bomber struck at a seder at the Park Hotel, 18 miles north of Tel Aviv, killing 30 and wounding 140 people. Had the bomber blown himself up at an empty Dizengoff Square in the heart of Tel Aviv, no one would have been killed other than the bomber.

Pizza Meter, Jerusalem, September 9, 2003

A suicide bomber attempted to enter a Pizza Meter store but was rebuffed by a security guard at the store entrance. So the bomber scurried over to the Café Hillel coffeehouse next door. There a guard tried to prevent the bomber from entering, but the terrorist managed to get several yards inside the coffeehouse. Seven people were killed (including the security guard) and over 50 wounded.

The Israel National Police forensics team analyzes the scene after Café Hillel (Jerusalem) suicide bombing attack on September 9, 2003. (*Credit*: Moshe Milner for Israel Government Press Office)

The flexibility built into the suicide bomber's "delivery system" is far greater than the most sophisticated missile guidance systems, giving a lone individual the kind of last-minute decision-making capability that no technology built into more powerful weapons can possess.

As humans, suicide bombers can use their brains in the final stages of an attack, decide that danger looms at one target, and switch immediately to another target. No other terror weapon has such flexibility. Unattended packages holding explosives are essentially stationary objects that cannot change position in light of some new piece of information. The same holds true for car bombs.

For instance in the spring of 2001, a bomb had been placed in a car near the Jerusalem District Police Headquarters at 9 a.m., on a Sunday, ordinarily rush hour on one of the busiest streets in Jerusalem. Though the bomb exploded, no one was hurt because Jews were getting ready for the Jewish holiday of Shavuot that began in a few hours. As a result of the approaching holiday, they were not in downtown Jerusalem. Had terrorist organizers realized that the downtown street would be empty, they would still not have been able to race to move or temporarily disarm the bomb for later use, for the risk of being caught would have been too high.

Choice of Targets

Not only do suicide bombers have an advantage of last-minute flexibility. They also have a wide choice of targets that allows them to create the perception that they might strike anywhere in the future.

Having a wide selection of targets does not suggest that the suicide bomber acts randomly. The bomber does not put on a suicide belt, walk down the street, search for an unsecured target, melt into the crowds, and then detonate the bomb. The suicide bomber knows exactly where he is attacking. His organizers have methodically selected his target in advance. They make sure to pick different kinds of targets: one time, a pizza parlor; another, a train station; a third occasion, an open-air market. The idea is to keep civilians frightened of going to any kind of place.

If suicide bombers attack only buses and not cars, people will stop taking buses and travel only by car, even though statistics show that it is statistically safer to ride in a bus than a car. In 2003, there were 482 Israeli traffic accident deaths, the lowest in 21 years, while in 2002, Israel's worst year of terror during the Second Intifada, there were 456 terror-related deaths. In short, Israel's fewest traffic deaths annually (2003) were still higher than Israel's worst year of terror (2002) [2]. Yet, despite these statistics, people still avoided buses because of the threat of terror and rode in the more dangerous (statistically) private cars.

Ease of Blending into Crowds

Another advantage for suicide bombers is that they know how to blend into crowds. Unlike the unattended package, which often in Israel stands out and gets noticed by people, the suicide bomber can insinuate himself unnoticed into a crowd. That makes locating him in time to stop the attack that much more difficult. Once he penetrates the crowd, once he gets through whatever security might exist, he is free to commit his dastardly deed.

Cheap and Easy to Carry Out

It may not seem a huge advantage, but a suicide bombing is relatively cheap and easy to carry out. This means that bomb makers can produce their lethal weapons without worrying about excessive costs or complicated and dangerous bomb-making procedures. It also means that suicide bombing becomes a cheap way of inducing panic. A conventional military operation costs far more. An individual soldier has to be housed, fed, and trained. The basic weapon that a soldier uses is far more expensive than a suicide bomb. All of these costs come at considered expense to the sponsoring government. In contrast, a suicide bomber requires no long-term housing, no feeding, and only a brief amount of training. The major cost is making the bomb, but that is not a great expense. Unofficial estimates put the cost at roughly $150 for an attack [3].

Relatively speaking, a suicide bombing is considerably easier to execute than a complex military campaign. The suicide bomb is simple to make, although sometimes organizers have difficulty getting their hands on the explosive material needed for the bomb. The learning curve for putting the bomb together safely can be long, but bomb makers in the West Bank did not need an advanced degree in physics, engineering, or chemistry to make a bomb.

Relatively speaking, a suicide bombing is considerably easier to execute than a complex military campaign.

Knowing some of the fundamentals of chemistry and electricity certainly helps the bomb makers. Because the bomb making was dangerous, many work accidents occurred. Slowly, by trial and error, bomb makers eventually learned how to make their bombs safe, and suicide bombings began to have a successful detonation rate.

Random rocket attacks launched by terror groups have achieved little due to the inaccuracy of the rockets. The same lack of achievement arose with terrorist shootings on the West Bank: When Palestinian terrorists shot at Israelis, they rarely killed anyone. But when suicide bombers launched attacks, they routinely killed five or six Israelis. With modern explosives producing greater yields, permitting greater destruction, and getting smaller, the suicide bomber was getting more bang for the buck—and for a small cost.

Attracting the Media

Engaging the media and trying to win the propaganda war against the enemy is crucial to the terrorists. Thus it is a great advantage when suicide bombers strike successfully in a Western urban environment, as they attract far more media attention than other terrorists. The suicide bomber's willingness to take his life—the supreme sacrifice for a cause—dramatizes the event like no other act of terror can. That drama—plus the ruthlessness and the frightening randomness of the deed—appeals to journalists, especially television reporters and photographers. In short, suicide bombing is made for television.

Terrorists have learned how to exploit the media's great interest. The suicide bomber has a face that his organizers will quickly display to news agencies soon after the bombing. Hence, within a few hours of the bombing, thanks to television and the Internet, the face is televised around the world. The suicide bomber will gain fame, if only for a day or so, and that fame attracts more and more support, including financial aid, for the cause—and more and more recruits.

Why do the media consider suicide bombings newsworthy? For one thing, suicide bombings are quite rare in Western societies, certainly compared to other forms of terror; yet casualty rates in suicide bombings are far higher than in other forms of terror. Besides, the irrationality and the counterintuitiveness of the act of suicide bombing lure the media. The notion that a seemingly crazy person blows himself up counts as high drama.

It is worth noting that in Iraq, Pakistan, and Afghanistan, where suicide bombings have occurred with great frequency, the media has devoted far less attention to those bombings than to the Western bombings that are the focus of this manual. Our explanation is that the Western media has collectively decided that non-Western suicide bombings, because "foreigners" perpetrated these acts, have no relevance for the West and no strong interest for a Western audience. The corollary is that Israel, Turkey, and England are not "foreign," and suicide bombings in those countries are therefore relevant. Americans can easily identify with Jerusalem, Istanbul, and London. Many have visited one or more of these cities. Some Americans may even have relatives or friends living in those foreign cities. Few Americans, however, have any such personal connection with Afghanistan or Pakistan.

Some argue that with so many suicide bombings occurring in Israel in the 1990s and the early 2000s, surely the media should have tired of these events once the bombings started to taper off in 2003. But that did not happen. Even as the bombings subsided over the next few years, the media still flocked to suicide bombing scenes.

We have examined the advantages and disadvantages that a suicide bomber has over other forms of terror, whether car bombs, shootings, or knifings. But how do we judge whether a suicide bomber has been effective? We take up this question in the next chapter.

NOTES

1. George Patton, quotation from BrainyQuote Web site, http://www.brainyquote.com/quotes/authors/g/george_s_patton_2.html.
2. Israel Police Division of Traffic provided these statistics to Gil Kleiman to distribute to the media in 2003.
3. Bruce Hoffman, "The Logic of Suicide Terrorism," *Atlantic*, June 2003, http://www.theatlantic.com/magazine/archive/2003/06/the-logic-of-suicide-terrorism/2739/.

9

Effectiveness
What Makes a Suicide Bombing Successful?

Understanding what the organizers of suicide bombings consider to be an effective bombing is important. The more we know about what the facilitators think makes for an effective suicide bombing, the better prepared law enforcement authorities will be in guarding, securing, and protecting their targeted populace.

It is clear that suicide bombing is an incredibly successful terrorist tactic. Let's start with some statistics: Between 2000 and 2008, 543 Israelis were killed by suicide bombings, nearly half (46.7 percent) the number of deaths (1,161) from Palestinian terror in those years.

Between 2002 and 2008, 543 Israelis were killed by suicide bombings, more than half the number of deaths (1,161) from Palestinian terror in that time.

AN INEFFECTIVE SUICIDE BOMBING

Before we look at what constitutes an effective suicide bombing, let's determine what is an ineffective suicide bombing. From the terrorist groups' perspective, the least effective suicide bombing is one that takes place in an unpopulated place where a bomb detonates by accident, killing no enemy civilians. If no one is harmed and no one hears of the incident, the bombing is a failure. But that does not happen often.

THE 14 WORST PALESTINIAN SUICIDE BOMBINGS
AGAINST ISRAELIS BASED ON 16 OR MORE
DEATHS PER INCIDENT (1994–2004)

October 19, 1994
22 killed
75 injured
Bus in Tel Aviv

January 22, 1995
19 killed
69 injured
Beit Lid junction near
Netanya

March 3, 1996
19 killed
7 injured
Bus in Jerusalem

July 30, 1997
16 killed
178 injured
Mahane Yehuda market
in Jerusalem

June 1, 2001
21 killed
120 wounded
Outside disco in Tel Aviv

March 27, 2002
30 killed
140 injured
Park Hotel in Netanya

June 5, 2002
17 killed
38 injured
Bus at Megiddo junc-
tion near Afula

June 18, 2002
19 killed
74 injured
Bus in Jerusalem

January 5, 2003
23 killed
120 injured
Near Central Bus
Station in Tel Aviv

March 5, 2003
17 killed
53 injured
Bus en route to Haifa
University

June 11, 2003
17 killed
Over 100 injured
Bus in Jerusalem

August 19, 2003
23 killed
133 injured
Bus in Jerusalem

October 4, 2003
21 killed
60 injured
Restaurant in Haifa

August 31, 2004
16 killed
100 injured
Two buses in Beersheba

112

WHY ARE SUICIDE BOMBERS SO SUCCESSFUL?

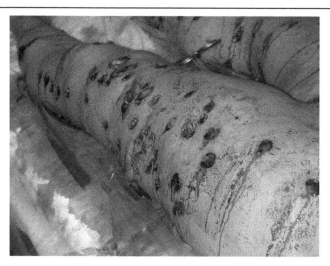

Photo of effect of fragment on a victim's leg. (*Credit*: Gil Kleiman photo collection)

What are the reasons for the high rate of success? One reason: suicide bombers face enormous pressure from their leaders to carry out the mission no matter what. The suicide bombers' sponsors tell them that, whatever target they ultimately choose, they must blow themselves up. Why? The bombers need to show that they can penetrate into the enemy's inner sanctum and inflict damage.

One piece of mistaken conventional wisdom has it that the nature of suicide bombing—a single attacker with a relatively small amount of explosives, often causing relatively few casualties—limits the bomber's prospect of success. But even if it's a simple fast-food stand, and he "only" kills three, the bomber knows that he must blow himself up. Despite the relatively small number of casualties, the attack will be listed as a success for the terrorists and a failure for the police.

A second reason for suicide bombers' high rate of success: Bombers can carry out their missions even if they arouse suspicions or are about to be subdued. Traditional criminals do not have that luxury in committing crimes: If a burglar finds that houses in a certain neighborhood have tight security, he is likely to bolt rather than to risk a botched burglary and being caught. In contrast, a suicide bomber will blow up no matter what, and as long as he causes casualties, the attack ranks as a success.

A third reason: Suicide bombing facilitators are careful not to send bombers into the field without the best possible intelligence and equipment. By the time a suicide bomber is sent on a mission, the sponsors have searched for the location and the number of enemy checkpoints, recruited and trained the best possible candidate for that mission, and obtained the correct kind of explosives.

A fourth reason: Organizers of suicide bombers know that for a mission to be successful, more must be done than convince the bomber to blow himself up and kill the maximum number of casualties. Conscious of their need to create as much havoc and fear among the wider population, planners take steps prior to the attack to make sure that the suicide bombing obtains the greatest publicity imaginable.

They prepare a video with the future bomber explaining himself and his cause to the audience. They seek out targets that will provide for maximum casualties, aware that the more dead and wounded, the more publicity the event will attract. The facilitators try to target certain kinds of civilians: Children killed in a suicide bombing are bound to get more television "air time" than if soldiers are killed; elders killed by a suicide bomber while attending a Passover seder will surely receive greater television coverage than a bomb attack against an Israeli military jeep on the West Bank.

However improbable, a suicide bomber killing an Israeli prime minister will gain far more television coverage than killing an average Israeli. Announcing that a suicide bombing will happen within a certain time frame in revenge for the Israeli killing of a Palestinian leader will attract a great deal of media attention as long as the attack happens within the time frame previously declared.

THE CHOICE OF TARGETS

One important factor determining the success of a suicide bombing is the target site: A suicide bomber blowing himself up at a low-level target like a restaurant may seem a far less significant event than killing a cabinet minister or blowing up a government building. But targeting a restaurant has its value to suicide bombing organizers. For one thing, a restaurant is easier to attack than a government building or a cabinet minister. Government buildings will be well guarded with security guards and even bomb detection devices at all entrances. Not all restaurants will have highly trained guards posted outside their premises. Finally, there are far more restaurants than government buildings; far more people visit restaurants than visit major tourist spots.

The number of potential victims is far greater if the choice of targets includes restaurants and other public spaces—malls, outdoor markets, department stores, railroads, and bus stations. So striking at a restaurant, even if the casualties are few, will strike fear in the population.

Civilians versus Soldiers

It appears that no suicide bombing attack could be more effective than one that targets enemy soldiers. Killing and wounding soldiers seems the best way to send a message to the enemy that "we can get to you and you are not as secure as you think." But, counterintuitively, evidence suggests that suicide bombers avoid soldiers as targets. Organizers prefer targeting civilians because soldiers, by definition, are professionally trained and more likely to detect bombers before they strike. Soldiers are also trained to overcome their fears and, when encountering a suicide bomber or anyone else posing a threat, they are trained to confront and disarm the person. Civilians, on the other hand, have no such training.

Attacking civilians ensures that the wider community will feel fearful. A civilian who hears of a suicide bombing against other civilians in a restaurant will think: "That could have been me sitting in that restaurant." But a civilian who learns of a suicide bombing targeting soldiers, is likely to say: "That could not have been me."

To be sure, Palestinian Arabs killed and wounded Israeli soldiers during the Second Intifada, but the suicide bombers did not target soldiers per se. They targeted civilian targets. Even had the terrorists wanted to target Israeli soldiers, they would not have been able to attack them easily. Every Israeli soldier on a bus or train is looking for suspicious persons, making it dangerous for a suicide bomber to approach any soldier.

It proved difficult to target Israeli soldiers in tanks, on patrol, or in jeeps with machine guns because soldiers, generally speaking, do not ride in such conveyances or go on patrol in civilian surroundings. Only on the West Bank has there been a large Israeli military presence. But sponsors of suicide bombers, while striking at Israeli soldiers on the West Bank here and there, preferred to penetrate into Israel to launch attacks against civilian targets. Did suicide bombers target Israeli police? Not specifically.

To the suicide bomber, attacking civilians is not only easier than taking on soldiers, it is also legitimate. Civilians are, in the view of Palestinian

115

terror leaders, potential soldiers (if they are children), actual soldiers (Israeli men spend a month a year on reserve army duty into their 40s), or supporters of the military (retirees). One specific slice of the Israeli civilian population that is a particularly legitimate target for suicide bombers are the several hundred thousand Jewish settlers who live on the West Bank. Those settlers, as Palestinians put it, are occupying their land; targeting settlers is one effective way of trying to weaken Israel's will. These settlers know that they are a popular target for suicide bombers and other terrorists. That is why, when they travel in Israel proper, ride the buses, walk the streets, or visit malls, settlers carry automatic rifles with them.

High-Level versus Low-Level Targets

To the facilitators of suicide bombers, striking at low-level targets is far more effective than going after high-level ones. Accordingly, planners spend far less time plotting to "take out" a high-level target than a low-level one, because their aim is to instill fear and instability in the wider population, and the best way to do that is to strike at the civilian population directly.

Killing a high-level target like the prime minister, the defense minister, or the army's chief of staff, while seemingly attractive for the terrorists, results in little more than the public feeling anger and frustration. The assassination will not arouse a general sense of vulnerability in the civilian population because it is clear that the prime minister was targeted because he was the prime minister. The public is not going to feel seriously threatened by a senior political leader's murder, for no citizen would say, "If they can get the prime minister, they can get me." Killing the prime minister does not increase the odds that civilians will be harmed via suicide bombing attacks.

On the other hand, the general public will recoil in fear after hearing that suicide bombers have attacked any one of a number of public places such as restaurants, buses, malls, open-air markets—all of which the public uses on a widespread and continuing basis.

DISRUPTING THE ROUTINE

Sometimes the fear that suicide bombers generate can permeate an entire city or, better still for the terrorists, an entire nation. That fear disrupts routines for millions, causing them to take actions that they would not take under normal circumstances. These disruptions, some small, some big, are one important way of measuring the effectiveness of a suicide bombing. The more fear, the more civilian life is disrupted—and the more the suicide bombers achieve their objectives.

By that criterion, 9/11 was astonishingly effective for al-Qaeda and its 19 suicide bombers. Many citizens slipped into shock and paralysis, and the authorities did little to help them adjust to new security needs required after the attack. All non-emergency civilian aircraft in the United States as well as Canada were grounded, resulting in thousands of passengers being stranded around the world. American stock exchanges were closed. The Federal Aviation Administration closed all international flights to American airspace; 500 flights had to be turned back or rerouted to other countries.

Twelve days after the attack, New York City remained empty of shoppers and tourists, and those who were within the city still seemed dazed. Smoke still hovered over much of the downtown areas of the city. Broadway theaters, which had completely shut down immediately after 9/11, were still closed. Few visited stores anywhere in the city. First responders were still the only residents to be found in a number of five-star hotels [1].

Some New Yorkers changed their routines radically: A small number of New Yorkers fled the city for seemingly safer locations far from large urban centers. Others, living in constant fear that more commercial airlines would strike New York's skyscrapers, remained home rather than go to work.

New York City mayor Rudolph Giuliani understood how vital it was not give the suicide bomber/hijackers any excuse to claim victory. He urged New Yorkers to return to normal quickly; he pleaded with residents to return to Broadway theaters; he asked foreign tourists to visit the city; and he urged work crews to clean up the stricken World Trade Center site as soon as humanly possible despite the many health risks involved. But New Yorkers were too numb to respond to his pleas. The authorities did little to assuage that numbness and simply allowed Americans a period of near paralysis, playing into the hands of al-Qaeda. In time, once the fear of another mega terror attack subsided among New Yorkers, they went back to their default mode—normalcy.

Another way to gauge the effectiveness of a suicide bombing is whether the bombers have forced the enemy government into an overreaction. For instance, President George W. Bush grounded all civilian aircraft during 9/11, and he shepherded legislation through Congress that approved new, tough methods to strengthen the government's intelligence-gathering capabilities. The president, however, did not take harsher steps, as might have been expected. He did not impose martial law on New York City or Washington, D.C., both 9/11 targets. Nor did he call for revising the military draft, turning the all-volunteer army into a conscripted force. And, rather than raise taxes, a step often taken when a country is under attack, he lowered them.

The president did take military action, and a few critics called what he undertook an overreaction. On October 7, 2001, he sent armed forces into Afghanistan in order to weed out al-Qaeda operatives living in government-protected sanctuaries there. (A decade later American troops were still there, and al-Qaeda activists were still plotting suicide bombings.)

Bush also sent the American army into Iraq on March 20, 2003, to disarm that country of weapons of mass destruction, and to end Iraqi leader Saddam Hussein's support for terrorism, especially his harboring of al-Qaeda. (Though the United States toppled Saddam Hussein from power, no weapons of mass destruction were found; and no evidence of Iraqi ties to al-Qaeda came to light.)

Israelis have long understood that disrupting their routines, while inevitable in the immediate days after a suicide bombing, does little but play into the hands of the suicide bombers. Eager to show the terrorists that they have not been effective, Israelis refuse to change their routines permanently. And so Israelis make a special point of quickly removing all signs of the bombing attack despite the urgings of some to "let the world see what the terrorists are doing to us."

Bodies are quickly removed from the suicide bombing site; the injured are expeditiously taken to hospitals. Emergency service crews take away human and other debris from the bombing scene with great haste. Within a matter of hours, most traces of the suicide bombing are removed.

TRYING FOR A POLITICAL IMPACT

One way to judge the effectiveness of a suicide bombing is its political effect. While terror leaders understand the great value of launching suicide bombers against public facilities, it is still tempting for them to try to kill a political leader: There is great symbolic value in such a bold step. But political leaders are the most protected of all possible targets, and suicide bombers have to "make do" almost all of the time with low-profile targets.

Ironically, when Israeli Prime Minister Yitzhak Rabin was shot and killed on November 4, 1995, it was not a Palestinian suicide bomber who launched the attack; it was a right-wing Israeli named Yigal Amir, who believed that in killing the prime minister, he could disrupt the Israeli–Palestinian peace process. That peace process, begun two years earlier with the Oslo Accords, had it borne fruit, would have led to the creation of a Palestinian state on the West Bank and the dislodging of many Jewish settlers there—developments that Amir, his Jewish settler friends, and the Israeli political right rigidly opposed.

Had an Arab, whether a suicide bomber or not, killed the prime minister, it would have been regarded—both by Israelis and Arabs—as a major terrorist success. It would have been viewed as highly effective because of its political impact.

Although Palestinians have not tried to assassinate Israeli political leaders via suicide bombing, the tactic has been used in other countries such as India, where on May 21, 1991, a Tamil Tiger suicide bomber killed Rajiv Ratna Gandhi, who had served as prime minister until December 1989.

There are other ways that a suicide bombing can have an important political impact and thus be considered quite effective. One would be for a suicide bomber to cause a policy change in the enemy's government.

Example

The particularly lethal (30 deaths) Park Hotel suicide bombing in Netanya on March 27, 2002, led Israel to launch a major military offensive.

Until the Park Hotel attack, the government of Prime Minister Ariel Sharon had shown restraint in the face of one suicide bombing after another. Refusing to be "lured" into a direct war with the terrorists, Sharon was concerned that the Israeli Defense Forces (IDF) would suffer many casualties in such a war. He hoped to solve the "Palestinian problem" through negotiations. But the Park Hotel attack was so lethal and resonated so widely with Israelis, many of whom, like the victims, had been sitting at their own Passover seder tables, that Sharon felt he had to take military action. Suicide bombing, an almost daily occurrence until then, had reached a "critical mass."

On March 29, 2002, Sharon—vowing to unleash Israel's maximum power to "let the army win" and "to destroy the infrastructure of terrorism"—launched Operation Defensive Shield, the largest military operation by the IDF on the West Bank since the 1967 Six-Day War.

STRIKING A TARGET A SECOND TIME

To show how much they care about ensuring the effectiveness of their missions, suicide bombing planners sometimes send bombers to a target that had already been hit but where the casualties were deemed not high enough.

119

With this "second time around" approach, the terrorists signal that they want to "get it right," to make sure that their message is understood: You cannot provide enough security to protect yourself against our suicide bombers.

Examples

At the Hasharon Shopping Mall in Netanya on July 12, 2005, a suicide bomber blew up, resulting in two deaths; a second suicide bombing at the same location on December 5, 2005, caused five deaths.

At the Rosh Ha'ir Restaurant in Tel Aviv on January 19, 2006, a suicide bomber's explosive device malfunctioned, killing only the bomber; a suicide bombing against the same target on April 17, 2006, resulted in 11 deaths.

Shwarma I—inside Shwarma Rosh Ha'ir suicide bombing site in southern Tel Aviv on January 19, 2006. (*Credit*: Moshe Milner for Israel Government Press Office)

BACK-TO-BACK SUICIDE BOMBINGS

When suicide bombers blow themselves up in back-to-back fashion—standing near one another, detonating their bombs a few minutes

120

apart—terrorists consider this tactic far more effective than a single bomb-ing. The sheer audacity and the compounded lethality of the twin deeds give suicide bombers a tactic that is even more frightening and unsettling than a one-bomber approach.

No suicide bombing illuminated that point more than 9/11, which was four highly coordinated suicide bombing attacks: two against the World Trade Center, a third against the Pentagon, and the fourth an abor-tive attempt to hit either the White House or the U.S. Capitol.

Back-to-back suicide bombings can take place at the same bombing site, with bombers blowing themselves up one after the other. Or they can occur within hours of each other at different locations. That was the case when suicide bombers blew themselves up in two separate events dur-ing a six-hour period on September 9, 2003. The first bombing occurred outside an army base near Rishon Lezion, killing nine and wounding 30. Six hours later, a Palestinian suicide bomber blew himself up inside the Café Hillel coffee shop in Jerusalem, killing seven people and injuring another 50.

ATTACKING ON CERTAIN DAYS

Suicide bombers like to choose certain memorial days to carry out attacks, creating a greater emotional tie between the wider Palestinian commu-nity and the suicide bomber. These "memorial day" suicide bombings are effective in that they link the bomber to all of those people who are com-memorating the day. That is why Israelis keep a vigilant watch on these "memorial days." For example, organizers might plan a suicide bomb-ing for the anniversary of the assassination on March 22, 2004, of Sheikh Ahmed Ismail Hassan Yassin, founder and spiritual leader of Hamas. Or a Palestinian suicide bombing might be planned for a Jewish holiday: For instance, on the Jewish holiday of Purim on March 4, 1996, a suicide bomber blew himself up at the Dizengoff Center (Tel Aviv), killing 13 Israelis (12 civilians and one soldier) and injuring 130 others.

"Memorial days" are not the only special days for Palestinian suicide bombers. They choose Sundays over other days of the week to carry out suicide bombing attacks, as Sunday, the first day of the week in Israel, means larger crowds at bus stops, restaurants, and open-air markets. On a Sunday afternoon, March 31, 2002, a suicide bomber blew himself up at the emergency medical center in Efrat, in the Gush Etzion block on the West Bank, south of Jerusalem. Six Israelis were injured.

121

GRISLY SCENES HELP MAKE SUICIDE BOMBINGS EFFECTIVE

Creating as grisly a scene in the aftermath of a suicide bombing is one more way that suicide bombers can assure the effectiveness of an attack. Whether the site is a restaurant, an open-air market, or a bus station, the visual images from the attack stick in peoples' minds for a long time. Here is Mordecai Dzikansky's recollection of arriving at a suicide bombing on October 4, 2003, at a popular restaurant in Haifa called Maxim, where Israelis and Arabs routinely gathered.

> I raced to the scene, arriving at 4 p.m. When I drove up to the site, I saw that blood and flesh were strewn about. Dead bodies were in seats and lay on the floor. A mangled baby carriage was outside the back of the restaurant. The entire restaurant had been destroyed. Its rear windows were completely blown out, as was the center of the drop ceiling, indicating where the bomber stood at the moment of detonation. I came across the torso of the suicide bomber—headless. Within seconds I spotted her head. I learned later that she calmly sat down, ate a meal, paid for it, and then blew herself up. Cars parked as far away as fifty feet were damaged. The death toll had reached 21, including four children; another 60 had been wounded. It was one of the bloodiest of all Palestinian suicide bombings yet. Among the victims were two families and four children, including a two-month-old baby. [2]

"I saw that blood and flesh were strewn about. Dead bodies were in seats and lay on the floor. A mangled baby carriage was outside the back of the restaurant."

TIMING OF POLICE RESPONSE DETERMINES EFFECTIVENESS

Another factor that determines the success of a suicide bombing is whether law enforcement responds promptly to the bombing attack. Too slow a response suggests to the perpetrators that law enforcement—and the whole fabric of society—has been weakened by previous suicide bombings.

Law enforcement officers are judged on how quickly they identify a suicide bomber. It's not that the public is crying out to know the name of the bomber, but the failure to identify the bomber quickly reflects badly on law enforcement's ability to cope with a suicide bombing.

If the media ask a police spokesman five hours after an attack whether it was a suicide bombing or not, and he still cannot say with 100 percent certainty, either police have lost control of the situation, or they are purposely lying to downplay the event. To the general public who look to the police as protectors, a show of uncertainty by the police makes the suicide bombing seem that much more effective.

In the past few chapters, we have looked at the advantages and constraints that affect suicide bombers, and we have examined what it is that makes for an effective suicide bombing. None of this would matter if the weaponry that the suicide bomber carries into the mission were inadequate. In the next chapter, we look at that weaponry.

NOTES

1. Coauthor Robert Slater was in New York on September 23, 2001, and took note that the city had still not returned to normal life.
2. Mordecai Dzikansky recollected his visit to Maxim's Restaurant on October 4, 2003, in a conversation on November 21, 2010.

10

Weaponry
The Armaments of Suicide Bombers

The suicide bombers of 9/11 brought no explosives on their planes, relying instead upon box cutters and knives. In contrast, the suicide bombers and the bomb makers who are the focus of this manual—those on the ground—face a variety of considerations in putting together the bombs to be used in their missions. In this chapter we discuss those considerations: How do the sponsors prepare the bomb? What explosives are the easiest and the hardest to manufacture; the most and least accessible; the most potent; the most stable and least? The answers to these questions determine in large part what kind of bomb the suicide bomber will use for the mission. We start with this important question: What makes a suicide bomber a human bomb?

THE SUICIDE BOMBER IS THE BOMB

Think of the suicide bomber as a human missile. As he carries out his mission, he is not detached from the bomb: He *is* the bomb. He is a very lethal weapon. Unlike an actual missile that costs hundreds of thousands of dollars, he does not travel at great speed. But, as he hones in on his target, he can do what no missile can do: He has the human eye and the instinct to make last-minute decisions to maneuver to a different, better target.

The suicide bomber is essentially a human head attached to a bomb. The brain inside that head can "lead" the device in any direction; it can calibrate its movements as it gets closer to a target. And what a frightening weapon the suicide bomber is. No more frightening image exists in warfare than that of a young man—explosives encased with ball bearings, nails, screws, or bolts inside a vest worn around his chest; his fingers wrapped around the detonator switch; a half-smiling smirk on his face—about to blow himself up. The "package"—this human bomb—sends out the kind of chilling fear that a tank or a fighter jet does not.

WE DO NOT SHOW HOW TO BUILD A SUICIDE BOMB

This chapter on bomb making is meant for security professionals to help them defend against suicide bombings. Its purpose is not to explain to a suicide bomber's sponsors how to make a bomb. We have spent a great deal of time thinking about how to achieve a balance between the information in this chapter falling into the wrong hands and the need of police officers to know how to apply this information to protect against suicide bombers.

All of the material we cover in this chapter comes from publicly available sources in newspapers, magazines, the Internet, and elsewhere; therefore we are providing nothing that is not publicly available already. The information that we convey will not enable a suicide bomber to construct

We do not provide specific instructions on how to build a bomb.

and detonate a bomb because our information is theoretical, not practical. We do not provide specific instructions on how to build a bomb.

Our task in this manual is to train law enforcement personnel, who do not need to know the details of how to build a bomb. However, they do need to know the type of the explosives in the bomb in order to identify a would-be suicide bomber and what he is carrying.

A law enforcement officer who comes upon a suspected suicide bomber would not be able to see the interior of the bomb, with its wires, battery, and detonator. However, during routine searches of houses and offices, the officer might recognize various bomb components, and that familiarity could help in identifying a potential suicide bomber. An officer who comes across an unidentified object should know not to touch it, as it may be dangerous; the officer should know to call for help.

Terror groups have already made use of the Internet to show how to make a sophisticated suicide bomb vest, along with demonstrating its kill range, using a mannequin instead of a human being. On December 22, 2004, the American news network, the National Broadcasting Company (NBC), revealed that it had obtained a detailed 26-minute video entitled

"The Explosive Belt for Martyrdom Operations" from a militant Islamic chat room on the Internet. The video showed how to make an explosive vest largely from common off-the-shelf materials [1].

If the suicide bomber is to perform like a human missile, the explosives must allow the bomber to

List of Explosives
Nitroglycerin
Dynamite
RDX
TNT
PETN
ANFO

Arrive at the best spot to cause massive lethal damage
Arrive undetected at the target
Detonate the bomb successfully

A BRIEF HISTORY OF EXPLOSIVES

Nitroglycerine, a heavy, oily explosive liquid made by nitrating glycerol, has been used in bomb making since the 1860s. It is sensitive to shock, which could cause it to explode; over time, it becomes increasingly unstable, making it quite dangerous to transport. In its liquid form, a premature detonation may occur when the liquid is sloshed around.

In 1863, German chemist Joseph Wilbrand invented a high explosive known as TNT (trinitrotoluene). At first used as a yellow dye, it was so hard to detonate that its potential as an explosive was not recognized for a few years. Once recognized as valuable, however, TNT became one of the most popular explosives for military and industrial applications. One of its most appreciated characteristics was its insensitivity to friction and shock, thereby reducing the risk of accidental detonation. Nitroglycerine, compared to TNT, was easier to detonate, but was flawed in that it was sensitive to shock and friction.

In 1867, four years after the discovery of TNT, Alfred Nobel, a Swedish chemist and engineer, tried to improve the stability and, hence, the safety of nitroglycerine. Nobel's breakthrough was to mix nitroglycerine with an absorbent inert substance: dirt. He called the more stable nitroglycerine dynamite, and it became an explosive that was safer and easier to handle than existing explosives. The creation of dynamite was a major step forward in the development of usable explosives.

Dynamite was not the perfect product Nobel had hoped it would be: Sometimes the nitroglycerine leaked from the dirt, producing unstable dynamite. As a result, dynamite was used primarily in places where explosives could cause little personal harm, such as in mining, quarrying, and the construction industries.

Many types of commercial dynamite are on sale in 2011. Some have been made less sensitive to shock and friction by limiting the amount of nitroglycerine used and replacing it with other substances. Although sometimes used in warfare, its instability has kept it from being commonly used in the military sector.

Eventually, the military industries improved on Nobel's dynamite by producing very potent and stable explosive products such as RDX (Research Department Explosive); C4 (Composition C4), a plastic explosive 1.24 times more powerful than TNT; and detasheet (detonation sheet). These improved explosives were widely used in military and industrial applications.

Each explosive had its advantages and uses. Though less potent than C4, TNT is cheaper, so that if someone wants to blow up a large building, TNT would likely be the explosive of choice, although Nobel's dynamite was more powerful than TNT; bomb makers preferred TNT because of its greater stability.

One example of how bomb makers made decisions as to what kind of explosive to use came on April 30, 2003, when Mike's Place in Tel Aviv was hit by a suicide bombing. Seeking a powerful device, the bomb maker would have liked to include fragments in the explosive device. These fragments are pieces of metal wrapped around the main explosive that travel at bulletlike speeds once the bomb explodes and do the actual killing and most serious injuries.

These pieces of metal are wrapped around the main charge and travel at great speed; these fragments are the main cause of casualties.

But the explosive needed to be compact to help ensure that no one would discover the suicide bomber in advance of the attack; the goal was to obtain a stable and pliable explosive that could be fitted to the bomber's body without attracting anyone's curiosity. So, the bomb maker decided not to use metal fragments but instead chose a detasheet-like product—a very high-grade military explosive that was pliable, powerful enough to kill even without the fragments, stable, and compact.

WHAT GOES INTO A SUICIDE BOMB?

Here are the critical components of a suicide bomb:

1. *Firing system*: the detonator that initiates the explosive chain that leads to the explosion of the main explosive charge.
2. *Main explosive charge*: The explosive material: a substance containing much stored energy that can produce an explosion when detonated correctly.

3. *Fragments*: metal pieces, behaving like lethal projectiles, that travel at high velocities and are the main cause for dead and wounded.
4. *Electrical system*: the system that ignites the detonator and starts the explosive chain.
5. *Camouflage*: the material that disguises both bomber and the bomb and allows the bomber to get in close to the prey.

Let's examine each of these five elements:

Firing System

The firing system is the detonator that initiates the explosive chain that will later set off the main explosive charge. Making the right kind of detonator is crucial. Bomb makers need to employ a detonator—a tiny explosive—because many explosives will not blow up without being detonated. The detonator must be quite sensitive, because only a very sensitive explosive can be set off by heat or friction generated by the electrical system's firing system.

Bomb makers create detonators that are so small that, if they blow up by accident, not much damage occurs other than the loss of a finger or, at worst, a hand. Unlike the detonator, the explosive substance for the main explosive charge cannot be too sensitive; otherwise, any spark or movement could set off the entire bomb.

Frequently, terrorists confront the problem of finding a proper detonator. "Proper" in this case means that the detonator is stable enough to use—not too unstable to explode prematurely—while remaining sensitive to heat or friction. If a suicide bomber carried explosives that were overly sensitive, every time he jumped or fell, threw a bag on the floor, or smoked a cigarette, he would be in danger of blowing up. So sensitive explosives are used only at the start of the explosive chain.

The detonator must be embedded or attached to the main explosive charge for the explosive chain to work. It must be in direct physical proximity to the main explosive charge. Any separation between the detonator and the main explosive charge would mean that the explosion of the detonator would not transfer to the main charge. A corollary to this latter proposition is that one way of rendering an explosive device semi-safe is to separate the detonator from the main charge. But such a measure is extremely risky and requires a highly skilled bomb tech.

Main Explosive Charge

The main explosive charge is the material containing much stored energy that, upon detonation, releases a large amount of energy and heat. When set off by a detonator, the material expands faster than the speed of sound, producing light, heat, sound, and pressure. The main explosive charge is a measured quantity of explosive material and the largest explosive component of the bomb.

TATP bomb laboratory. (*Credit*: Gil Kleiman photo collection)

The main explosive charge should be stable and insensitive to shock, and friction. An explosive charge called TATP (triacetone triperoxide peroxyacetone), an organic peroxide that takes the form of a white crystalline powder with a distinctively acrid odor, was popular among Palestinian bomb makers because it was easy to produce, powerful, and could be initiated without a detonator.

But when bomb makers began experimenting with it, its instability proved hazardous. TATP turned out to be very sensitive to friction. Bomb makers and nearby civilians were involved in numerous "work accidents" when TATP exploded inadvertently. With its high susceptibility to accidental detonation by shock, friction, or heat, TATP is known as the "Mother of Satan" among certain Islamic terrorist organizations.

Though the Palestinians began using TATP in 1980, by the start of the Second Intifada in September 2000, Palestinian bomb makers had learned how to make TATP stable and the explosive was widely used, mostly as the main explosive charge and sometimes as a detonator. The Palestinians relied upon TATP because it was available to them and other better explosives were not. TATP had the important advantage of avoiding detection by early airport scanners.

Among the incidents where TATP was used or suspected of being used were:

December 22, 2001
   Richard Reid of al-Qaeda (the "shoe bomber") targeted American Airlines Flight 63 from Paris to Miami with a bomb concealed in his shoe using a TATP detonator. He was caught before he could detonate his bomb.

July 21, 2005
   TATP was used in explosives in four attempted bomb attacks on London's public transport system. Only the detonators of the bombs exploded, so there was no loss of life.

September 5, 2006
   Homemade TATP was found during the arrest of seven suspected terrorists in Vollsmose, a neighborhood in the Danish city of Odense.

September 4, 2007
   Homemade TATP was found during the arrest of eight suspected al-Qaeda collaborators in Copenhagen, Denmark.

December 25, 2009
   Umar Farouk Abdulmutallab (the "underwear bomber") of al-Qaeda tried to detonate a bomb containing TATP hidden in his underwear after boarding Northwest Airlines Flight 253 en route from Amsterdam, Holland, to Detroit, Michigan. He was subdued before he could detonate the bomb; no one was hurt.

September 2010
   A pen bomb exploded in Charlotte, North Carolina, at the Turning Point Academy School. Police said a large amount of TATP was found inside a student's home.

September 10, 2010
   A TATP bomb accidentally exploded, injuring the bomb maker in a toilet at the Hotel Jørgensen in Copenhagen.

Fragments

These pieces of metal are wrapped around the main charge and travel at great speed once the bomb explodes; the pieces of metal—or fragments—are the main cause of casualties. The suicide belt, using shoulder straps and covering the bomber's stomach, contains a number of cylinders filled with explosives surrounded by fragments. When filled with explosives and fragments, the suicide belt can weigh between 11 to 44 pounds and is often concealed under thick clothes and a heavy coat.

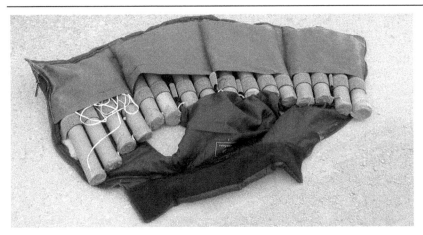

Suicide bomb belt; the belt contains PVC (plastic) piping as opposed to metal pipes. (*Credit*: Gil Kleiman photo collection)

Suicide bomb makers generally cannot obtain powerful explosive charges and therefore have to rely on fragments to do the killing. The fragments have to be made of a material strong enough to withstand the pressure, the force, and the heat created by the explosive charge. To avoid metal detectors which might pick up fragments, it is tempting for sponsors to use glass as fragments; however, glass melts or disintegrates into sand and is thus of no use as a fragment explosive.

Metal is the fragment of choice: bolts, small thick wire, nuts, nails, screws, ball bearings, or a cut up metal known as "rebar" (reinforcing bar) used to reinforce concrete. Palestinian bomb makers had been able to obtain "rebar" from Palestinian construction workers, and therefore used it routinely. The most widely used and dangerous fragments are steel balls, usually a little less than half an inch in diameter.

132

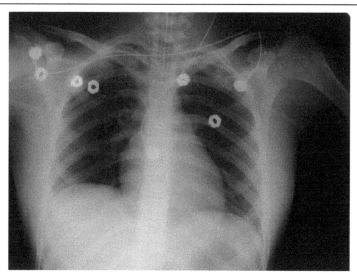

X-ray of a suicide bombing victim from a bomb containing bolts (metal fragments). (*Credit*: Gil Kleiman photo collection)

Various kinds of fragments: bolts, nails, and ball bearings. (*Credit*: Gil Kleiman photo collection)

133

The fragments must be able to withstand the explosive charge yet be strong enough to penetrate a human being. They must be small in order to get the largest amount of fragments inside the device. The more fragments, the more the potential casualties.

Until the mid 1990s, Palestinian bomb makers used more explosives and fewer fragments, convinced that the explosives killed. Realizing that the fragments produced 90 percent of the dead and wounded in a suicide bombing, the bomb makers altered the ratio and put in fewer explosives and more fragments. The number of victims rose dramatically.

It seemed logical that bomb makers would seek other more lethal fragments than metal, such as chemical fragments, including rat poison, hepatitis B, and AIDS. Bomb experts insisted, however, that none of these add-ons would prove of value: Fragments were enough to kill and, at any rate, these add-ons could not survive the heat and pressure of the explosion.

Electrical System

Creating the electrical system for the bomb is the easiest part of the bomb's assembly. For a suicide bomb, no sophisticated electrical equipment is required as it would be for a remote radio control, or proximity device, all of which can be "programmed" to explode when someone approaches or when exposed to light.

All that is required for a suicide bomb to explode is to press the detonator switch, which sends an electric spark to the detonator, causing the sensitive explosives in the detonator to explode. That explosion produces an explosive chain that ultimately leads to the explosion of the main charge.

While approaching the target, the suicide bomber keeps the electrical switch in an "up" or "off" position, not permitting the electrical current to flow through the battery and ignite the electrical match inside the detonator. When it is time to detonate the bomb, the switch is pushed down, allowing the electrical current to flow through the battery, igniting the electrical match, a device that uses an externally applied electric current to ignite a combustible compound. Igniting the electrical match produces a small spark, which sets off the sensitive explosives in the detonator.

Sometimes the main explosive charge is so stable that the small explosion of the detonator is not sufficient to start the explosive chain, requiring a "booster" (or intermediary charge) to enlarge the explosive effect of the detonator.

The bomb's electrical system works no differently from one that turns on a flashlight or any of thousands of other devices. But instead of turning on a light, it turns on an electrical match. The components of the electrical system are exactly what one would find in a flashlight: batteries, electrical wires, an on-off switch, and an electrical match (rather than a light bulb) inserted in a detonator.

The genius of the suicide bomb is its simplicity, unlike missiles, which are expensive and require sophisticated tracking technology (none of which the suicide bomber needs). The suicide bomber has no need for a GPS system or a gyroscope as the missile does. The bomber needs only a thumb to set off the electrical current that will ignite the bomb.

Once the on–off switch is turned on, in a matter of milliseconds, there's a small boom—sounding like "puck," which is the sound of the detonator exploding, and milliseconds later, the main explosive charges goes off. If the would-be suicide bomber hears the "puck" but doesn't feel the big boom, he knows that the detonator, but not the main charge, has gone off. This "dud" might injure the bomber slightly, but he will survive.

Example

When suicide bombers attempted four separate attacks on the London public transport system on July 21, 2005, their four bombs proved to be duds. Only the bombs' detonators exploded, resulting in no loss of life. One person was slightly injured, suffering an asthma attack triggered by the incident. This fortuitous "dudding" may have been due to the low quality of hydrogen peroxide used in the devices. Possibly, the suicide bomb makers purchased a diluted, hence inferior, version from a drugstore.

Camouflage

To reach a spot where the suicide bomber can cause mass casualties requires the bomber to camouflage both himself and his bomb. Camouflage allows the suicide bomber to fit into his surroundings and go undetected.

The suicide bomber has much camouflage, apart from a suicide belt, from which to choose: a knapsack, guitar case, attaché case, duffel bag, plastic bag, computer bag, loaves of bread, beer cans, even Similac cans—all of which have been used in suicide bombings in Israel. Which of these camouflaged items he uses depends on his surroundings: Knowing that his target is a bus filled with college students, he will camouflage the bomb in a knapsack.

Certain camouflage may prove burdensome: To conceal the bomb, the suicide bomber might place the bomb belt under his coat. But the sheer bulkiness of the bomb could give him away. A heavy-set suicide bomber, already bulky and uneager to show more bulk, may well camouflage the bomb elsewhere on his body. For example, suicide bomber Asif Muhammed Hanif, who perpetrated the Mike's Place suicide bombing (killing three and wounding 50), was so heavyset that he placed his explosives device on his back to avoid detection and to make it easier to get around.

An Arab may employ a disguise—a long black coat, side curls, even a fake long beard—to allow him to appear as an Orthodox Jew, thereby not arousing suspicion. Or, an Arab may try to emulate a typical Israeli teenager: wearing earrings, dying his hair, sporting a T-shirt, a motorcycle jacket, and jeans—all in order to fit in with an Israeli crowd.

Najibullah Zazi, arrested in 2009 for planning suicide bombings in a New York City subway station, did not employ any camouflage at all, though he certainly looked like a suicide bomber from "central casting": an Arab, a Muslim, dark-skinned, with a bit of a militant's beard. But he felt no need to change his appearance because, with no suicide bombings in New York City during the eight years since 9/11, no one was on high alert for Middle Eastern–looking would-be terrorists. [2]

Sometimes, a would-be suicide bomber does not need a special disguise; if his target is a Middle Eastern–looking community, then his "camouflage" need only be Middle Eastern.

Example

A female suicide bomber, dressed in typical Arab garb, blew herself up at a bus stop outside French Hill in Jerusalem on September 22, 2004. She killed two police officers. It was not unusual to see people dressed as she was in that neighborhood.

"POOR MAN'S ALTERNATIVE"

When high-powered explosives are not available and the bomb maker is unable to produce improvised explosives, the fallback option is what is called the "poor man's alternative," i.e., smokeless powder. Not an explosive at all, the alternative is an incendiary or low-explosive device composed of the smokeless powder found in bullets or match heads.

Fast-burning smokeless black powder: an incendiary used as a "poor man's alternative" to conventional explosives. (*Credit*: Gil Kleiman photo collection)

Placed inside pipe bombs, these incendiary devices, once packed inside the tight confines of a closed pipe, "explode," but they have none of the force that high-explosive devices generate. These alternatives contain fast-burning substances that, when under pressure in a closed pipe, burn in very similar ways to explosives. The end result: The outer metal container that is under pressure from the fast-burning substance disintegrates, and fragments fly out at high speeds, very similar to an explosion. It can be as life threatening as the more powerful explosives.

A police officer must be conscious of these kinds of bomb devices. Searching through someone's house, an officer may find one or more items that suggest someone may be planning to make a "poor man's alternative" device: piles of match heads on a table; large numbers of bullets; empty bullet shells; cans of black (smokeless) powder when no bullet-making machines are present; black powder without powder scales; metal; or PVC (polyvinyl chloride, a widely produced plastic).

THE EASE OF ACQUIRING EXPLOSIVES

Palestinian bomb makers needed a readily available explosive charge that would mimic military-grade devices. Bomb makers favor inexpensive bomb-making materials that are easy to acquire. If the necessary explosive materials were easily available but cost $100 million, they would be in trouble. The bomb must be inexpensive and easy to make; it must be potent; and it must be safe until it is detonated.

Explosives the Suicide Bomb Maker Tries to Access

Let us examine the three kinds of explosives that are potentially available to suicide bombers: military-grade, commercial, and improvised explosives.

Military-Grade Explosives

The most stable, most compact, and most powerful devices, these high-grade devices deliver the greatest bang for the buck. Military-grade explosives are often compact because of the military's need to put an explosive charge in a missile head or a shell that requires limited space and a small amount of weight and volume. Accordingly, military leaders spend much money on producing explosive material that is both small and potent.

All of these features make military-grade explosives the most expensive to produce. But the military can afford the highest-grade explosives made by weapons factories. Suicide bomb makers cannot. Even if they could, there is no open market where military-grade explosives are sold. They can be found only at military bases, certain storage places, or mine fields.

Gaining access to military bases requires inside assistance, stealthy execution, and perhaps outright thievery. For terrorists to obtain military-grade explosives, they would have to make secret deals with military sources that willingly exchange cash from the sponsors for the hard-to-get explosives. But it is quite impossible that Palestinian terrorists could make such deals with Israeli military sources.

Makers of suicide bombs sometimes locate high-grade (i.e., military) explosives in mine fields. Digging up an old mine and cutting open its casing carries great danger and risk. Therefore, there were times when terrorists used an entire anti-tank mine as the main explosive charge, placing the detonator directly into the mine, using the mine as the main explosive charge.

Commercial Explosives

With military-grade explosives very difficult to acquire, suicide bomb makers made do at times with commercial explosives. The latter had the advantage of being powerful, stable, and quite accessible, but at times not compact.

By purchasing commercial explosives, the bomb maker was relieved of having to make the explosive himself. Instead, all he had to do was to walk into a store, armed with a fake license, and walk out with ready-made explosives. (Normally, building contractors can purchase commercial explosives but only under severe restrictions; licensing arrangements are routine.)

138

Commercial devices had one disadvantage: They tended to be bulkier than military-grade ones. A bulky suicide belt could make wearing camouflage more difficult and more noticeable. But commercial bomb manufacturers hardly took the needs of the suicide bomber into account.

Because quarry managers require explosives that can dig a hole in the ground, they have no limits on the volume of the explosive material that goes into the hole. As a result, explosives manufacturers do not invest a lot of money in order to make their explosives compact, making the explosives more expensive.

In canvassing for commercially available explosive material, bomb makers have turned at times to ANFO, ammonium nitrate/fuel oil. It is stable and user friendly, showing up sometimes in improvised explosive devices. It is known as a fertilizer bomb.

ANFO is the most widely used explosive in civil construction, metal mining, coal mining, and quarrying, accounting for 80 percent of the 6 million pounds of explosives used in North America each year. It is not appropriate for suicide bombing, however, because the bomb maker needs a large amount of ANFO to get the same "bang for the buck" that he could get from a smaller amount of TNT or dynamite. Hence, when it came to terror, ANFO would only be found in a car bomb.

Terrorist bomb makers have preferred TNT if they can get a hold of it, but they have often had to settle for ANFO. At times they did get their hands on TNT, as in the high-casualty October 1983 truck bomb attack on the American marine barracks in Beirut when two suicide bombers blew themselves up using 12,000 pounds of TNT, killing 241.

Middle East terrorists have not used ANFO, although other terrorists have: the Irish Republican Army (IRA); FARC, the Revolutionary Armed Forces of Colombia—People's Army; Euskadl Ta Askatasuna (ETA); the Basque Homeland and Freedom group; and Ramzi Yousef, a main operative in the 1993 World Trade Center bombing.

A more sophisticated variant of ANFO, known as ANNM (ammonium nitrate and nitromethane), was used in the 1995 Oklahoma City bombing (a truck bombing).

Weighing the pluses and minuses, a bomb maker would be disinclined to use commercial explosives unless he could obtain a high-end product close to military levels of quality, which is all but impossible. Still, at times bomb makers are forced to seek out and use commercially obtained explosives when it is too complicated to make the bomb on their own.

139

Improvised Explosives

If a bomb maker had access to military-grade explosives, he would always opt for them. However, since they are not easily accessible, he will seek out commercial explosives; but off-the-shelf explosive materials are not always easy to purchase. So the bomb maker is forced to improvise bombs that he produces that are called improvised explosives.

It is much more expensive to make an explosive device that is potent, stable, compact, and pliable. Such an explosive is more expensive than one that requires only stability and potency.

During the First Intifada (1987–1992), because of tight security at Israeli checkpoints, Palestinians had no access to military or commercial explosives, so they turned to improvised explosives such as TATP. Because the explosive is improvised, the potential for producing new improvised explosives is limitless. New developments in the terrorist world are occurring all the time. Palestinians used EGDN (ethylene glycol dinitrate), a powerful improvised explosive, starting in 2001, in 20 terror incidents.

To stay on top of monitoring would-be suicide bombers, law enforcement officers need to know where bomb makers would go to purchase the ingredients to make improvised explosives. People do not buy improvised explosives; they make them from products that are purchasable and, when put together, produce a bomb. A good example of a bomb maker and would-be suicide bomber who purchased these items from everyday stores was Najibullah Zazi.

Planning to carry off a suicide bombing against a New York City subway train, he nearly built a suicide bomb based on the purchase of bomb ingredients acquired commercially. Zazi wrote notes on what he needed to buy to make triacetone triperoxide peroxyacetone (TATP) [2]. According to a government memorandum, during the summer of 2009 Zazi undertook Internet searches for hydrochloric acid, and bookmarked a Web site about "Lab Safety for Hydrochloric Acid" [3]. He also "searched a beauty salon website for hydrocide and peroxide." After these Web searches, Zazi and a few associates purchased "unusually large quantities of hydrogen peroxide and acetone products from beauty supply stores in the Denver metropolitan area."

One associate purchased a 1-gallon container of a product containing 20 percent hydrogen peroxide as well as an 8-ounce bottle of acetone. A second associate purchased an acetone product, and a third bought

140

32-ounce bottles of Ion Sensitive Scalp Developer, a product containing high levels of hydrogen peroxide.

Because of the benign nature of the products he and his associates bought on the commercial market, Zazi seemed harmless to other customers and clerks. No one had been trained to become suspicious of someone purchasing numerous dual-purpose (benign and harmful at the same time) products containing large amounts of hydrogen peroxide.

ASSEMBLING THE BOMB

Starting in 1994, when Palestinians launched their first suicide bombings against Israel, bomb makers multitasked: They procured the explosives; made the device; put together the bomb belt or other means of camouflage; recruited the would-be suicide bomber; trained him; found his target; and sent him on his way. Eventually, mutlitasking proved unworkable: There were too many mom-and-pop bomb makers, some who did their jobs well, others who did not.

Seeking to improve their suicide bombing planning, terrorists dropped multitasking in favor of a system where individuals performed one task in the overall planning. Thus, one person would be responsible for getting the explosive materials; one for making the bomb; one for putting the wires together; one for making the fragments; one for recruiting potential suicide bombers; one for deciding on targets; and one for driving the suicide bomber to the target. No longer was someone a jack-of-all-trades.

In 1993, Yahya Abd-al-Latif Ayyash appeared. Nicknamed "the engineer" because of his bomb-making skills, especially his ability to assemble a bomb made of homegrown ingredients, he became the bomb maker for Hamas. Others took on one specific task each in the chain of planning suicide bombings. Ayyash made bombs; he had no idea who would use them, when, or where.

In the early 1990s, Ayyash sent a letter to the Hamas leadership arguing, "We paid a high price when we used only slingshots and stones (during the First Intifada). We need to exert more pressure, make the cost of the occupation that much more expensive to human lives, that much more unbearable" [4].

He lived to be 30, assassinated on January 5, 1996. This Israeli-sponsored targeted assassination, meant to reduce Palestinian terror, led instead to an increase in such acts: in the two months after Ayyash's death, four suicide bombings occurred that killed 59 Israelis.

Ayyash's reputation among Palestinians was legendary. Streets in Jenin and Ramallah on the West Bank and in Beit Lahiya in northern Gaza, as well as a square in Jericho, were named after him.

For a period, Ayyash was Israel's most wanted man. Estimates put the number of Israelis killed by his bombs at 90. With TNT and other high explosives not available in the West Bank or Gaza Strip, Ayyash often employed acetone and detergent, both available household products that, when combined, created TATP.

Among the suicide bombings for which he supplied the bomb were: the Mehola Junction bombing that killed one person on April 16, 1993, the first suicide car bomb attack carried out by Palestinian terrorists on the Israeli-occupied West Bank); and the Afula car bomb attack on April 6, 1994, killing eight Israelis, which marked the first suicide bombing carried out by Palestinian terrorists against Israeli civilians in Israel proper. He also supplied bombs for suicide attacks near the Gaza Strip in April 1995 (nine killed); in Ramat Gan two months later (six killed); and in Jerusalem in August 1995 (five killed).

Israeli security personnel carried out a huge manhunt for Ayyash until Israel's Shabak carried out the assassination, convincing an Ayyash friend to turn over a cell phone containing a bomb to "the engineer." As soon as Ayyash turned on the cell phone, the Shabak detonated it, and Ayyash died at once.

Until now, we have looked at the various aspects of suicide bombing from the perspective of the suicide bomber and the terror organization. In the next chapter, we look at the decisions taken by the U.S. federal government and the city of New York to protect America—including New York City—against further terror after 9/11.

NOTES

1. "On December 22, 2004…" NBC, "Web video teaches terrorists to make bomb vest." December 22, 2004.
2. Affidavit of FBI Agent in support of criminal complaint and arrest warrant in United States v. Najibullah Zazi, U.S. District Court for the District of Colorado, September 19, 2009. http://tomdiaz.wordpress.com/2009/09/20/the-case-against-terror-suspect-najibullah-zazi-fbi-affidavit-reveals-elegant-work/.

3. September 24, 2009: United States District Court Eastern District of New York, United States of America, against 09-CR-663 (RJD) Najibullah Zazi, Defendant, Memorandum of Law in Support of the Government's Motion for a Permanent Order of Detention.
4. "We paid a high price:" *New Yorker Magazine*, "An Arsenal of Believers: Talking to the 'human bombs.'" November 19, 2001. http://www.stephensp. Ocatch.com/articles/articles…/_hassan_arsenal_Believers.do

Section IV

Defending against Suicide Bombings

11

Responses to 9/11
Federal Government

We now shift gears. Having spent the first part of this manual dealing with the phenomenon of suicide bombing, we now discuss the various ways that law enforcement professionals can use to defend against that phenomenon.

Until 9/11, the United States had no trouble identifying its enemies. When the United States was attacked, it did not have to figure out against whom to launch a counterattack. This was the case with Nazi Germany and the Japanese in World War II; with the Chinese and Soviets after that war; and with the North Koreans and North Vietnamese in the 1950s and 1960s.

WHO IS THE ENEMY?

But when the unprecedented act of crashing commercial airlines into skyscrapers and the Pentagon occurred, at first the United States could not say with certainty who its foe was. Its intelligence officials conjectured that it might be al-Qaeda, but few had heard of that terror organization; and no one could say with certainty that Osama bin Laden and his associates had committed the horrific act.

Even when the U.S. intelligence community concluded on September 11 that al-Qaeda had carried out the attacks, it still seemed unimaginable that cave dwellers in Afghanistan had secretly planned and executed the most devastating mega suicide bombing in American history. The events of 9/11 left Americans bewildered, frustrated that insufficient attention had been paid to whoever had carried out the attacks, and baffled as to how to retaliate against an enemy willing to send suicide bombers against high-profile targets on American soil.

President George W. Bush grasped that the 9/11 attacks were bound to cause historical shifts in the way the United States sought to defend itself, and he realized that the suicide bombings were a declaration of war against the United States requiring an immediate military response. The attacks were so gruesome, so overwhelming that the immediate reaction of the president, even before knowing who the enemy was specifically, was to go to war against terror. But terror was a phenomenon, not a nation against whom one could go to war. Still, by the afternoon of September 11, George W. Bush told his senior military commanders that he planned a major military strike that would do far more than put "a million-dollar missile on a five-dollar tent" [1]. His authority for launching a war came from Article II of the U.S. Constitution and from House and Senate resolutions authorizing the president to lead the country into battle against nations and/or organizations that he deemed the 9/11 perpetrators.

Responses by President George W. Bush to 9/11

American attacks on Afghanistan and Iraq
New focus on global terror
Strengthening America's infrastructure
Augmenting intelligence
A new Department of Homeland Security
Sweeping new intelligence powers
USA PATRIOT Act (Uniting and Strengthening America by Providing Appropriate Tools Required to Intercept and Obstruct Terrorism)
Dealing with Guantanamo detainees

PLANNING: A MILITARY STRIKE

But a military strike against whom?

Traditionally, nations went to war against other nations, but there was no indication that a nation had ordered 9/11. Some American movie and spy novel addicts thought the 9/11 villains reminded them of SPECTRE, the murky organization that was James Bond's nemesis. The acronym stood for "Special Executive for Counterintelligence, Terrorism, Revenge and Extortion."

A novelist or scriptwriter could get away with creating an entity that had no fixed address, no affiliation with a nation, but to the tough-minded politicians and military commanders, a stateless, faceless enemy pulling off a 9/11 attack seemed preposterous. But the facts were clear: 19 hijacker/suicide bombers representing a little-known organization had executed the attack. The organization was affiliated with no state and was as elusive as it was nihilistic, jihadist, brutal, and animated by hatred, with its main agenda instilling fear and chaos among so-called infidels. Once President Bush learned that an amorphous, jihadist, anti-American group called al-Qaeda was behind the attack, he took on the trappings of a small-town sheriff: He wanted al-Qaeda's leader, Osama bin Laden "dead or alive" [2]. To the president, such an outcome seemed richly deserved: Not only had bin Laden masterminded 9/11, but in August 1996, he had also issued a fatwa, saying that the murder of Americans was obligatory for every Muslim. Between 1996 and 2001, bin Laden had built training camps for 10,000 terrorists in Afghanistan.

He took on the trappings of a small-town sheriff: he wanted al-Qaeda's leader, Osama bin Laden "dead or alive."

Though outraged and determined to destroy bin Laden and al-Qaeda, Bush and his military commanders proceeded cautiously, not entirely sure how best to target an enemy who hid in caves, had no homeland, and seemed no more than a guest in many countries. To make it easier to resolve the question of who to bear arms against, the president decreed that any country that harbored terrorists would be considered as much of an American enemy as the 9/11 attackers themselves. Notably excluded from the Bush doctrine was Saudi Arabia, no doubt due to its status as America's chief oil supplier.

Eventually, America's focus centered on Afghanistan and its Islamic fundamentalist Taliban rulers who provided a safe haven for bin Laden and his al-Qaeda terrorists. By September 15, President Bush was meeting with his national security team at Camp David and planning for an American invasion of Afghanistan. On October 7, nearly a month after 9/11, the president launched a military strike against Afghanistan, hoping to cut off al-Qaeda's main support system by eradicating the Taliban.

The Untied States succeeded in ending Taliban political rule, but al-Qaeda removed itself to neighboring Pakistan before America could wipe it out. Over the next decade, the United States continued to root out Taliban fighters in Afghanistan until its planned departure from Afghanistan in 2011. The United States sought to capture or kill Osama Bin Laden from soon after 9/11 but he proved elusive, presumed to be hiding in some remote spot either in Afghanistan or Pakistan. Finally, a breakthrough occurred when a Bin Laden courier, whom American intelligence agents had been searching for, turned up in a compund 35 miles north of the Pakistani capital of Islamabad. That led to eight months of further intelligence that resulted in May 2011 in a helicopter attack by U.S. military and intelligence operatives on the compound. During the attack, the operatives came upon Bin Laden and killed him.

Determined to uproot al-Qaeda wherever it appeared, Bush opened a second military front on March 20, 2003, against al-Qaeda, sending American troops into Iraq to topple Saddam Hussein, believed to be a strong supporter of bin Laden's terror group. To justify the American invasion, the president argued that the U.S. military aimed at disarming Iraq of weapons of mass destruction (meaning nuclear, biological, and chemical weapons) and to end Saddam Hussein's support for terrorism. American forces crushed his regime within three weeks of its invasion of Iraq.

American troops captured Saddam on December 13, 2003, nine months after the U.S. invasion. He was turned over to the Iraqis, who tried and convicted him and then sentenced him to death. He was hanged on December 13, 2006. Iraqi insurgents continued to fight against American troops. On August 13, 2010, the last American combat troops left Iraq, leaving 50,000 U.S. troops behind, acting as advisors. No connection between Saddam Hussein and al-Qaeda was ever established.

A NEW APPROACH TO TERROR

Until 9/11, the American government and its intelligence agencies had not taken international terror seriously as a direct threat to the United States. Even terror attacks against American targets thousands of miles from the United States were regarded as little more than painful, tragic blips on the screen.

When al-Qaeda attacked two American embassies in East Africa (1998) and the USS *Cole* (2000), the American reaction was moderate. In the East African attacks, 11 were killed in Dar es Salaam, Tanzania, and 212 were killed in Nairobi, Kenya, in simultaneous suicide truck bombings. These attacks did bring Osama bin Laden onto the FBI's radar screen for the first time: He was placed on the FBI's Ten Most Wanted list. While harbored and refueling in the Yemeni port of Aden, the USS *Cole* fell victim to a suicide bombing that killed 17 sailors.

After the attack on the embassies, President Bill Clinton launched cruise missiles at al-Qaeda sites in Afghanistan; but the training camps had been mostly abandoned; the long-distance strikes appeared ineffective. Following the USS *Cole* attack, the United States did not respond militarily.

After 9/11, U.S. intelligence services decided that the two al-Qaeda suicide bombings hardly bespoke a systematic build-up to a mega suicide bombing on American soil. When Hezbollah terrorists bombed the Marine barracks in Lebanon in 1983, President Reagan withdrew American forces.

150

As the phenomenon of suicide bombings spread from Lebanon and Sri Lanka in the 1980s to Turkey, Chechnya, Kashmir, and Israel in the 1990s, the United States still regarded these bombings as local events and not a terror tactic that could metastasize to the United States.

With 9/11 came the dramatic and frightening evidence that terror could no longer be treated dismissively as little more than a "foreign" occurrence; indeed, as those in the World Trade Center and Pentagon learned, Americans on American soil could become victims as instantly as those in the East African embassies or on the USS *Cole*.

The al-Qaeda terrorists on 9/11 did not launch a coup attempt against the United States or try to assassinate President Bush. However, their more "moderate" tactic of employing suicide bombers to kill Americans at high-profile targets was enough for the United States to take global terror seriously for the first time. It became clear to Bush that he must employ a whole new approach to terror—and do so urgently.

Certainly President Bush got the message immediately; but did others? On the surface, the idea that a new, implacable enemy had surfaced as a credible threat to the United States seemed absurd, tragically comic. Al-Qaeda had not "invaded" America by sending in a few divisions. It had launched 9/11 with "only" 19 attackers. But American intelligence agencies began to worry whether al-Qaeda was planning more 9/11-like attacks. That fear paved the way for the most important revamping of American security services since the post–World War Two period.

COSTLY NEW PRIORITIES

The financial cost of the new priority that the American government would give to terror would be high. Intelligence agencies would have to be expanded. A new home security apparatus would need to be organized. Security would have to be increased at the nation's infrastructure sites, and airline security would need urgent improvement. But few worried about the costs.

Despite the growing urgency to deal with global terror, no senior official raised a voice publicly in favor of dropping the volunteer army policy in favor of an enlisted one; since 1973, the United States had not conscripted soldiers. Nor had anyone suggested ordering factories to stop building civilian products and start manufacturing military ones. Though both wars in Afghanistan and Iraq would cost billions of dollars, President

Bush preferred not to raise taxes that would have paid for those wars. The most he asked of citizens was to volunteer and to give to charities.

In time, however, the U.S. government imposed a different kind of cost on civilians, becoming far more intrusive. Its intelligence agencies scrapped long-held personal freedoms in the name of foiling terrorist plots. Policy makers strongly believed that they had a license to expand intelligence and security powers regardless of that personal cost.

THE DAY AFTER: SEPTEMBER 12, 2001

As early as the day after 9/11, President George W. Bush concluded that he possessed that license. He woke up September 12 to a nation believing that another terror attack seemed imminent. Out of such fear, families purchased gas masks and hoarded food and water; workers in skyscrapers stayed home; sporting events were postponed. In New York City, people tried to carry on normally, driving their cars, walking down streets, but they could not stop worrying that another mega terror event might occur in their midst very soon.

No longer would the focus of George Bush's nine-month presidency be on domestic matters: deciding on budget priorities, reducing unemployment, and improving the performance of the private marketplace. Now the focus would be on war, specifically on getting the United States ready for a historical shift in attitude, policy, and action regarding American security.

As the scope of the 9/11 attacks became increasingly clear, President Bush set three goals for himself and the nation. The first was to prevent terrorists from hitting again. Fears had heightened that al-Qaeda might soon turn to biological, chemical, or even nuclear weapons for the next attack. The second was to enlist the support of American citizens to keep the terrorists from shutting down the economy or from dividing the country. Given the numbness, even paralysis felt uniformly around America, it seemed likely that few would return to work quickly. Bush wanted everyone back to work as soon as possible.

The third was to convey to Americans that the nation would be engaged in a new kind of war with an unknown face. At a CIA briefing that morning, Bush received the first confirmation that bin Laden had been behind 9/11; it came from intelligence intercepts of al-Qaeda members in Afghanistan, congratulating one another. Bush asserted that America would be fighting an unconventional war against an enemy that had no permanent home: It was still not clear how this new war would be fought.

152

AUGMENTING INTELLIGENCE

Bush suggested that the defeat of the terrorists would come from improving American intelligence, engaging American troops against not only al-Qaeda but also its host nations, and freezing terrorists' bank accounts. The terrorists would have to be deprived of their safe havens. Hearing from the FBI, Bush learned that most of the 19 9/11 hijackers had been identified, as had their dates of arrival in America, where they had stayed, and how they had carried out the attacks. It was impressive intelligence work, but hardly sufficient to dent the future plans of al-Qaeda. Bush told FBI Director Robert Mueller that he wanted the FBI to focus on preventing attacks, not just investigating them after they occurred.

The president understood that his first task was to strengthen America's defenses against further terror attacks. New measures were quickly adopted: increasing security at bridges, nuclear power plants, seaports, and other vulnerable infrastructure sites; adding air marshals on planes; requiring airlines to fortify cockpit doors and tighten visa and screening procedures for passengers; and deploying National Guard forces to airports.

Bush began to prepare the nation for war. Later on September 12, Bush told the press: "The deliberate and deadly attacks which were carried out yesterday were more than acts of terror. They were acts of war."

"The deliberate and deadly attacks which were carried out yesterday were more than acts of terror. They were acts of war."

Some who had complained that American military involvement in Vietnam had cost too many lives (58,267)—and had dragged on for too many years—questioned whether the president should have declared war, but he countered that four coordinated attacks by terrorists seeking to kill as many Americans as possible certainly obligated America to make such a declaration. Cynics feared that the United States, in declaring war, would battle against all 1.6 billion Muslims in the world, but Bush pointed out that America would go to war only against al-Qaeda. By making that qualification, he hoped to calm the same kind of American hysteria that had sent Japanese Americans to internment camps during World War Two.

Nerves were so frayed that when a bomb threat against the White House was delivered on that Wednesday—the "day after"—Bush ordered White House staff evacuated, but he went on with his business, refusing to give in to terrorists. No bomb was found.

VISIT TO GROUND ZERO

On Thursday, September 14, Bush traveled to Ground Zero—the site of the World Trade Center—where he greeted first responders, and found them fanatical in their anger at al-Qaeda. One of them urged: "George, find the bastards who did this and kill them." Another shouted: "Do not let me down." A third: "Whatever it takes." As the president began his off-the-cuff remarks, someone asked him to speak louder, to which Bush replied: "I can hear you. The rest of the world hears you. And the people who knocked these building down will hear all of us soon." The crowd began chanting: "USA, USA, USA."

"I can hear you. The rest of the world hears you. And the people who knocked these building down will hear all of us soon."

REVAMPING HOME SECURITY

To get a bead on the terrorists, Bush and his administration understood that government efforts at home security would have to expand and, at the same time, become more efficient. Before 9/11, home security agencies functioned independently of one another. Case in point: In March 2002, six months after 9/11, the Immigration and Naturalization Service (INS) notified a Florida flight school by mail that it had approved student visas to Mohammed Atta and Marwan al-Shehhi, the two pilots who had crashed airplanes into the World Trade Center. Streamlining these dysfunctional agencies was in order.

Bush asked Pennsylvania governor Tom Ridge to coordinate the 180,000 employees who worked for those federal home security agencies. Ridge became the first director of the Office of Homeland Security, a White House post, in October 2001. His mandate was to develop and coordinate a broad national strategy to protect against future attacks. It soon became clear that the White House post should be morphed into a cabinet department. On January 24, 2003, nearly 16 months after 9/11, the Department of Homeland Security was created with Ridge as its first secretary and the same mandate: Keep the terrorists at bay.

MASSIVE NEW POWERS

Other parts of the government created new agencies to improve the fight against terrorism: The FBI established a National Security Branch that centered on stopping terrorist attacks; the Defense Department set up a Northern Command to defend the homeland; and the Treasury Department designated a team to disrupt terrorist financing.

As part of these broadened powers, the government gave intelligence services sweeping new authority to track down and capture would-be terrorists (including suicide bombers), and it established tough new security arrangements at airports. Just as significantly, it scrapped the old attitude that a terrorist was just another form of criminal who should be prosecuted as a criminal. The boldness and scope of 9/11 made the 19 hijackers seem far more than common criminals. Treating them as such, prosecuting them for murder—had they lived—hardly seemed a deterrent to future terrorist attacks; only a war against them seemed logical.

AN ANTHRAX SCARE

Tensions and fears over an imminent second terror attack were at the maximum a week after 9/11, when a second nightmare seemed to be happening. On September 18, five letters, each containing anthrax and with a Trenton, New Jersey, postmark, were mailed to ABC News, CBS News, NBC News, and the *New York Post*—all in New York City—and the *National Enquirer* in Boca Raton, Florida. Two U.S. senators—Tom Daschle of South Dakota and Patrick Leahy of Vermont, both Democrats—received anthrax letters, dated October 9. Anthrax is an acute disease caused by bacteria, and most forms of the disease are lethal. Prior to the creation of a vaccine, it had killed thousands of people and animals.

A major investigation followed, especially given the fears of a second mega terror event. It took until April 2005 for the FBI to focus on an American scientist named Bruce Edwards Ivins as the prime suspect in the anthrax scare. He had been working at the government's biodefense laboratories at Fort Detrick in Frederick, Maryland. The FBI informed Ivins in June 2008 that he would soon be prosecuted for disseminating the anthrax, murdering five people and injuring 17 others, but on July 27, he allegedly committed suicide by taking an overdose of acetaminophen. Ten days later, federal prosecutors announced that Ivins had been the sole guilty party of the anthrax crimes.

Despite the anthrax letters and the subsequent deaths and injuries, Americans breathed a sigh of relief that the plot had been homegrown. As we view it, disseminating anthrax widely is the ultimate example of a successful terror attack: It is low-cost; it achieves the biggest bang for the buck;

and it causes global panic. Why? Billions of people are vulnerable: We all get mail. But not everyone visits the World Trade Center or the Pentagon. To be killed on 9/11, one had to be in one of those buildings on a specific day; to die from anthrax, one could be home, at the office—anywhere.

CHANGING SECURITY DOCTRINES

After 9/11 and the anthrax scare, it was self-evident that America's long-established security doctrines had to be revised completely to deal with suicide bombers and other forms of terror.

Take airport security. The only precaution taken at airports before 9/11 was to match each piece of luggage to a passenger out of fear that someone might plant a bomb in a bag without boarding the plane. It had been taken for granted that no terrorist would board a plane with luggage containing a bomb, since the terrorist would not want to die in the explosion.

Or take the American attitude toward international events. Whereas few Americans thought what went on overseas could impact them, after 9/11 terror around the world took on a new urgency, with American intelligence taking a much stronger interest in overseas terror organizations and leading terrorist figures.

But how and where could American intelligence start to track down terrorists? With governments supporting terrorism and the terrorist organizations themselves hiding behind total secrecy, U.S. intelligence agencies had no option for the first 18 months after 9/11, other than to simply count—and hence identify—a "who's who" of international terror. All the while, overseas terror groups were growing and becoming more menacing.

While security doctrines were changing, a new augmentation of American intelligence agencies was occurring: Given the amorphous and secretive methodology of the terrorists, intelligence efforts had to be significantly increased—more people, more resources—but no one could be sure that bulking up was the answer. One example: 50,000 intelligence reports were being produced a year, many of them simply ignored because there was so much overlap on subject matter.

THE PATRIOT ACT

With the anthrax scare at its height toward the end of October 2001, President Bush sought to improve counterterror efforts drastically by overhauling procedures that had kept law enforcement and intelligence personnel from sharing vital information with each other. The legislation written to fill that gap was called the USA PATRIOT Act, and it was signed by the president on October 26, 2001. It required law enforcement and intelligence agencies to share information with one another, making available to investigators the fruits of tools such as roving wiretaps that had until then only been used to catch drug traffickers and mob bosses—but not terrorists.

The act also authorized new financial measures to freeze terrorist assets, and it provided judicial and congressional oversight to protect civil liberties. Civil rights groups constantly complained that the act allowed the government to be too invasive into peoples' private lives, especially because—so these groups charged—all the PATRIOT Act had done was to catch second-rate criminals who appeared to be planning terrorism. Another controversial provision of the act permitted the government to seek warrants to look at business records of suspected terrorists: apartment leases, credit card receipts, and library records. Though First Lady Laura Bush, a former librarian, complained to her husband that she didn't like federal agents snooping around libraries, he allowed the provision to stand.

So much criticism arose, especially surrounding the government's right to conduct roving wiretaps, that reauthorization of the act, required in 2005, was in question, but it was reauthorized. In early 2010, important provisions of the PATRIOT Act were approved by an overwhelmingly Democratic Congress.

A DEFECT IN THE FOREIGN INTELLIGENCE SURVEILLANCE ACT

Another matter to be fixed within the American intelligence system arose from a defect in the 1978 Foreign Intelligence Surveillance Act (FISA) that forbade the National Security Agency (NSA) from monitoring communications inside the United States without a court order. Under this arrangement, it was easier to monitor al-Qaeda communications outside the United States than inside. The Bush administration argued that this had led American intelligence to miss key intercepts that might have provided an ample warning of 9/11 that, in turn, might have prevented the attacks. Bush understood that whether al-Qaeda agents were communicating in or out of the United States, American intelligence agents had to be able to intercept those calls without wasting valuable time to get a court order.

Consulting with his White House counsel and the Justice Department, Bush was told that he needed no revision of FISA, but could simply authorize the NSA to monitor all al-Qaeda communications, as authorized by the congressional war resolution and his constitutional authority as commander in chief.

THE ROAD TO GUANTANAMO

The attempted suicide bombing of an American commercial airliner—in December 2001, two months after 9/11—led to a fierce debate in America over how and where captured al-Qaeda detainees should be tried. The question was whether the trials should be held in U.S. district courts, giving defendants the same protections afforded to all American citizens, or via military tribunals that offered far less constitutional protection.

A month earlier, on November 13, 2001, President Bush had signed a military order that authorized the creation of military tribunals for the detention, treatment, and trial of certain noncitizens in the war against terrorism. In the executive order, President Bush argued:

> Given the danger to the safety of the United States and the nature of international terrorism,...it is not practicable to apply in military commissions under this order the principles of law and the rules of evidence generally recognized in the trial of criminal cases in the United States district courts.

He further asserted:

> Having fully considered the magnitude of the potential deaths, injuries and property destruction that would result from potential acts of terrorism against the United States and the probability that such acts will occur, I have determined that an extraordinary emergency exists for national defense purposes, that this emergency constitutes an urgent and compelling government interest, and that issuance of this order is necessary to meet the emergency.

The order defined the individuals subject to the order as al-Qaeda members; individuals who had engaged in, aided, or abetted acts of international terrorism; or individuals who had knowingly harbored such international terrorists. From the Bush administration's viewpoint, for the 9/11 perpetrators and other al-Qaeda operatives to gain access to U.S.

federal district courts, they would have had to be engaged in an armed conflict with an international character. Bush argued that the American war with al-Qaeda was no ordinary war between nations.

Inasmuch as ordinary prisoners of war have no access to federal courts, the Bush administration argued that unlawful combatants (al-Qaeda terrorists) did not have the right of such access to those courts either. Certainly, the administration wanted to punish some of the detainees via military tribunals, but its real goal was to hold and interrogate the detainees in the hope of getting valuable intelligence from them on future al-Qaeda operations against the United States.

What might have been the first test of the status of these al-Qaeda combatants came on December 22, 2001, when Richard Reid (the "shoe bomber"), a member of al-Qaeda, managed to get on American Airlines Flight 63 from Paris to Miami with a bomb concealed in his shoe. When the plane was close to Boston, passengers complained of smelling smoke in the cabin. A flight attendant sought out the source, and she found Reid trying to light a match. Warned that he was not permitted to smoke, Reid promised to stop. Minutes later, a flight attendant noticed that Reid had a shoe in his lap, with a fuse extending from the shoe, and a lit match in his hand. She tried but failed to grab Reid, and several passengers eventually subdued him. It appeared that the explosive failed to detonate due to a one-day delay in the takeoff, causing Reid's shoe to become too wet for the detonator to ignite. Reid's attempted suicide bombing has changed security protocols at American airports. Passengers now have to remove their shoes for inspection prior to boarding a flight.

When Richard Reid was arrested, he was placed into the American criminal justice system, most likely because military tribunals had not yet been set up in the wake of Bush's November announcement creating them. Charged with "interfering with the performance of duties of flight crew members by assault or intimidation," which carried a jail sentence of up to 20 years and a $250,000 fine, he was indicted by a grand jury on January 16, 2002, and charged with criminal counts related to his terrorist acts. Pleading guilty to all eight counts on October 4, Reid was sentenced to life imprisonment without parole. During the sentencing hearing, Reid contended that he was an enemy of the United States and in league with al-Qaeda, a soldier of God under Osama bin Laden's command.

"You," Judge William Young countered, "are not an enemy combatant; you are a terrorist.... You are not a soldier in any army; you are a

"You're big, but you're not that big. You are no warrior. I know warriors. You are a terrorist." terrorist. To call you a soldier gives you far too much stature. We do not sign documents with terrorists. We hunt them down one by one and bring them to justice....You're big, but you're not that big. You are no warrior. I know warriors. You are a terrorist."

For President Bush, the Reid court case highlighted a broad gap in his fight against terror. Noting that Reid, by being placed in the U.S. criminal justice system, had been given the same constitutional protection that any American charged with a crime received, Bush said that Reid was "not a burglar or bank robber; he was a foot soldier in al-Qaeda's war against America.... By giving this terrorist the right to remain silent, we deprived ourselves of the opportunity to collect vital intelligence on his plan and his handlers."

What Bush did not say publicly was that trying the al-Qaeda detainees in military tribunals meant that the CIA could use special interrogation methods such as water-boarding—or simulated drowning. Using these methods, the CIA could attempt to force terrorists to divulge future terrorist plans more freely than if the accused combatants enjoyed the constitutional protections afforded in U.S. district courts.

The Bush administration had no interest in criminally charging terrorists, which would give them access to a court to challenge their detention. Instead, Bush's legal team came up with the idea of placing the detainees in a facility that was not on American soil, thus depriving them of access to American courts. The decision was taken in 2002 to hold detainees at a naval station on the southern tip of Cuba at Guantanamo Bay. Though on Cuban soil, the United States controlled the facility. The Justice Department concluded that the Guantanamo Bay detention camp could be construed as outside American legal jurisdiction. Hence, the detainees were not entitled to appeal or to be tried in U.S. district courts.

On January 11, 2002, the first 20 of the eventual 779 detainees arrived at the detention center. The issue of where the detainees should be tried remains litigious. Three Supreme Court cases focused on the rights of the detainees. The administration's justification for its seeking military tribunals as the proper venue for these combatants was that America was at war. Lawyers for the Bush administration argued that it was free to imprison the detainees indefinitely and do with them what it wanted, including torture and execution.

As George W. Bush was about to leave office on January 20, 2009, a resolution to the issue of where to try the detainees was left to President Barack Obama. Obama had made clear in his presidential campaign that he favored closing the Guantanamo Bay facility. On January 22, 2009, two days after Obama replaced Bush as president of the United States, the new president signed an order to suspend the work of Guantanamo military trials. He favored U.S. district court trials for the detainees. Obama said he would shut the facility down within a year, but finding venues in the United States to house the detainees who would face trials on American soil proved to be quite difficult. By the end of 2009, 220 prisoners remained at Guantanamo.

By July 2011, many of the 779 detainees brought to Guantanamo had been released without being charged. The remaining 172 detainees are classified as "enemy combatants." (By December 2008, some 60 detainees had been cleared for release, but due to difficulties in repatriating them, they remained at Guantanamo.)

Then on March 7, 2011, in a sharp reversal of his administration's policies toward the Guantanamo detainees, President Obama issued an order approving the resumption of military trials for those detainees. The new presidential order countermanded his original decision to suspend military tribunals soon after coming to office in January 2009. Though Obama continued to pledge to close Guantanamo Bay, his decision sanctioning military tribunals was a tacit admission that it had proven too difficult to hold trials for the detainees on American soil.

NOTES

1. George Bush, *Decision Points* (New York: Crown, 2010), 135.
2. CNN Web site, "Bush: bin Laden 'Wanted Dead or Alive,'" September 17, 2001, http://articles.cnn.com/2001-09-17/us/bush.powell.terrorism_1_bin-qaeda-terrorist-attacks?_s=PM:

12

Responses to 9/11
The New York City Police Department

For the handling of homeland security, almost all American cities, large and small, deferred to the federal government. All major cities—from Los Angeles to Chicago to Miami—knew that they were as vulnerable to suicide bombing and other forms of terror as New York City had been. But they also knew that they did not have the resources to do what the feds could do, and therefore had little reason to try to duplicate the federal government's efforts.

The best course seemed to be to stay in close touch with federal officials and benefit from the improvements in their intelligence and security apparatuses. For any American city to set up its own security would prove costly and would duplicate unnecessarily what the federal government could accomplish more easily and efficiently. Only one city disagreed with this "leave it to the feds" approach to American homeland security: New York City.

Before 9/11, the New York City Police Department (NYPD) had organized intellectual exercises about how it would handle terror in vulnerable locations around the city, but, persuaded that such scenarios would play out only in novels or Hollywood movies, the NYPD brass filed those plans in drawers. Terror, typhoons, and earthquakes—all terrible disasters—did not seem likely to become New York events. Accordingly, the NYPD concentrated on chasing after serious criminals. Through its aggressive efforts, the department was able to reduce those crimes in frequency, especially murder, rape, and drug cases.

At the start of 2002, three and a half months after 9/11, the newly elected mayor of New York City, Michael R. Bloomberg, took office, replacing Rudy

Giuliani. As one of his first decisions, Bloomberg appointed Raymond W. Kelly as the new police commissioner. Bloomberg's genius in selecting Kelly was to pick a practitioner, someone with military and federal government experience, who had risen through the police ranks and was not just another paper pusher.

A NEW PROACTIVE POLICE COMMISSIONER

NYPD Police Commissioner Ray Kelly (left) and Mordecai Dzikansky on February 23, 2004, at NYPD headquarters at a private ceremony where Dzikansky was promoted to detective first grade. (*Credit*: Mordecai Dzikansky photo collection)

Viewing the federal government's attempts to bolster homeland security through the lens of a practitioner, Kelly believed that, for all their expanded efforts, the feds could not and would not take on the day-to-day responsibilities of defending New York City from future terror attacks. New York City's budget could not rival that of the federal government, nor could its intelligence team rise to the level of the FBI or the CIA. But none of that mattered to Kelly.

Would the Feds, in light of 9/11, provide preferential treatment to New York City in bolstering its security? Even if Washington officials said they would give that preferential treatment, Kelly would have still worried that the feds would not and could not be there when New York needed them. The only way for New York City to guarantee that the city would get the maximum protection against terror, in Kelly's view, was for the NYPD to take matters into its own hands. His proactive stance was a bold move but, in his view, it was what was best for the city.

In deciding to take on the security burden, Kelly was blessed with the kind of manpower and resources that no other American city possessed. Even so, only a New York City, with its proven vulnerability to terror, could even think of taking an aggressively proactive stance. Certainly Kelly had to know that by adding counterterror to tasks already assigned to the NYPD, he was increasing their responsibilities. But he felt it crucial that the cops search for terror suspects and suspicious activities as well as chase traditional criminals.

In the immediate aftermath of 9/11, the NYPD was consumed with identifying bodies or remains, and city government was still in shock, so that little thought was given to preparing New York City for further terror attacks. Apart from the recovery process, other "routine" tasks— homicides, the anthrax scare, tracking down tipsters—monopolized its time. Still, Kelly insisted on turning the NYPD upside down.

Reorienting Manpower and Resources

What Kelly understood was that after 9/11, New York's protectors would have to rise to a new level of vigilance. That would not be easy, especially with regard to the "hardening" of local landmarks. Local law enforcement in New York and elsewhere in America would primarily rely on private security to secure local landmarks and public buildings.

The New Counter Terrorism Division

The NYPD had in the past been concerned about crime against its subways and bridges, but that concern toward vital transportation links grew far more intense after 9/11. As part of reorienting the priorities of the NYPD, Kelly understood that he had to strengthen the NYPD's counterterrorism and intelligence operations. His greatest innovation was to create the Counter Terrorism Division (CTD) within the NYPD, the first unit of its kind in local law enforcement in the nation.

The NYPD would now have two intelligence units: the new CTD and its already existing Intelligence Division. The Intelligence Division (ID) gathered information and shared what was relevant with the CTD, which then implemented new NYPD tactics based on that ID-provided information. The ID also shared the information with other relevant NYPD units.

The CTD reflected the new overhaul of priorities within the department: raising the interest in potential terror against New York. To minimize casualties in the event of a terrorist act, the CTD saw fortifying vulnerable buildings in New York against terror attacks as one of its most important tasks.

Prior to 9/11, almost no thought had been given to what people and institutions could do proactively to minimize casualties at a terrorist incident. The commissioner changed the existing ID from a secret-service style operation that mostly escorted and protected visiting dignitaries into one of the most sophisticated and advanced police intelligence units in the world. Among American local police enforcement, the NYPD Intelligence Division became the gold standard, its senior officers realizing that the keys to terror prevention are intelligence-driven investigations.

THE NYPD GOES OVERSEAS

Making decisions on his own, without having to consult the feds, Kelly believed that New York would benefit from senior NYPD officers spending time abroad and analyzing terror, especially suicide bombings. Though far from New York City, the NYPD overseas liaison officer would search for any piece of information that would help the NYPD better protect New York.

After placing officers within the Toronto, Canada, Police Department and in Interpol (Lyon, France), he then placed an officer in Israel, a country suffering through one suicide bombing after another in 2002. Approached to become the NYPD liaison with the Israel Police, Mordecai Dzikansky began his assignment in early 2003. Commissioner Kelly had only a general idea of what Dzikansky and the other ten liaisons to overseas police departments might accomplish.

Kelly's attitude was: Let's get boots on the ground and then let's see if we can gain information that would be valuable in fighting terror in New York. The assignment would be for three months at a minimum; if too little value came from it, the liaison would get on the next plane back to New York.

Dzikansky felt there was no time to lose. He realized the only way to learn was to become operational: to go to terror scenes to get real-time, first-hand information as events were unfolding. Providing his analysis to the NYPD brass and relevant NYPD units, he hoped they would adapt lessons learned in Israel that would make New York City's public places better prepared for terror. The police would have a road map in place for becoming proactive. Merely responding to terror events was clearly not enough.

NEW PROGRAMS TO FIGHT TERROR

From 2002, when Commissioner Kelly took office, the NYPD instituted numerous programs designed to defend the City against terror, including suicide bombings:

> *Patrol: Surge drills.* Officers from around the city form caravans (up to 80 cars in less than an hour) and converge on a high-profile location. This familiarizes officers with potential targets throughout the city and disrupts enemy planning or surveillance efforts. Locations can be adjusted based on intelligence estimates, and officers are situated to respond to other events throughout the city.
>
> *Transit: Bag searches.* To the NYPD, even after 9/11, utilizing security guards to check bags at every public building in the city was unrealistic. However, Kelly and his senior staff knew that Israeli security guards had saved many lives at suicide bombings, but as long as New York remained free of suicide bombings, few saw a strong need for armed security guards with metal detectors positioned at all public places. Without recurrent suicide bombings, New York's residents would find the searches intrusive.
>
> That was why New York was unlikely to respond positively to a proposal for random security checks at all public sites. The

politicians would worry that armed security guards posted at all Broadway theaters would deter tourism. The libertarians would argue that even random security checks violated an individual's civil rights.

Two weeks after the July 7, 2005, London bombings, the NYPD instituted random bag searches for the New York City transit system. That decision set off a major legal battle with the New York Civil Liberties Union (NYCLU). Two weeks later, responding to the NYPD's new policy, the NYCLU filed a lawsuit to stop the practice. Explaining the lawsuit, Donna Lieberman, the NYCLU executive director, observed: "Our very real concerns about terrorism do not justify the NYPD subjecting millions of innocent people to suspiciousless [sic] searches in a way that does not identify any person seeking to engage in terrorist activity and is unlikely to have any meaningful deterrent effect on terrorist activity" [1].

Filed in federal court, the suit argued that the NYPD was violating the Fourth Amendment right of commuters to be protected against unreasonable searches and seizures. Finding that "the risk of a terrorist bombing of New York City's subway system was real and substantial," U.S. District Judge Richard M. Berman ruled on December 2, 2005, that random bag searches were constitutional; they were not as intrusive as alleged by the NYCLU. Justice Berman noted that "the threat of terrorism is great and the consequences of unpreparedness may be catastrophic," arguing that it would be folly not to allow random searches. [2]

Transit: Train sweeps. Over a dozen officers began inspecting an entire train by entering into all of its cars simultaneously. Officers observed people and packages. Passengers were continually reminded to report suspicious objects and activity via regular announcements over the loudspeakers and in print ads posted throughout the transit system.

Emergency services units. NYPD officers specially trained in heavy weapons and tactics were deployed to sensitive locations where terrorists were most likely to be conducting surveillance or preparing to strike. Possible suicide bombing targets included Wall Street, Times Square, cruise ship docks, and special events.

Camera surveillance. The NYPD was pursuing the latest technology for both fixed and movable camera monitoring.

Operation Hercules. Intelligence analysts identified the city's most vulnerable targets. Teams of officers from specialty units randomly appeared at these locations to disrupt surveillance and reconnaissance efforts. The operation was designed to force enemy planners to contend with an unpredictable but robust police response. The operation also called for police officers to alert local merchants to question and report suspicious persons to the authorities. The operation was designed to force enemy planners to contend with an unpredictable but vigorous police response.

The Shield Program. The NYPD began working hand-in-hand with private security firms, offering a series of NYPD briefings for private security managers aimed at protecting New York City from terrorist attacks.

Harbor operations. On a daily basis, harbor boats and divers checked the underwater support structures of the city's bridges for sabotage and explosives.

Operation Nexus. The NYPD enlisted the assistance of businesses in the New York City metropolitan area and educated them to pay attention to anyone suspicious. For example, someone might try to secure large amounts of bomb ingredients from a beauty products store, or seek to learn how to fly a plane, specifying routine flying and takeoffs, but no landings.

Interagency cooperation. NYPD intelligence investigations were shared with those of other agencies, including the FBI, state police, the Drug Enforcement Administration, and representatives from neighboring jurisdictions. Databases and investigations were coordinated.

Cyber unit. Native language speakers monitored extremist Web sites worldwide. These investigators actively attempted to infiltrate these sites, hoping to gain their trust and to be invited to private areas on the Internet.

See Something, Say Something. A citywide advertising campaign that featured announcements at every subway and train stop as well as in television and radio commercials. It was clear, especially after the 2004 Madrid train bombings, that passengers on public transport had to become more alert. Lack of public alertness had allowed the Madrid terrorists to place their bomb-filled luggage on luggage racks and elsewhere on commuter trains, and then disembark. Nobody seemed alarmed that people boarded with bags and then left without them. Though Madrid was not a case

See Something, Say Something: A citywide advertising campaign with announcements at every subway and train stop as well as in television and radio commercials.

of suicide bombings, the principle of "see something, say something" still applied.

Having examined in this chapter and the last one what the federal government and New York City have done to defend against further terror post-9/11, we turn in the next chapter to what kinds of telltale signs law enforcement officers and citizens alike should look for in confronting possible would-be suicide bombers.

NOTES

1. ACLU Website: NYCLU Sues New York City Over Subway Bag Search Policy. http://www.aclu.org/racial-justice_prisoners-rights_drug-law-reform_ immigrants-rights/nycl
2. MSNBC.com, "N.Y. subway bag searches ruled constitutional," 12-2-2005. http://www.msnbc.msn.com/id/10301189/ns/us_news-security/t/ ny-subway-bag-searches-ruled-constitutional

13

Detection
What Makes a Suicide Bomber Seem Suspicious?

What makes a would-be suicide bomber or his accomplices (sponsors, intelligence-gathering operatives) appear suspicious? Before we get to the specifics of how to identify someone as suspicious, let's take careful note: There is no way of identifying a would-be suicide bombing simply from physical appearance.

Looking at the situation in Israel, one should not assume that every potential terrorist looks like the stereotypical Middle Easterner. During the mid-1990s, the conventional wisdom had it that Palestinian suicide bombers would be male, roughly 25 years old, single, and religious Islamists. But with suicide bombers displaying so much diversity (women suicide bombers, teenage suicide bombers, Arab men dressed as Orthodox Jews, and Arab women dressed as Israelis), we say with great confidence that physical profiling (as opposed to behavioral) is not a useful tool for uncovering would-be suicide bombers.

We do not advocate ignoring physical appearance altogether in seeking out potential suicide bombers: If someone shows up at an airport or a bus terminal with a kaffiyeh around his head, holding a sign that says "Kill the Jews," security professionals should give him a thorough physical examination and insert his name into computers to check him for possible terrorist links.

Profiling suspicious behavior and actions is another matter. Prior to 2002, Hamas and its military arm, the Izz al-Din al-Qassam Brigade, and the Palestinian Islamic Jihad took responsibility for virtually all of the suicide bombers sent against Israel, all of whom were young unmarried males. But, in 2002, the al-Aqsa Martyrs Brigade began to choose men and women, villagers and townspeople, bachelors and married people. Suicide bombers have been young and old, educated or not, from poor families and wealthy ones too.

We need to demystify the notion that only Arab males of a certain age, single and religious, become suicide bombers: A suicide bomber can be white, black, Hispanic, or Asian. He may have been born Jewish, Christian, Buddhist, or a Muslim and become radicalized as a teenager. He may have become a radicalized Muslim convert nurtured in that notorious breeding ground for terrorists: the U.S. prison system. A suicide bomber can be a foreigner or homegrown. After encountering numerous disguised suicide bombers, Israel's law enforcement officials broadened the visual profile of the suicide bomber to all sizes and shapes, male or female, nonreligious, old and young:

On April 30, 2003, a British citizen, 22 year-old Asif Mohammed Hanif, not an Arab at all, blew himself up outside Mike's Place, a well-known pub along the Tel Aviv seaside promenade. He killed three civilians and wounded 50. During the same incident a second British citizen named Omar Khan Sharif, 27, tried unsuccessfully to blow himself up. Both were British Muslims of Pakistani origin.

Head of suicide bomber, Asif Muhammad Hanif, after attack at Mike's Place in Tel Aviv on April 30, 2003. (*Credit*: Gil Kleiman photo collection.)

On August 19, 2003, a Palestinian Arab suicide bomber from a Hamas cell in the West Bank town of Hebron disguised himself as a Hassidic Jew and boarded a double-length Jerusalem bus crowded with Orthodox Jewish families returning from the Western Wall. He blew himself up, killing seven children and 16 adults, wounding another 130. Taking credit for the bombing, Hamas noted that the bomber was not a Hassidic Jew but, rather, a 29-year-old mosque preacher from Hebron. The lesson: An Arab suicide bomber will use local dress or disguise to blend into the surroundings. If he is well disguised, the only way to identify the bomber will be either via intelligence-driven information or by watching for suspicious behavioral patterns.

On March 24, 2004, at the Hawara checkpoint south of the West Bank town of Nablus, a 14-year-old Palestinian boy, Hussam Abdu, wearing an explosive belt, was intercepted. Israeli sappers deployed a remote-controlled robot to pass scissors to Abdu to cut the explosive belt from his body. Abdu said later that he had received the equivalent of $25 to carry out the suicide attack. The lesson: 14-year-olds, not just 25-year-olds, might be suicide bombers.

At times, Palestinian terrorists dress as emergency personnel, employ ambulances—considered neutral in war zones—and try to get through Israeli checkpoints, concealing weapons to be used in an attack in Israel proper. It is yet another kind of camouflage Arab terrorists employ to deceive Israeli security personnel.

On March 26, 2002, Ahmed Jibril, a Tanzim terrorist, was detained at an Israeli Defense Forces (IDF) roadblock near Ramah Bridge, south of Ramallah. Jibril worked as an ambulance driver for the Palestinian Red Crescent (PRC), the Palestinian version of the American Red Cross. He was arrested while driving a PRC ambulance that contained an explosives belt and explosives. Jibril admitted that Mahmoud Titi, a Tanzim leader in Samaria, told him to deliver the items to Tanzim operatives in Ramallah. Besides Jibril, a woman and three children, aged six months and three and four years old, were in the ambulance. The explosives belt held 16 pipes containing approximately 22 pounds of explosive materials. The belt was hidden under the mattress of the stretcher on which one of the children was lying.

Sometimes, suicide bombers try to disguise themselves but the disguise does not entirely deceive. This happened to a suicide bomber, dressed in Orthodox Jewish garb, who was forced on May 18, 2003, to prematurely detonate his bomb after a passenger with security training sensed something was wrong.

Inside the bus after a suicide bomber blew himself up on May 18, 2003, in Jerusalem. (*Credit*: Avi Ohayon for Israel Government Press Office)

Perhaps it was the odd way the bomber was wearing his yarmulke (Jewish prayer hat) and tzitzit (Jewish ritual fringes). The passenger was about to confront the suicide bomber, but the bomber managed to blow himself up, killing eight and wounding 26. Had it not been for the alert passenger, who was seriously injured and died seven years later, the bomber might have harmed many more people on the bus. By observing and confronting the bomber, the passenger saved lives, since more passengers would have gotten on the bus by the time the bomber was planning to explode his bomb.

Still, the passenger, a highly trained combat shooter, could not best the suicide bomber. The passenger's only hope would have been to surprise the bomber by shooting him between the eyes. But the bomber's toggle switch proved quicker than the passenger's trigger. Had the passenger snuck up on the bomber, he might have gotten the upper hand, but he didn't. He just simply lost the "draw." As for the concern that, by shooting at the bomber, the passenger might have killed nearby Israeli civilians, the passenger's combat training called for him to shoot even if it meant killing innocent civilians, which has happened in the past.

Because a potential suicide bomber can wear a disguise, it makes no sense to decide that someone looks suspicious because of what he or she is wearing. Now that it has been established that a potential suicide bomber will not necessarily come from central casting, we need to focus on other ways to catch the bad guys.

As for security checks at Israel's Ben-Gurion International Airport, near Tel Aviv, once security professionals realized that suicide bombers came in all sizes and shapes, they began to rely upon behavioral profiling, checking whether people acted suspiciously rather than looked suspicious by virtue of their physical appearance and garb. As part of the behavioral profiling, security officers analyzed passenger documentation and responses to questions posed to all passengers.

At Ben-Gurion, racial profiling is employed along with behavioral profiling. All security workers have a military background, which helps them analyze security risks. Because no Jewish person has carried out a terrorist attack against aircraft at Ben-Gurion, a large portion of departing passengers do not require intense screening.

Ben-Gurion security guards resort to physical profiling only if there is cause to be suspicious. Security begins at the entrance to the airport, where vehicles are stopped and armed guards check passengers before permitting entry. Guards determine which cars and passengers require more scrutiny than others. Luggage of course is put through machines in search of suspicious items.

American security professionals have been reluctant to use behavioral profiling, concerned that the practice makes it too easy for a terrorist to slip through the security net. One can appreciate the American avoidance of behavioral profiling. There are simply too many people departing on American airlines and too many different kinds of would-be terrorists for American security officers to rely on behavioral profiling.

Israeli security teams, it must be said, have a far easier task in using behavioral profiling than do the Americans given that Israel's enemy is defined. Any Arab showing up at a public location and acting the slightest bit suspicious puts Israeli security personnel on the highest alert. Israelis do not permit West Bank and Gaza Palestinians to fly out of Ben-Gurion International Airport.

Israeli security teams, it must be said, have a far easier task in using behavioral profiling than do the Americans given that Israel's enemy is defined.

They take a ground route to Amman, Jordan, and fly from there. Israeli Arabs, who are permitted to fly out of Ben-Gurion, complain that they are scrutinized far more extensively than Jewish Israelis. That is not surprising:

First, they are Arabs; and second, some Israeli Arabs have been involved in helping suicide bombers reach their targets.

It is our firm view that American security personnel should not be seduced into believing that behavioral profiling is sufficient. We now offer advice on what makes a person suspicious and what to do when confronted with a suspicious person or object.

LIST OF SUSPICIOUS CHARACTERISTICS FOR A POSSIBLE SUICIDE BOMBER

Loitering for long periods without any apparent purpose

Recording, videotaping, photographing, or sketching infrastructure that has no tourist value

Alone, perspiring; conceals his hands, perhaps leaving one hand in his pocket

When he speaks, he is hesitant

He may communicate furtively with someone else

Avoids getting too close to security personnel

Concealing something under bulky clothing that is inappropriate for the season

Has an item protruding from clothing

Constantly checks to make sure that some item hidden under his clothes is still there

SITUATION #1: THE SUSPICIOUS PERSON

You are in a crowd of people, whether outside on a sidewalk, at a bus stop, inside in a mall, sports stadium, or restaurant. Suddenly you look at someone in the crowd, and for one reason or another, you become suspicious of him. While instincts can often be right in detecting someone out of place or not quite right, here are specific examples of suspicious activity to be aware of and report:

A person is loitering for long periods without any apparent purpose.

An individual is concerned over the authenticity of his credentials/ identity passes.

A person is recording, videotaping, photographing, or sketching infrastructure that has no tourist value, such as transit system tunnels, bridges, or highway overpasses.

Someone is making alarming statements that you overhear.

A person is found in work areas that are off-limits to nonemployees (e.g., rooms with access to electrical systems, ventilation areas, emergency stairwells).

The person might not be a potential suicide bomber, but he could be a suicide bomber sponsor seeking pre-attack intelligence. While people may exhibit these behaviors and not be terrorists, they are certainly indicators that might require further examination and action.

What else makes a would-be suicide bomber look suspicious?

The person is alone, perspiring. He may conceal his hands, perhaps leaving one hand in his pocket. When he speaks, he is hesitant. He may communicate furtively with someone else: If a sponsor, he might be gathering intelligence; if a potential suicide bomber, he might be consulting a sponsor on which crowd to penetrate.

Perhaps a would-be suicide bomber is talking to someone else; they appear to be in private conversation. Or they both avoid getting too close to security personnel.

Maybe a would-be suicide bomber is concealing something under bulky clothing that is inappropriate for the season: a large hat, scarf, or some other piece of clothing that hides his face or body. Perhaps he is wearing a uniform that does not seem to fit the surroundings.

Or he is wearing religious garb unnaturally. Perhaps you notice someone inside a synagogue with a tallit (prayer shawl) draped over his shoulders but he is not wearing it properly or he is fidgeting with it; you may notice someone in a church sloppily dressed, not in his "Sunday best."

A person may have an item protruding out from clothing such as a wire with a toggle switch running through a sleeve. He may constantly check to make sure that some item hidden under his clothes is still there. His body may smell of chemicals, excessive perfume, or cologne to hide certain smells that emanate from a bomb.

We must be careful not to accuse, at least in our minds, anyone who seems nervous of being a potential threat. All of us look nervous at one time or the other. We must come across some other suspicious sign before deciding that the person qualifies as a possible threat. Perhaps he is sweating or has trouble looking into people's eyes, or walks strangely because of something hidden in his clothes, or his gait is not natural, or he appears utterly focused as if in a trance.

It would also be suspicious for a would-be suicide bomber or handler to make repeated attempts to avoid police or security, or to ask certain questions such as: "When do the largest crowds gather at this spot?" "Do the police come here often?" "What kind of security is there in the building?"

It makes sense to search for suspicious people not only inside a sensitive building, but also while someone is standing in line to get into that building. Suicide bombers search for wherever a large crowd gathers—inside or outside a building. Let's say you are at a baseball game, and you are one of 50 people waiting in line to enter the stadium. Look around for anyone seeming suspicious. Don't wait until you get inside to look for suspicious people.

Bottom line: When large crowds gather, you should not be totally relaxed. Vendors who sell products or provide services need to be alert for suspicious people. If someone enters a store and asks to buy numerous items that could be used for improvised explosives, such as hydrogen peroxide, that should be a red flag.

Other red flags: Someone checks into a hotel for a long time but has no luggage and pays in cash; someone buys a one-way plane ticket and pays in cash. Someone doing surveillance on a building might appear suspicious, standing in front of a church or some other public institution for an inordinate amount of time; he might be taking photos, perhaps videotaping places to ascertain the amount of surrounding security, to learn the best time to launch an attack, or to identify the best location to stand when setting off an explosive.

Remember that the people who know the "cadence of life" best on a specific street corner in front of a specific store in a specific city—those who live or work there, security guards, local store employees, building staff—should be listened to if they identify someone or something suspicious. Far better than outsiders, they know what passes for unusual behavior.

What Are Your Options?

If you (a civilian) come across someone you think might be suspicious, what are your options?

1. You can ignore what you see, make a quick exit, and live with your conscience if your instincts were correct.
2. You could observe the person for a while to see what he or she is up to.
3. You could carefully engage the person in conversation to see if he has some legitimate explanation for why he is at this spot.

4. You could call or otherwise notify the authorities, even if you do not feel comfortable doing so. For instance, if the suspect is about to enter a building that has a security guard, you can alert the guard that someone outside looks suspicious.

5. If outside a building with no security guard, you could look for someone of authority, a police officer most likely, anyone who can take charge of the uncertain situation. If you ask law enforcement personnel to become involved in evaluating whether your suspicions are true not just in this case, but in all cases, it is of the utmost importance that, when law enforcement officers do get involved, they take an interest in what the citizen has to say. If there is no response, citizens will simply stop calling.

6. Both a civilian and a police officer should be on extra alert when in or near major landmarks in a city: In New York, examples would be Grand Central Station, Pennsylvania Station, and the Empire State Building. Other sensitive spots would be financial institutions on Wall Street, trains, buses, religious institutions, and of course airports. Another possibility is a spot that has a large number of children, elderly or other such "soft" targets, where security might be low or nonexistent, but the potential for casualties high.

SITUATION #2: THE SUSPICIOUS AUTOMOBILE

What might make you think an automobile is suspicious?

It may be parked at a sensitive location for a long time such as a no-parking area. The car may seem weighted down, with the rear of the vehicle sagging. The license plate may look improvised or mismatched (e.g., a truck with passenger license plates). Someone may be sitting in a car for a long time, perhaps watching something for no apparent reason. Or, the car may contain objects that look suspicious: PVC pipe that could be used as an explosives container, chemicals, wires that protrude from certain areas, batteries, or timers.

There may be inappropriate additions to the body of the vehicle. A well-made car bomb, however, will be difficult to notice, as it will likely be well camouflaged. Once, in the 1980s, while on duty at the Lebanon frontier, a team of police mechanics inspected a car for a suspected bomb but found nothing suspicious. It was only as an afterthought that they conducted a more thorough inspection the next day and discovered that the on-off switch for the car radio was in fact a detonator. They quickly located the bomb in the gas tank and dismantled it.

What Are Your Options?

1. You can ignore the situation, walk away from the car, and hope that it is not wired to explode soon after you leave. That's hardly thoughtful.

You could ignore the situation, walk away frc the car, and hope that it is not wired to explo soon after you leave. That's hardly thoughtful.

2. You can try to find out from nearby people if the car belongs to one of them. We recommend this as your first course of action. Some quick questioning can bring the civilian's concern to a quick close without requiring the authorities to invest a good deal of time and effort only to find a false alarm.
3. You can approach the car and try to open it. But we strongly recommend against taking such a risky step.
4. You can call 911. This should be the second thing you do after not finding anyone who claims ownership of the car. If there is something suspicious about the car, and if someone gets into the car and drives off before the authorities show up, you should obtain as much information about the car and driver as possible: What does the driver look like? What is he wearing? Try to get the license plate, make, and model of the car, or any telltale markings such as a broken taillight. Share this information with the proper authorities!

On May 1, 2010, two alert vendors, Lance Orton and Duane Jackson, noticed a Nissan Pathfinder parked illegally on the south side of 45th Street between Seventh and Eighth Avenues in Times Square, one of the busiest locations in New York City. Near the car were the two vendors' T-shirt and handbag stands and the Viacom headquarters.

The engine was running, hazard lights flashing, and the driver nowhere to be found. The car was four miles north of the site of the World Trade Center. It had been abandoned 10 to 15 minutes earlier, according to the vendors, who noticed that the car was filling with smoke pouring from the back of the SUV, emitting sparks, and making popping noises; Jackson detected a cherry bomb or firecracker smell.

The vendors alerted police officer Wayne Rhatigan, who asked two other officers to take the rare step of evacuating Times Square. Bomb squad techs discovered that the SUV had been packed with three propane tanks, two five-gallon plastic jugs of gasoline, a clock, electrical components, and a canister of gunpowder. The techs were able to dismantle the bomb without anyone getting injured.

A Pakistani American, Faisal Shahzad, was arrested 53 hours after the incident. He confessed to planting the car bomb and on October 4, 2010, was sentenced to life imprisonment without parole.

SITUATION #3: A COWORKER EXHIBITS SUSPICIOUS BEHAVIOR

If you hear a colleague at work mouth off against America, keep in mind that someone bold enough to make incendiary statements may well be prepared to take violent action. This applies as much to general workplace violence as to terror. Within the American context, mouthing off against America or the American government is not a sufficient reason to think that someone might be a terrorist. But, this person should be considered suspicious if he couples his rant against America or the government with a call for violent action.

Americans are protected by the U.S. Constitution's First Amendment, which reads in part: "Congress shall make no law...abridging the freedom of speech, or of the press...." But if someone incites people to take violent action, he should be considered a possible terrorist.

The perfect example: the mass shooting at Fort Hood, Texas, on November 5, 2009, in which Major Nidal Malik Hasan was reported to have killed 13 people and wounded 30. According to news reports, Hasan had exchanged e-mails with Anwar al-Awlaki, seeking spiritual guidance about violence; al-Awlaki has been linked to radical Muslim terror and blessed the Fort Hood operation, likening a suicide bomber to a soldier who throws himself on a grenade to save his colleagues, and sacrifices his life for a "more noble cause." In one of the e-mails, Malik wrote al-Awlaki: "I can't wait to join you" in the afterlife, and asked him when jihad is appropriate.

If someone at work engages in erratic behavior such as becoming religious overnight, and makes statements espousing violence, this should be brought to the attention of the authorities. You may not feel the person's behavior is worth reporting to authorities right away, but he must be watched.

181

What Are Your Options?

1. Keep the person under observation.
2. If the person becomes very suspicious, speak to someone in Human Resources as well as notify the proper security authorities so that they can follow up on the person. Such reporting can be done anonymously.

SITUATION #4: PROTECTING PUBLIC FACILITIES

What should those in charge of public facilities do to deal with suspicious situations? In answering this question, we are not talking about government buildings and courthouses, which have done security screening upon entry for decades. We are referring mostly to locations where large numbers of people gather, such as sports stadiums, amusement parks, and the like. At such locations, those in charge have an inherent obligation to secure the facility as much as possible. The more security, the more likely that the terrorist, upon doing surveillance, will go elsewhere.

How often does a terrorist forgo a well-protected facility and pick an easier, softer target? Always! Time and time again, targets that are easy are chosen over hardened targets. The lesson is simple: Always harden your target.

With security in place, even if there is an intelligence breakdown and no one hears about a terrorist threat, at least the facility will be protected. With regard to smaller public facilities—restaurants, movie theaters, department stores, and the like—it is not realistic to expect security officials in American cities and towns to post security guards outside all of their public locations unless there is specific intelligence that a suicide bomber plans to hit a certain city or town.

We want to emphasize that the measures that we propose should be implemented even without an imminent threat. Most importantly, if you are an executive or an administrator at a public facility, if a wave of suicide bombings is threatened against America, do not rely solely on the police or federal, state, or municipal governments to help you minimize casualties. You must take responsibility for securing your own location. You must ask and find out what you can do to harden or fortify your facility.

What Are Your Options?

The more sensitive your location, the more measures you should install. By sensitive, we are talking about public facilities that are popular, well known, and attract large crowds. You can pick some or all of these options to implement:

1. Make sure professional security personnel are in place. You must have them (preferably armed) on location to keep anyone suspicious from doing damage outside or inside your building. If the building's person in charge hires someone with military experience, make sure that person has served in the field and not just in an office. Remember: five-and-dime security gets you five-and-dime safety.

   Those who qualify as proper security guards include retired correction officers, police officers, and even firefighters. Without this background, the person should at least be state-licensed as a security professional; he must be sharp and aggressive and know the job well. It is crucial that the location's security manager be a professional with security training and background.

   Once a serious threat of a suicide bombing materializes, all public locations should have armed security guards at all entrances and, even though it is expensive, x-ray machines at each entrance as well.

2. Anyone going into a building should identify himself by showing a driver's license, passport, or work ID. A record should be kept of all guests on the premises. If it is not practical for guards to personally interact with everyone entering a facility, an electronic card access system should be deployed. Lost or stolen cards should immediately be reported and purged from the system, and this requirement must be strictly enforced.

3. All bags should be screened. It is vital that those checking bags know how to conduct the best possible search: looking inside bags for suspicious items and feeling the weight of bags (overly heavy bags could mean the presence of explosives and fragmentation). But it is foolish for security guards to make a cursory search of a bag by simply hitting or shaking it. That kind of action just might trigger the very explosion that the guard is trying to prevent.

4. The sophistication of the screening technology should depend on the sensitivity of the location. The greater the sensitivity, the more

sophisticated the screening devices should be. Once the technology exists, it should be put in place as soon as possible. But the burden of detecting suspicious people or objects rests with the human element, the security guard.

An x-ray machine hopefully would detect unusually formed items such as a gun or knife or tiny pieces of metal used for fragments in an explosive device. An explosive trace detector machine, augmenting the x-ray device, would be able to pick up traces of explosives, not just metallic items. In order to make certain that all of these items are discovered, only highly trained security personnel should be operating these machines.

It is quite important for security officers in charge of public facilities not to get mesmerized into thinking that machines at building entrances are a 100 percent solution to bomb detection. In fact, as the following example shows, they are only as good as the person using them.

Example

In the spring of 2002, Israel police commissioner Shlomo Aharonishky and foreign press spokesman Gil Kleiman arrived at the Department of Justice in Washington, D.C., for a meeting with Attorney-General John Ashcroft. In Kleiman's hand as he approached security officers inside the building was a plastic bag containing a mock suicide bomb belt. It contained no explosives. Aharonishky and Kleiman planned to show it to Ashcroft as an indication of the kind of terror Israel had been facing of late.

Laying the plastic bag on the conveyor belt of the x-ray machine, Kleiman admonished the guards, "You guys should see this. You probably won't see something like this often." His intent was to educate these security professionals in what a suicide bomb belt looked like, something they may have not seen before other than in photos. The Israeli police commissioner and the spokesman were not pranksters or terrorists.

After the suicide bomb belt emerged from the state-of-the-art x-ray machine, to Kleiman's utter surprise, a guard handed the bag back to him, noting: "Oh, we see bottles of champagne here all the time." To the guard, the bag contained nothing more lethal than celebratory champagne.

"I didn't expect that response," Kleiman admitted to the guard. "Do you want to see what's inside the bag?" After Kleiman showed the guard its contents, the guard's jaw dropped. He took two steps back nervously, and ordered everyone, "Don't move."

The security guard informed Aharonishky and Kleiman that he had to call his supervisor who, after hearing the story, understood that the two Israelis had arrived for a meeting with Ashcroft and planned to show him the "champagne bottles."

"You guys should see this. You probably won't see something like this often."

"Oh, we see bottles of champagne here all the time."

When Aharonishky explained to the attorney general that suicide belts like this one had been used continuously against unarmed Israeli civilians, Ashcroft responded that there was a clear need for American security professionals to become more familiar with all aspects of terror.

5. In the event of a suicide bombing threat, make sure a building's occupants are on full alert. Hiring security personnel is not enough. You must raise the level of alertness of your occupants: Workers in office buildings, tenants in apartment buildings, must become your eyes and ears in looking for suspicious people and items. This means giving these people formal training. The more people who are alert for suspicious activity, the greater your chances of limiting the damage that a suicide bomber can cause.

6. You should have a plan if an attack, whether a suicide bombing or some other form of terror, is about to happen. Practice evacuation of the facility; the frequency of these drills is to be determined by how sensitive your location is.

7. Of great importance for security personnel is to be keenly aware of specific dates that might trigger a sense of revenge for potential suicide bombers. The attack, motivated by such revenge, might be in response to a Western attack against Iran's nuclear facilities; a tough Israeli response to an Arab riot on the Temple Mount in Jerusalem; or a targeted killing of a high-level Palestinian terrorist.

In the next chapter, we continue our discussion on how to reduce casualties arising from a suicide bombing.

14

Reducing Casualties
Private Security Guards and Hardening Buildings

CAN CASUALTIES BE REDUCED?

Ideally, the best way to combat a suicide bombing is to catch the suicide bomber before he carries out an attack. That prevents people from being killed or maimed and the wider community from becoming traumatized. This requires intelligence and undercover work. The more difficult, but not impossible, way of stopping a prospective suicide bomber is to identify and capture him as he tries to carry out an attack. The frequent inability to foil suicide bombings leads many to think that there really is not much one can do in dealing with a suicide bombing. We want to demonstrate that this attitude is simply not true.

If the wall of security—the behavioral profiling, the hiring of trained security guards, and the like—does not prevent a suicide bombing, the good news is that there are steps that can be taken in advance to reduce casualties. Israelis have taken many of these steps in their efforts to eliminate and reduce the withering effects of these bombings. By noting what Israel has done to minimize death and injuries as a result of suicide bombings, we hope to instill hope that others can control the situation to some extent, if not entirely.

PRIVATE SECURITY

Throughout the 1980s and 1990s, Israel's most blunt instrument was a private security program that proved reasonably useful as a last-minute defense against suicide bombers. However, it is quite hard for a security guard to be 100 percent successful, and even 100 percent alertness means that the guard may still die.

With their military background and a feeling that they were protecting their families, however indirectly, Israeli private guards were prepared to "take the bullet," which in their cases meant keeping a suicide bomber from getting inside the premises even if the bomber blew himself up next to the guard. At this stage, American private security guards do not have the same mind-set that Israelis guards do: willing to put their lives on the line to protect civilians. If terrorists begin a suicide bombing campaign in the United States, one assumes that American guards would "take the bullet," if required, as their Israeli counterparts have sometimes been forced to do.

Success for the security guard means preventing the suicide bomber from entering the premises and, indeed, alert security guards have stopped suicide bombers before they could get inside. If the suicide bomber gets inside the premises, he will almost always kill and wound more people than if he had blown himself up outside. Ideally, the guard will identify and stop the bomber from blowing himself up. But realistically, success for the guard means reducing or preventing as many deaths and wounded as possible.

Despite their limitations, security guards represent a last line of defense. The creation of a professional private security program proved of immeasurable help in Israel's fight against suicide bombings. After the Palestinians began employing suicide bombing as a weapon of choice against the Israelis in the mid 1990s, Israel had to employ any tactic it could to fight the bombers.

The favored Middle Eastern terror tactic in the 1970s and 1980s was airplane hijackings in which the Palestinian goal was to free the passengers in exchange for the release of Palestinian prisoners in Israeli jails. The defense against hijackings was greater vigilance against potential hijackers. Inasmuch as Palestinian terror was confined to the skies, there was no need for a private security guard to be posted at every central bus station, department store, office building, and the like. Even when Palestinians launched suicide bombings in Israel, security professionals assumed that bombers would be highly selective, targeting only such high-profile figures as the prime minister, cabinet members, and the army chief of staff or other symbols of power, such as the electric grid and gas and port facilities.

The prime minister's office and home in Jerusalem along with the Knesset were turned into military fortresses, but few other buildings were given such high-level security. Though Israel's security outlook required the outlay of millions of Israeli shekels to protect these high-profile targets, Israeli security officials look back upon that expense as largely a waste because the terrorists wound up not attacking symbols of power. When Palestinian terrorist organizations unleashed their suicide bombers against Israeli targets, they aimed at places where Israelis gathered in large numbers.

These locations had great advantage for the suicide bombers. Each coffeehouse or restaurant had far less security than that provided to a prime minister. For Israelis to guard each and every place where people gathered seemed frustratingly useless. If a suicide bomber found too much security at one coffeehouse, he could easily find another with weaker security down the block. However, once suicide bombings against public places began in earnest in the mid-1990s, placing security guards at their entrances seemed increasingly necessary. In addition, the Israel Police, which had the chief responsibility in the fight against domestic terror, flooded the streets.

The police minister at that time, Roni Milo, even ordered all police cars to keep their flashing lights on their car roofs on at all times—not just when heading for an emergency—to give Israelis the impression of an omnipresent and large police presence in the streets, thus calming their nerves. In fact, the tactic may have backfired by causing the public to believe that the police cars were on their way to another suicide bombing, which is not exactly what the police minister had in mind.

In Israel, security guards were trained to study the behavioral patterns of potential suicide bombings, but even the most professional guard could at best prevent the suicide bomber from blowing up inside the premises. Guards did identify would-be suicide bombers as they tried to enter a restaurant or bus terminal; on a few occasions, realizing he had been spotted, the bomber prematurely detonated his bomb, killing the guard, who died a hero having saved numerous lives inside the premises.

Requiring Israeli youth to serve as security guards after serving in the army would have added a harsh burden to those young people. The Israel government ordered its young men and women to join the army at age 18 and serve three years for men, two years for women. After serving in the military, Israel's youth wanted to travel or attend a university, not guard public places. Besides, the Israel government was unable to take on the financial burden of hiring and training a professional group of security guards. Accordingly, the government enacted laws that passed the financial burden on to the private sector.

As a result, the government relied on private security companies to supply the needed personnel. The Israel Police took responsibility for creating the training doctrine for the private guards, overseeing its implementation, and the hiring of trainers who ran courses and performed background checks on potential security guards. Israel benefited greatly from the fact that most private security guards had recently graduated from the military and were willing to work at affordable rates.

All schools were required to have secure physical barriers with an armed guard stationed at all entrances. According to law, trained security guards were posted at shopping mall entrances, restaurants (of a certain size), hotels, and most other public venues such as event spaces where weddings, bar mitzvahs, and Passover seders, were held.

As security guards appeared outside many public facilities from supermarkets to movie theaters, checking bags of visitors, no one complained that their right to privacy had been invaded. No one thought the threat of suicide bombers was a fantasy. It was the norm for Israelis to wait in line for mandatory (as opposed to random) security checks of their bags for explosives. Guards used metal detectors, but they did not ask men to take off their belts or request men and women to remove their shoes, instead relying almost entirely on spotting someone suspicious. X-ray machines were used mainly at government offices, airports, and central bus and train stations.

In the same way that American-based security guards have been trained how to stop a shoplifter from leaving a store, Israeli guards, in meaningful contrast, have learned how to keep a potential suicide bomber from entering the premises or from blowing himself up in a crowd outside a public place. Israeli security officers have a shorthand way of describing the contrast: In America the security guard faces "in." In Israel, the security guard faces "out."

In America, the security guard faces "in." In Israel, the security guard faces "out."

On a number of occasions, Israeli security guards, whether relying upon a visual read or metal detectors, have been successful in identifying suicide bombers as they approached a target. Though the bomber sometimes detonated his explosives outside the target, many lives were saved by the guards' careful screening technique. However, a guard's lax

190

behavior at the Maxim Restaurant in Haifa on October 4, 2003, showed that weak security could be devastatingly lethal.

Should intelligence agencies supply private security guards with information about potential suicide bombers? For years, these agencies debated the question among themselves. American intelligence does not provide classified information to private security guards concerning terrorists about to carry out an act of violence. But in Israel, the police routinely pass on what Americans would consider classified intelligence to senior executives at private firms. Those executives then pass the intelligence on to their security guards. Routinely armed with normally classified intelligence about potential suicide bombers, well trained to detect suspicious behavior, and highly motivated, these private security guards often proved their on-the-spot value. Some examples:

April 24, 2003; train station, Kfar Saba: A suicide bombing occurred at the entrance to the brand-new Kfar Saba train station northeast of Tel Aviv. At 7:20 a.m. the bomber arrived, hoping to get into the station, where numerous Israelis were waiting on platforms for arriving trains. Sensing that the man was suspicious, a security guard refused to let him into the station, demanding to see his identity papers. The bomber changed his plan and set off the bomb there and then, killing the security guard and wounding nine others.

April 30, 2003; Mike's Place, Tel Aviv: A suicide bombing had taken place at 12:45 a.m. when a terrorist approached Mike's Place and blew himself up at the entrance to the bar, killing three people, and wounding another 60, including a security guard named Avi Tabib, who had properly identified the bomber as suspicious, and had kept him from entering the restaurant, where many more people had congregated.

The guard faced terrible odds. Even had he put the bomber through a metal-detection scanner, the detasheet (detonation sheet) explosive that the bomber was carrying would have gone undetected. After the guard grabbed the bomber, the man realized that he could not get into the restaurant; he set off his explosives near the entrance, killing "only" three people and injuring the guard.

July 11, 2004; Caffit Restaurant, Jerusalem: Malak Nasser A-Din, a 41-year-old Hamas terrorist, stood outside the popular café, Caffit, on Emek Refaim Street, planning to kill the security guard and then rush into the café and detonate his bomb. Instead, spotting the guard, the would-be bomber suddenly walked away and was subsequently arrested.

Apart from private security guards, Israel has enjoyed the advantage of an enlisted civilian public that has stayed on full alert, even during so-called quiet periods. In addition to private security guards, Israeli bus drivers, unarmed and devoting full attention to driving carefully, have sometimes played a significant role in identifying suicide bombers and taking action against them to reduce casualties in a bombing.

Example

On August 31, 2004, a pair of suicide bombings occurred within minutes of one another in the southern Israeli city of Beersheba. Seven people had been killed on Bus #6, and another five had been killed on Bus #12. Four people died of injuries later—16 dead in all. Another 100 had been wounded.

Both suicide bombers, sent by Hamas, had blown themselves up inside the buses, with Bus #6 about half a block behind Bus #12; the driver of Bus #12, after hearing the explosion on the other bus, had the foresight to pull off to the side of the road, all the while yelling to passengers that there had been a terror attack. He feared that a similar event could happen to his bus as well. Once on the side of the road, he opened up the doors, urging passengers to exit. When the second bomber did explode his device, he was standing at the center of the bus near the rear exit doors. Had he detonated his bomb seconds earlier, he would have killed or maimed many more passengers.

TECHNICAL ANALYSIS OF SIMULTANEOUS SUICIDE BUS BOMBINGS

Mordecai Dzikansky
NYPD

Date: August 31, 2004

Times: 14:55 hours (bus no. 6) and 30 seconds later (bus no. 12)

Locations: Inside local bus no. 6 in the southern city of Beersheba and inside no. 12 bus, traveling about 100 meters (328 ft) north of the first bus

Victims: Seven killed on no. 6 bus and five killed on no. 12 bus; four passengers evacuated to a nearby hospital later died of their injuries; 90 injured in total

Bomber's positions at detonation:

Bus no. 6: bomber was standing in the front third of the bus, facing front

Bus no. 12: bomber was standing in the rear third of the bus, facing back (likely to watch bus no. 6 explosion)

Camouflage: Suicide belt/vest worn on the bombers' midsections (covered by clothing)

Explosive material: High explosives—nitroglycerin and TATP; fragmentation (weights unknown)

Explosive effect:

Bus no. 6—bomber's body ripped apart; head, shoulders and legs severed, but remained intact; all parts found near point of detonation

Most injuries were to people located in the front of the bus; many head and upper torso injuries

Most bus damage occurred in the front of the bus; most windows shattered; front seats all mangled; air conditioning unit caught fire, resulting in additional injuries and damage to bus

Bus no. 12—bomber's body: head found detached underneath nearby seat; left hand ripped off (left hand was closest to IED); legs found connected to groin but severed from torso

Most injuries were to people located in the rear of the bus; many heads and upper torso injuries; some bodies in vicinity of bomber were ripped apart

Most bus damage occurred in the rear of the bus; most windows shattered; back seats mangled

Suicide bombings in a closed environment are a preferred location by terrorists, since only a small explosive charge is needed to maximize casualties and damage.

Simultaneous/multiple suicide bombings are not uncommon in Israel and also a tactic used in the 9/11 attack on the United States.

HARDENING PUBLIC AND PRIVATE PLACES

Placing security guards outside entrances to public places provides "last-minute" security. To reduce casualties, security guards have to act at the last minute or even the last few seconds before a suicide bombing. But Israelis learned that acting *before* a suicide bombing can reduce casualties as well.

One way to take action long before a suicide bomber sets off on a mission is to harden (or fortify) a public place; the object of hardening the place is to reduce casualties should a suicide bomber blow himself up, whether in a car or standing outside the venue near or inside a crowd.

The security officer is always trying to find an answer to a perceived threat as opposed to threats that are unrealistic. If word reaches security officers that a terrorist has a nuclear weapon, the officer does not need to harden a target. Certain threats like the threat of a nuclear weapon simply have no reasonable answer. The security officer's job is to take responsibility and provide professional answers to reasonable threats based on available resources.

The far more realistic threat, as the Israelis discovered, is from suicide bombers. Before the mid-1990s, Israel paid scant attention to the hardening issue, as the wave of bombings only began in 1993. After that, a wave of suicide bombings against Israel drove its security officials to think about fortifying, or hardening, public and private places against that specific threat. Between 2000 and 2002, when a second wave of suicide bombings was hitting Israel, this time on a weekly basis, the government learned the hard way that it had to step up its hardening efforts against suicide bombings quickly.

HOW SHOULD ONE HARDEN A FACILITY?

The professional security officer decides what is the best way to harden a target. Each target should be hardened according to the specific threats faced and the available resources. Israeli security officers always describe a security program as an individual process peculiar to each site, or "tailoring a security suit."

There are specific steps that should be taken to "harden" facilities:

1. Perform background checks on all employees.
2. Search people coming into a public building.

3. Install a good camera system that photographs both inside and outside a building to determine if someone is engaging in surveillance near the building.
4. View monitors regularly; then send recordings and information about anyone suspicious to law enforcement.
5. When and if possible, building managers should put in place physical barriers, such as planters or cement blocks, that can block an explosive-laden vehicle from getting close to its intended target. The barriers will almost certainly minimize casualties and building damage.
6. Attention should be given to all exterior building windows and the possible secondary blast effects. Solutions run the gamut from different types of glass to add-on film to interior fragment reducers such as blast curtains. Exterior building windows should be covered with blast-resistant film to mitigate shattering from the blast effect of explosives.
7. If the building, especially a sensitive one, has a garage, cars entering should be checked, including car trunks, to make sure that they are not carrying explosives. The height of roofs in a parking garage should be lowered to prevent large vehicles (which could potentially carry enough explosives to take down a building) from entering,

Fortification of schools is a top priority in Israel, and there are valuable lessons to learn from the Israeli experience. Here is what the Israelis learned: Guards need to be placed outside all school entrances. Security and building maintenance officials must learn how to check a school building's heating, ventilation, and air conditioning systems, since terrorists might try to place explosives or chemical or biological agents inside them. Access to these systems must be limited and controlled. All exterior doors and operable windows should have alarms and motion sensors.

A gate or fence should be installed along the perimeter of a school. Schoolchildren should be taught "terror awareness" at an early age; youngsters should be instructed not to pick up anything from the ground and to report anything suspicious to teachers. What they find just might be an explosive. In Israel, such instruction begins in prekindergarten. Israelis know that it is never too early.

Teachers, principals, and security guards are responsible for security functions in Israeli schools. Those are the only school personnel who should carry the obligation of ensuring the safety of schoolchildren.

THE LESSON OF ISTANBUL

While on assignment in Israel, Mordecai Dzikansky visited Istanbul soon after suicide bombing attacks rocked the city. The first of the two Istanbul incidents occurred on November 15, 2003, at 9:26 a.m., when a suicide bomber struck at Neve Shalom, the city's largest synagogue. Five minutes later a second suicide bomber attacked the Bet Israel synagogue.

Dzikansky found indisputable evidence that hardening a target prior to a suicide bombing reduces casualties significantly. That lesson offered New York City—and the rest of America as well—a way to reduce casualties in such a bombing.

Upon arriving in Istanbul, Dzikansky wanted to know whether either target had been hardened, and if so, which had fared better. As it turned out, Neve Shalom, which had 11 dead and 125 wounded, had been fortified; Bet Israel, with 12 dead and almost twice as many wounded (220) had not been.

Seventeen years earlier, on September 6, 1986, Arab gunmen had entered Neve Shalom and killed 22 worshippers. The Palestinian terrorist and founder of Fatah, Yasser Arafat, had been blamed. Inasmuch as suicide bombers were employing a tactic of striking twice at the same place, fortifying Neve Shalom made much sense.

Because of the 1986 attack, all sorts of security improvements had been put in place: bullet-proof entrances, security checks of congregants, six large pillars outside the building to act as barriers against direct hits, video cameras installed to monitor people and the street. Bet Israel had not made any of these improvements.

The pillars at Neve Shalom worked, keeping the truck from getting closer to the synagogue, preventing deaths, and limiting injuries inside. The video camera recorded the truck as it came to a slow crawl and then, while still moving, exploded in front of the Neve Shalom synagogue. Heavy structural damage was sustained, but far less than at the Bet Israel bombing site.

Bet Israel, in contrast to Neve Shalom, was left porous: The street at its main entrance was closed off to vehicular traffic, and security personnel were stationed at the door. But the street at its back entrance was open to traffic. Though five security officers and one police officer had been stationed at the back entrance, all six were killed when the bomber blew himself up. Nor did Bet Israel have pillars at either of its two entrances, allowing the bomber to get close to the building.

In the next chapter we look at actual planned and executed suicide bombings post 9/11. We look at events that law enforcement officers were able to foil as well as events that law enforcement did not prevent.

15

Suicide Bombings
Law Enforcement Successes and Failures

After 9/11, many Americans were certain that more terror attacks, already in the final planning stages, were imminent. And yet over the next decade through late May 2011, "only" 39 such planned attacks were uncovered and made public; all 39 attacks were foiled.

In this chapter we look at six planned suicide bombing incidents in the decade after 9/11, all in the West. Three were prevented; three were not. The three that were foiled we call law enforcement successes; the three that were not foiled we call law enforcement failures. With regard to one of the three plots that were foiled—the "underwear bomber" case— law enforcement officials met with only mixed success: The fact that the bomber was able to board the plane with a bomb was certainly an intelligence and security failure; that he was subdued by passengers before exploding the bomb was a civilian success.

With the existence of a great deal of open-source material, especially court documents and media interviews, we are able to write about sensitive intelligence affecting these cases. Two of the foiled cases that we document were aimed at New York City; they illustrate that the New York City Police Department (NYPD) has been willing to invest its resources into low-level, early-stage probes, conscious that the federal government did not have the resources on the ground as the NYPD did.

"These kinds of homegrown, lone-wolf incidents start way below the level the federal government would focus on," said David Cohen, the NYPD's deputy commissioner for intelligence. "If we weren't doing it, nobody would be" [1]. Agreeing, NYPD Commissioner Raymond Kelly suggested that New York City had no choice but to be proactive in stopping terrorists: "Yes, we want to work with other agencies, and yes, we have detectives placed overseas," he said. "But in New York City, we're on our own. We have to protect our own turf" [2]. While Cohen and Kelly would have everyone believe that the NYPD could replace the federal government in taking proactive steps against terror, both would readily acknowledge that it takes everyone working together and exchanging information to keep New York City and other parts of the United States safe.

We start with two law enforcement successes and one mixed success: first, the case of Assam Hammoud and the plot to blow up the PATH subway lines linking New Jersey and New York; second, the case of Umar Farouk Abdulmutallab, known as the "underwear bomber" and his planned suicide bombing on a plane over Detroit (a mixed success); and third, the case of Najibullah Zazi and his attempt to kill himself and others in the New York subway system.

Six (out of 39) suicide bomb plots against the United States (9/11 to May 20, 2010)

Richard Reid attempts to detonate explosives hidden inside his shoes on a flight from Paris to Miami (December 2001).

James Elshafay and Shahawar Martin Siraj are arrested for plotting to bomb a subway station near Madison Square Garden before the Republican National Convention (August 2004).

Eight men including Assam Hammoud are arrested for plotting to attack train tunnels between New York and New Jersey (July 2006).

A group of 24 men are arrested in London for plotting to blow up U.S.-bound commercial airliners with liquid explosives (August 2006).

Najibullah Zazi and at least four others are arrested for purchasing chemical explosive materials, allegedly to bomb the New York subway system (September 2009).

Umar Farouk Abdulmutallab, a Nigerian student, allegedly attempts to detonate explosives on a Detroit-bound international flight on Christmas Day (December 2009).

LAW ENFORCEMENT SUCCESSES

Assam Hammoud and the Plot to Blow Up the PATH

Assam Hammoud's plan was to stage a suicide bombing in October or November of 2006 on the PATH (Port Authority Trans-Hudson) rail system below the Hudson River. The PATH links Manhattan with New Jersey. One report had the target as New York City's Holland Tunnel. But before he could carry out the plot, Hammoud, 31, and two other suspects were arrested abroad, Hammoud in Lebanon. Ranked as the most credible terror threat at the time, the plot was also considered one of the hardest to frustrate. No one in law enforcement could conceive of placing inspectors at every subway or commuter train.

A professor at the Lebanese International University, Hammoud studied economics and finance in Canada in the late 1990s for six years. Arrested by the Lebanese Armed Forces in West Beirut on April 27, 2006, Hammoud was handed over to the United States on July 7, and only then did the FBI announce that he had been captured two months earlier and had confessed to the plot. Noting that the plotters were moving forward with their plans, the FBI indicated that the would-be bombers were about to enter the phase of monitoring targets, establishing a regimen for the attack, and then acquiring the resources needed to carry it out. Newspaper reports said that Hammoud had been released on bail in June 2008, indicating that U.S. prosecutors believed they would face difficulties proving that he was planning a concrete plot.

Confessing to the plot, Hammoud said that he had done basic weapons training in the Palestinian refugee camp Ain al-Hilweh near Sidon in South Lebanon. He had planned to visit Pakistan for four months of training before heading for the United States to plan and execute the mission. Hammoud, also known as Amir al-Andalousi, pledged allegiance to al-Qaeda and Osama bin Laden. Police had identified eight people on three continents as suspects in the case.

The suspects planned to use backpack explosives to carry out the mission. The plot was still in its early stages; the suspects had not performed reconnaissance or obtained weapons. They had not even arrived in the United States. Politicians praised intelligence agencies for uncovering the plot when it was still in its talking stages. American law enforcement worked with six intelligence agencies abroad to crack the planned attack.

The PATH system maintains three Hudson River tunnels, two of which connect New Jersey with Lower Manhattan through the former World

Trade Center site. A third goes to midtown Manhattan via Greenwich Village. Security experts have long considered the tunnels a soft target for terrorists. In 2006, the PATH carried 215,000 passengers daily

The plotters reportedly hoped to flood Wall Street as a result of bombing the Holland Tunnel, but experts doubted that the blast, two miles from Wall Street, would have flooded areas above water level. Still, a bomb placed in a PATH train could breach the tunnel, flooding lower Manhattan.

Law enforcement officials pointed out that a recessed foundation at the former World Trade Center site—known as "the bathtub"—protected the buildings and the subway tunnels from the Hudson River. If an explosion affected the "bathtub" that protects lower Manhattan from the Hudson, the results would be devastating.

Authorities were able to sniff out the plot by monitoring Internet chat rooms. No evidence was found to substantiate the plot other than chat about it on the Internet. Upon making public the details of the planned suicide bombing, Port Authority police officers began guarding the Holland Tunnel entrance in New York, pulling over vans and trucks every few minutes, and searching the backs of the trucks. Before September 11, one searched passenger said, he would have thought such behavior on the part of law enforcement a sign of paranoia. But after 9/11, he believed the potential existed for anything, and he had no objection to the searches. Other passengers complained that security near the tunnel was not tight enough even with the searches.

With at least a dozen relatives of Hammoud accused or convicted of terrorist-related incidents, they and Hammoud had been dubbed the Hezbollah–Hammoud Syndicate. New York's tabloid press nicknamed Hammoud the "Playboy Plotter," publishing photos of him holding a drink amidst several attractive blond women despite professing to be an Islamic fundamentalist.

Umar Farouk Abdulmutallab: The "Underwear Bomber"

Known popularly as the "Underwear Bomber," Umar Farouk Abdulmutallab is a Nigerian citizen who, on December 25, 2009, tried to detonate plastic explosives hidden in his underwear while flying on Northwest Airlines Flight 253 from Amsterdam to Detroit, Michigan. He was 23 years old.

The youngest of the 16 children of one of the wealthiest men in Africa, the former chairman of First Bank of Nigeria, Alhaji Umaru Mutallab, Umar Farouk Abdulmutallab grew more devoutly Islamic during his childhood years in Nairobi. He condemned his father's banking profession as "immoral" and "un-Islamic" for charging interest. At school he defended the Taliban.

In Internet postings he disclosed that he had sexual fantasies that were uncontrollable: "The bad part of it is sometimes the fantasies are a bit worldly rather than concentrating in the hereafter." But, as for his "jihad fantasies," he described in a posting on February 20, 2005, how "the great jihad will take place, how the Muslims will win inshallah (God willing) and rule the whole world, and establish the greatest empire once again."

He studied engineering and business finance at University College in London starting in the fall of 2005. Three years later he earned a degree in mechanical engineering. He was president of the school's Islamic Society. MI5, the United Kingdom's domestic counterintelligence and security agency, learned of him and his radical connections with Islamic extremists.

Reaching 21, he asked his parents to let him get married, but they refused, saying he had to wait until after he had earned a master's degree. From January to July 2008, Abdulmutallab studied in a master's of international business program at the University of Wollongong in Dubai.

In April 2009 he received an American multiple-entry visa that was valid through June 2010 in order to attend an Islamic seminar the following August 1 to 17 at the Almaghrib Institute in Houston. When he tried to return to Britain in May 2009 for a six-month "life coaching" program, British authorities viewed the program as fictitious and rejected his visa application. His name was placed on a security watch list, but, significantly, the United Kingdom did not share the information with other countries. Their reason: The application had been rejected not for reasons of national security, but to prevent immigration fraud.

In August 2009, Abdulmutallab arrived in Yemen to study Arabic, the only African among 80 students at San'a's Institute for the Arabic Language. Visiting a mosque every morning, he spent hours each day reading the Koran in his room. After less than a month at the institute, he began attending lectures at Iman University. He told classmates that his greatest wish for Islam was for Sharia law, the sacred law of Islam, to be followed around the world. While in Yemen, he met with al-Qaeda operatives who gave him weapons training. He also made a video in which he justified his actions against "the Jews and the Christians and their agents."

When he informed his father that he wanted to study Sharia and Arabic in a seven-year course in Yemen, his father threatened to cut off his funding, but it was a meaningless threat, as Abdulmutallab was getting everything for free. In October 2009 he broke off relations with his father and asked forgiveness for any wrongdoing he would commit in the future.

British intelligence sent U.S. law enforcement authorities a cable on November 11, 2009, indicating that a man named "Umar Farouk" (his last name was not given) had been in touch with a senior al-Qaeda talent recruiter named Anwar al-Awlaki. He had connections to three of the 9/11 hijackers, the 2005 London underground bombers, as well as those who carried out terrorist attacks carried out in Fort Dix, New Jersey, and Fort Hood, Texas. Meeting al-Awlaki, Abdulmutallab pledged to support jihad. Over the next few months, the two men communicated with one another, with al-Awlaki providing spiritual support to the Nigerian.

Eight days later (November 19) Abdulmutallab's father reported to two CIA officers at the U.S. Embassy in Abuja, Nigeria, that his son had exhibited "extreme religious views" and might be in Yemen. As a result, Abdulmutallab's name was placed in the United States' 550,000-name Terrorist Identities Datamart Environment (TIDE) located at the American National Counterterrorism Center in McLean, Virginia. But American authorities failed to add his name to the FBI's 400,000-name Terrorist Screening Database. Meanwhile, his U.S. visa was not revoked. While the State Department wanted to revoke Abdulmutallab's visa, American intelligence officials decided not to let the revocation go forward for fear that this would have interfered with a broader probe into al-Qaeda.

Abdulmutallab left Yemen on December 7, 2009, flew to Ethiopia, two days later to Ghana, and then, on December 24, on to Lagos, Nigeria. Before he left Yemen, he had obtained plastic explosives that had been sewn into his underwear as well as a syringe from an al-Qaeda associate who was a bomb maker.

On Christmas Day 2009, Abdulmutallab traveled to Amsterdam, boarding Northwest Airlines Flight 253, which was headed for Detroit. Prior to boarding, passengers noticed a "smartly dressed Indian man" beseeching Abdulmutallab to get on the plane even though the would-be suicide bomber said he had no passport. Abdulmutallab was led away but eventually boarded the plane. The passengers, when interviewed, had no explanation how he managed to board.

Passengers smelled a foul odor, heard popping noises, and noticed that Umar Farouk Abdulmutallab's trouser leg and the wall of the plane were on fire.

As the flight neared Detroit, Abdulmutallab spent 20 minutes in the bathroom and, returning to his seat, covered himself with a blanket. An instant later, passengers smelled a foul odor, heard popping noises, and noticed that his trouser leg and the wall of the plane were on fire.

Passenger Jasper Schuringa, a Dutch film director, jumped on Abdulmutallab, subduing him; meanwhile, flight attendants used fire extinguishers to douse the flames. Abdulmutallab was taken to the front of the airplane cabin. Passengers noticed that he had burns on his legs and was no longer wearing trousers.

A flight attendant asked him what he had in his pocket. "Explosive device," Abdulmutallab answered, sounding proud. The device that had been sewn into his underwear was a six-inch packet containing an explosive powder, pentaerythritol tetranitrate (PETN). It is one of the most powerful high explosives and was serving as the primary explosive. Also in the packet was triacetone triperoxide (TATP), the detonator. PETN and TATP were the same two explosives that "shoe bomber" Richard Reid had used in his abortive 2001 attack.

Abdulmutallab later told authorities that he had received the device in Yemen and had marched to al-Qaeda 's orders. Al-Qaeda claimed the attack was revenge for the American role in a military offensive against al-Qaeda in Yemen.

Two days after the attack, Abdulmutallab was released from a hospital where he had been treated for first and second degree burns to his hands, his right inner thigh, and genitalia, all sustained during the attempted bombing. He was sent to a federal prison in York Charter Township, Michigan, to await trial. On December 26, he was charged in the United States District Court for the Eastern District of Michigan with two criminal counts: attempting to blow up and placing a destructive device on a U.S. civil aircraft. Eleven days later, four counts were added in a grand jury indictment, including the attempted use of a weapon of mass destruction and the attempted murder of 289 people. Incarcerated at the Federal Correctional Institution in Milan, Michigan, if found guilty, he could receive a life sentence plus 90 years in prison.

At first, Abdulmutallab cooperated with investigators, but then ceased talking until the FBI arranged for two of his Nigerian relatives to visit with him. He then began cooperating again. Some politicians were incensed that he was read his Miranda rights.

In March 2010, Anwar al-Awlaki released a tape in which he said, in part:

> To the American people…nine years after 9/11, nine years of spending, and nine years of beefing up security, you are still unsafe even in the holiest and most sacred of days to you, Christmas Day.… Our brother Umar Farouk has succeeded in breaking through the security systems that have cost the U.S. government alone over 40 billion dollars since 9/11.

203

On April 6, 2010, the *New York Times* reported that President Obama had authorized the targeted killing of al-Awlaki [3]. Nearly a year later al-Awlaki was believed to be alive and hiding in Yemen.

Though the "underwear bomber" failed to explode his device, he revealed dramatic flaws in American air security. Homeland Security Secretary Janet Napolitano acknowledged that aviation security had failed. President Obama ordered a review of detection and watch-list procedures, calling the systemic and human security failures "totally unacceptable." Security experts argued that, with so many red flags associated with him, Abdulmutallab should never have been allowed to board the plane. Members of Congress called upon Obama to cease attempts to repatriate Guantanamo detainees to Yemen.

One aspect of American security that seemed "totally unacceptable" was the chilling fact that Mordecai Dzikansky had shared two Israeli "underwear bomber" incidents with the NYPD quite some time before Abdulmutallab carried his underwear bomb onto a plane. Accordingly, the concept of an "underwear bomber" should have been on American radar. One incident occurred on August 31, 2004, when a Hamas male was caught at the Erez border crossing wearing underwear laden with nitrate-based explosives. The other was on June 20, 2005, when Wafa al-Biri was captured at Erez with 20 pounds of explosives in her underwear. We tell her full story in Chapter 4.

In summary, the "underwear bomber" case had mixed results. Thanks to a daring and alert plane passenger, the bomber was unable to blow himself up, what we would call a civilian success. But defects in the American intelligence system permitted him to board the plane with a bomb, and that is a clear-cut example of intelligence and security failure.

Najibullah Zazi and the New York Subway Plot

In 2009, Najibullah Zazi was a 25-year-old Afghan-born driver of a shuttle bus at the Denver International Airport. With his parents, two sisters, and two brothers he had moved in 1992 at age seven from Afghanistan to the Peshawar area of Pakistan, four years before the Taliban takeover of Afghanistan. In 1999, he and his family moved to the United States as legal residents, residing in a Flushing, Queens, apartment. His father, Mohammed Wali Zazi, worked as a New York City taxi driver.

Finding his studies at Flushing High School difficult, Zazi dropped out and, from 2004 to 2009, ran a coffee and pastries vending cart in the

Lower Manhattan Financial District. On his cart he displayed a "God Bless America" sign. In 2006, while in Pakistan, he entered into an arranged marriage with a 19-year-old cousin. He was 21 years old. Claiming that his trips to Pakistan were purely to visit his wife, in 2008 he received weapons and explosives training at an al-Qaeda camp there.

Along with two high school classmates—Adis Medunjanin and Zarein Ahmedzay—he was planning to carry out coordinated suicide bombing attacks at rush hour against the New York City subway system's two busiest stations—Grand Central and Times Square. He said his suicide mission was meant to draw attention to American military activities in Afghanistan.

Federal officials described the Zazi conspiracy as the most serious terrorist plot since 9/11. It had been discovered when Scotland Yard intercepted an e-mail from a senior al-Qaeda operative, instructing Zazi how to execute a suicide bombing. Starting in late spring 2009, Zazi began searching where to find ingredients for the explosives. He also rode the subway a number of times to the Grand Central and Wall Street stations, scouting for the best location to kill the maximum number of people. He and his fellow conspirators intended to obtain and assemble the remaining components of the bombs, and conduct the attack on September 14 (the most likely date), 15, or 16, 2009. If carried out, the Zazi suicide bombing could have killed even more than the Madrid train bombings (2004).

Unbeknownst to him, Najibullah Zazi had been under FBI surveillance since his 2008 Pakistan trip. The evidence the FBI had accumulated was strong enough for it to warn the NYPD to be especially vigilant for attacks against New York City's mass-transport system, stadiums, and hotels. But the evidence was not sufficient to charge the Zazis with terrorism.

NYPD officers showed Zazi's photo to Ahmad Wais Afzali, an Afghan-born imam of a mosque in Queens, Long Island. He sometimes acted as a police informant, but his loyalties were vague: The government informant tipped off both Zazis about the investigation [4]. FBI agents raided homes in Queens that Zazi had visited, seizing backpacks and cell phones, but, monitoring cell phone calls, they realized that their covers had been blown.

Zazi flew back to Denver, where he agreed to undergo FBI questioning. After three days of interviews, he ceased cooperating. Over the summer of 2009, the FBI listened to Zazi's phone conversations, learning that he and his three associates were buying large quantities of hydrogen peroxide and acetone products from beauty supply stores near Denver. Explosives built with hydrogen peroxide, easy to conceal and detonate, killed 52 people in 2005 in the London underground attack. The FBI overheard Zazi in August speaking about mixing chemical substances.

Security videos from a beauty shop showed Zazi pushing a cart full of hydrogen peroxide. He checked into a motel suite in the Colorado town of Aurora on August 28 and again on September 6 and 7 to experiment with heating chemicals in his room's kitchenette in an effort to create a bomb. Authorities examined the kitchenette and discovered traces of acetone, found in nail polish remover. Hydrogen peroxide, acetone, and acid, readily available in beauty supply stores, are components used in triacetone triperoxide peroxyacetone (TATP). As noted in Chapter 10, TATP was also used in the 2005 London underground bombings and the foiled December 2001 suicide bombing of "shoe bomber" Richard Reid.

Zazi later acknowledged that he had conducted several Internet searches for hydrochloric acid, and then had used notes he had written to construct an explosive (hydrogen peroxide) for the detonators. When mixed with other chemicals, hydrogen peroxide produces an improvised explosive (TATP), a highly sensitive and powerful IED that can be used both as an initiating explosive in a detonator and as a main explosive charge.

According to intelligence officials, on September 6 and 7, 2009, Zazi sought repeatedly to communicate urgently with another person to help him put together the safe mixture of ingredients to make the explosives. Two days later, Zazi drove 1,800 miles from his Denver area home to New York City, carrying with him a detonator and explosives, planning on carrying out one of three coordinated suicide martyrdom bombings on the New York City subway system. Unbeknownst to him, he was under FBI surveillance.

The day after he left Denver, two NYPD Intelligence Division detectives asked Imam Ahmed Wais Afzali to identify and provide information on three individuals whose photographs they showed him. Afzali identified Zazi, who had prayed at Afzali's mosque, and two of the other men in the photos.

Zazi was driving near New York City on the afternoon of September 10. He planned to spend the night at the residence of his childhood friend Naiz Kahn in Flushing, Queens, intending to obtain and assemble the remaining bomb components over the weekend. Once that was done, he and his two high school friends planned to carry out the suicide bombings. But, as Zazi crossed the George Washington Bridge heading for New

York City, he was pulled over by Port Authority Police, acting at the FBI's request, for what he was told was a routine drug search. Remarkably, the police searched his car and, finding nothing suspicious such as drugs or bomb materials, let him go. Pleased not to be taken into custody, Zazi thought the search too much of a coincidence and most likely a ruse.

The next day, figuring out what may have caused the car search, Zazi heard from his father that Ahmad Afzali had shown him photos of his son and the two other plotters. When his father learned from Zazi of the car search, he warned him to speak with Afzali urgently or to hire an attorney. Before Zazi could do one or the other, Ahmed Afzali called him, saying that the authorities had asked him about "you guys." He also asked Zazi for the telephone number of one of the other two men, noting mysteriously that he wanted to meet with the other plotter. Later that day, Zazi's rental car was towed because of a parking violation. Searching the car, FBI agents found a laptop with a JPEG image of nine handwritten pages on how to make initiating explosives, main explosive charges, fuses, and detonators. The pages were in Zazi's handwriting. In a panic, Zazi called Afzali, informing his that his car had been "stolen." Deciding that he was being watched, he believed that the watchers had taken his car. Afzali asked if there was anything that could be construed as evidence in the car. Zazi said no.

On September 14, Zazi flew back to Denver. That same day, at the Queens home, FBI agents found Zazi's fingerprints on an electronic scale and several AA batteries as well as a dozen black backpacks. The FBI issued an alert for everyone to be on the lookout for hydrogen peroxide-based bombs.

On September 16, Zazi volunteered to undergo questioning in the presence of his lawyer at the FBI's Joint Terrorism Task Force in the FBI Denver office. Confronted with the nine handwritten pages, Zazi insisted to his interrogators that he had downloaded the notes by mistake and had deleted them, suggesting that he must have accidentally downloaded the pages thinking it was a religious book. But during eight hours of interrogation, he eventually admitted to training in weapons and explosives at an al-Qaeda camp in Pakistan in 2008 and to e-mailing himself bomb-making instructions to use once he returned to the United States.

On September 21, law enforcement authorities arrested Zazi's father and charged him with conspiring, by pouring chemicals down a drain and shredding containers, to destroy evidence. Released on $50,000 bond to his home in Aurora, he was placed under house arrest and was ordered to wear an electronic bracelet. If convicted, he faces 20 years in prison and a $250,000 fine. That same day, Najibullah Zazi was indicted in the U.S. District Court for the District of Colorado on charges of conspiracy to use weapons of mass destruction and making false statements in a matter involving international and domestic terrorism.

The capture of Zazi and his father was a huge success for intelligence officials. The arrests should have been a cause for celebration, but FBI officials were frustrated: They had not intended to take Zazi and his father into custody so soon. But once the informant had tipped off Zazi and his father that law enforcement was on to them, thus preventing intelligence officials from monitoring their movements and discovering their connections to additional terrorist networks, the officials had no choice but to arrest them. "I don't need to f—k around for two more weeks and learn one more fact," said David Cohen, head of the NYPD Intelligence Division. "Sometimes the search for intelligence can get you killed" [5].

"I don't need to f—k around for two more weeks and learn one more fact. Sometimes the search for intelligence can get you killed."

On January 7, 2010, the FBI arrested Zazi's two high school classmates from Queens, Adis Medunjanin and Zarein Ahmedzay, on charges similar to Zazi's. On February 28, Zazi pleaded guilty to conspiring to use weapons of mass destruction, conspiring to commit murder in a foreign country, and providing material support to a terrorist organization.

Zazi's guilty plea was the result of a plea bargain with the prosecution. One report had it that Zazi had agreed to cooperate with the U.S. government after his two associates and father were threatened with being taken to court. As of July 1, 2011, Zazi was awaiting sentencing.

An interesting footnote about training and cross training with other security officials is that Mordecai Dzikansky and Gil Kleiman had just run a 10-day terror-training seminar for Colorado law enforcement and first responders, including bomb techs and SWAT personnel, four days prior to the arrests and searches in Denver with regard to the Zazi case.

The police found their course, in the words of one Denver police investigator, "unbelievably timely. It helped us." Just the fact that Denver and Aurora police were in the midst of a major terrorist investigation soon after learning about all aspects of suicide bombings gave the police an extra dose of self-confidence. Within a few days of returning home to Denver, they themselves were dealing with a major terrorist investigation (the Zazi case) that covered exactly these suicide bombing–related topics.

LAW ENFORCEMENT FAILURES

ISTANBUL: ATTACKS ON TWO SYNAGOGUES

List of suicide attacks in the West since 9/11

Casablanca—May 16, 2003; 25 dead
Istanbul—November 15, 2003; 23 dead
Sharm el-Sheikh—July 23, 2000; 90 dead
Moscow I—February 6, 2004; 41 dead
Moscow II—August 24, 2004; 89 dead
Moscow III—August 31, 2004; 10 dead
London—July 7, 2005; 52 dead

Two synagogues in Istanbul were the targets of suicide bombings in Istanbul, Turkey, in November 2003. The first of the two incidents occurred on Saturday, November 15, at 9:26 a.m., when a terrorist hit Neve Shalom, the city's largest synagogue, and five minutes later another bomber attacked the Bet Israel synagogue. A suicide bomber rammed the entrance of the Neve Shalom synagogue with his explosive-laden Isuzu minitruck, killing 11 and wounding 125. Twelve more people were killed and 220 injured at the Bet Israel attack. Again, a suicide bomber slammed an identical explosive-laden minitruck into the synagogue. In total (including deaths in hospital), 23 people, mostly Turkish Muslims, were killed, and another 300 people wounded in this double suicide bombing. Turkey, with 99.8 percent of its 76.8 million population Muslim, is one of the largest Muslim countries in the world.

Each truck carried 272 to 318 pounds of explosives that were hidden in containers. Turkish investigators concluded that World Islamic Jihad had done the bombings along with al-Qaeda and other terror groups. The two bombers were cousins.

Seeking to prevent further terror, Mordecai Dzikansky, then based in Israel as the NYPD Intelligence Division overseas liaison to the Israel National Police, alerted the NYPD to the bombings. New York immediately decided to step up patrols and provide other coverage of New York City synagogues that Saturday morning.

Five days later, on Thursday, November 20, shortly after 11 a.m., two suicide bombers detonated their vehicles at the London-based HSBC bank and the British consulate in Istanbul, killing 30 and wounding 400 others. Al-Qaeda took credit for the attacks. Most of the victims were Turkish Muslims. Among those killed was the senior British official in Istanbul, Consul General Roger Short. Turkish police believed that the terrorists might have timed their attacks to coincide with President George W. Bush's visit to England to meet with Prime Minister Tony Blair.

Turkish first responders gathering evidence after suicide bombing at Neve Shalom Synagogue in Istanbul on November 15, 2003. (*Credit*: Moshe Milner for Israel Government Press Office)

Moscow: Attack on the Russian Metro

On Friday, 8:32 a.m., February 6, 2004, during rush hour, a suicide bomber blew himself up in the Moscow Metro. Learning of the Moscow attack from Israel Radio, Mordecai Dzikansky called the NYPD and informed them of the attack.

With the identity of the Moscow terrorists still unknown (they turned out to be Chechen), it seemed plausible to the NYPD that a terror cell in America might turn copycat on the New York subway system. The explosion had occurred in the second car of a train leaving the Avtozavodskaya station. The attack was the bloodiest on Moscow's Metro, the world's busiest, averaging 8.5 million riders a day (larger than the Paris metro, which carries 6 million; the New York subway system, at 5.2 million; or the London Underground, at 3.4 million).

In that Moscow bombing, 41 people were killed and more than 140 injured. With probably 200 people on the targeted train car, the driver made a quick and wise decision: He got off the train and asked controllers to switch off electricity on the tracks so that passengers could safely leave the train. In doing so, he kept countless others from being harmed in the aftermath. Overall, 700 people were evacuated safely from the two train stations. Still, the Moscow Metro suicide bombing has to be considered a failure on the part of intelligence officials, who had not prevented it from happening.

London: The First Suicide Bombing in Western Europe

On July 7, 2005, a series of coordinated suicide bombings against London's public transport system occurred during the morning rush hour. The bombings were the work of four al-Qaeda militants who had detonated four bombs: three on London Underground trains, one right after the other, and the fourth on a double-decker bus in Tavistock Square. In addition to the four bombers, 52 people were killed in the attacks; another 700 were wounded. TATP was thought to be the explosive used in the bombings, though there has been no firm confirmation.

The incident was significant for a number of reasons: It was the deadliest terror act in the United Kingdom since the 1988 Lockerbie bombing of Pan Am Flight 103 that killed 270 people. It was also the deadliest bombing in London since World War Two. More people were killed in the London suicide bombings than in any single Provisional Irish Republican Army (IRA) attack in Great Britain or Ireland. And, the action marked the first suicide bombing in Western Europe during the modern era of suicide bombings.

Packed inside rucksacks, the bombs consisted of homemade, organic peroxide-based materials. As for motives, the bombers opposed British support of Saudi Arabia and British involvement in the Iraq War. They were strong admirers of Osama bin Laden.

The three bombs on the London Underground exploded within 50 seconds of each other. Law enforcement officers believed that one bomber vacated the Underground after his compatriots began blowing themselves up and wandered over to a bus and blew himself up there.

211

With respect to the four suicide bombers, Mohammad Sidique Khan, 30, lived in Beeston, Leeds, with his wife and young child, where he worked as a learning mentor at a primary school. His blast killed seven people, including himself. Shehzad Tanweer, 22, also lived in Leeds with his mother and father; he worked in a fish-and-chips shop. Tanweer's blast killed eight people, including himself. Jamaican-born Germaine Lindsay, 19, lived in Aylesbury, Buckinghamshire, with his pregnant wife and young son. His blast killed 27 people, including himself. Hasib Hussain, 18, lived in Leeds with his brother and sister-in-law. His blast killed 14 people, including himself. The four suicide bombers had traveled from Bedfordshire to Luton by car, and then on to London by train.

In a video that Shehzad Tanweer made, he declared: "What you have witnessed now is only the beginning of a string of attacks that will continue and become stronger until you pull your forces out of Afghanistan and Iraq. And until you stop your financial and military support to America and Israel." He argued that the non-Muslims of Britain deserved such attacks because they voted for a government that "continues to oppress our mothers, children, brothers, and sisters in Palestine, Afghanistan, Iraq, and Chechnya."

There had been no warnings of an attack like the London bombings or of when they might take place, but widespread media reports suggested that the bombers were under official scrutiny before the blasts. It was said that MI5 had checked out Mohammad Sidique Khan but decided he was not a likely threat; he was not put under surveillance.

Before the attack, a Syrian cleric had said in a newspaper interview that an al-Qaeda-affiliated group was on the verge of launching a major terror act. One report disclosed that FBI agents based in London had stopped traveling on the Underground, fearing terror attacks. Israeli chief of the Mossad—the national intelligence agency of Israel—Meir Dagan was quoted in a German magazine saying that the Mossad had been alerted to the attack six minutes before it began.

For much of the day of the attack, central London's public transport system was entirely closed. Bus services resumed at 4 p.m. the same day, and most mainline train stations reopened a short time after that. Thousands of people walked home or made their way to the nearest bus or train station. Most of the Underground apart from the affected stations began operating the next morning; some commuters chose to stay at home.

Most of the King's Cross railroad and Underground station was closed; the station's ticket hall and waiting area were turned into a make-shift hospital to treat casualties. While the station reopened later in the day, only suburban rail services could use it. Service on some lines was not restored for weeks.

Television films and broadcasts were postponed or cancelled for reasons of taste. One BBC Radio program recounting the story of an attempt by German secret agents to engineer a jihad against the British in the Middle East during World War Two was not broadcast.

The case studies described in this chapter invite the question: Do steps exist that a nation's military can take against suicide bombing? To answer that question, in the next chapter we look at what the Israel Defense Forces did to defend against suicide bombings in the early 2000s.

NOTES

1. *New York Magazine*, "Anatomy of a Foiled Plot," May 21, 2005.
2. Ibid.
3. *The New York Times*, "U.S. Approves Targeted Killing of American Cleric," April 6, 2010. http://www.nytimes.com/2010/04/07/world/middleeast/07yemen.html.
4. *The New York Times*, "Imam and Informant Tells Why He Lied," April 15, 2010.
5. *Newsweek*, "Inside the Zazi Takedown," September 26, 2009.

16

Israel
The Military Weapon

We have mentioned ways that Israel coped with the horrifying effects of suicide bombings, tactics that mitigated but did not entirely put an end to those bombings. Among the tactics: hardening (fortification) of public facilities, putting private security guards outside all public locations, and using intelligence agents to learn of planned suicide bombings.

However, the terrorists seemed to have the advantage when it came to suicide bombings. Israelis and Palestinians were so close to one another (though separated by impermanent frontiers and checkpoints) that a Palestinian suicide bomber could literally walk the two and a half miles from his home in the West Bank town of Kalkilya to the Israeli coastal town of Netanya and commit his act there.

The Israelis understood that to end the systematic wave of suicide bombings during the early 2000s, it would have to take a more offensive stance and, eventually, they might have to unleash the Israel Defense Forces (IDF). Israel had been reluctant to send its army into the West Bank to take on suicide bombers proactively, fearing heavy casualties that would arise from the inevitable house-to-house fighting between the IDF and Palestinian terrorists.

Prime Minister Ariel Sharon's government feared also that invading the West Bank would lead to heavy international condemnation against Israel for crossing a frontier, killing Palestinians, and imposing harsher measures against the Palestinian population than existed before. To that end, holding the full might of the IDF in reserve, Sharon continued to take a largely defensive posture toward suicide bombings. He began by putting the public on the highest alert.

PUBLIC ALERTNESS

The public was already ahead of Sharon. When suicide bombers were carrying out attacks on an almost daily basis against Israel starting in late 2000, it did not require much convincing for Israelis to buckle down and protect themselves. They went into a state of high-level public alertness automatically, knowing that they had no choice.

Israel had an enlisted population: Its citizens were used to being on alert, willing to obey stringent security rules, prepared to go through constant monitoring and the consequent delays in their schedules. They were taught from their earliest school days about the need for tight security and the need to identify suspicious objects and behavior. It was not unusual for a third-grader to notify his teacher of an unattended object.

The IDF was trained to stay on high alert against suicide bombers but was unable to be 100 percent effective in preventing those bombers from crossing into Israel via its porous borders. In the early days of the Second Intifada, the IDF erected checkpoints on the West Bank, but they were no more then a minor inconvenience for suicide bombers and their sponsors.

That period starting in late 2000 was a difficult and frustrating one for Israel. It had a powerful army, with many soldiers, sophisticated tanks, and an air force that ranked among the best in the world. And yet all that manpower and armor seemed powerless in the face of suicide bombers who, because checkpoints and roadblocks were, at that time, useless, penetrated the country seemingly at will. To add to the misery, within moments of a suicide bombing, Israel Television was on the air live from the scene of the bombing, sending footage that added to Israeli frustration, fear, and feelings of helplessness.

Public alertness could go only so far. Public frustration could only last so long. Most Israelis wanted, indeed begged, Sharon to take the country from a defensive posture to an offensive one. But he remained reluctant.

TARGETED ASSASSINATIONS

By early 2001, four months after the start of the Second Intifada, the suicide bombings began escalating, but not at a pace or lethality that would have forced Sharon to send the IDF into the West Bank to eradicate bomb makers and bombers.

In 2000, there had been four suicide bombings in Israel with no deaths, but the numbers increased in 2001, with 34 suicide bombings causing 85 deaths that year. On February 14, 2001, eight people were killed and 25 injured when a bus, driven by a Palestinian terrorist, plowed into soldiers and civilians waiting at a bus stop near Holon, south of Tel Aviv. On March 4, three people were killed and 60 injured in a suicide bombing in the seaside town of Netanya. Three weeks later, two teenagers were killed and four injured in a suicide bombing at a gas station east of Kfar Saba.

By early 2001, it was clear to Israeli leaders that they needed to take more aggressive measures against the suicide bombers. Sharon searched for a tactic that had the advantage of keeping the IDF out of the West Bank but striking a direct blow against the terror cells. He found such a tactic in targeted assassinations.

Aimed at Palestinian terrorist leaders, the tactic sought to "cut off the head" of the suicide bombing phenomenon without having to worry about heavy Israeli battle casualties. Those specifically targeted would be Sheikh Hassan Nasrallah, leader of the Lebanese-based Hezbollah, and Hamas's cofounder, Sheikh Ahmed Yassin, but not PLO leader Yasser Arafat. Killing Arafat could have led to unintended, negative circumstances for Israel, including Palestinian revenge attacks against Israeli leaders.

Launching a campaign of target assassinations against Palestinian terrorist leaders was so sensitive that Israel kept the operations highly secret, never confirming that it had played a direct role in someone's death. For all the secrecy, Israeli newspapers, after speaking privately with Israeli intelligence figures, published articles that documented in rich detail the assassinations, routinely attributing the deeds to Israeli hit teams. It may have seemed naïve on Israel's part to believe that denying its part in the targeted assassination campaign would keep the world from knowing that Israel had done these deeds. But at least Israel could be satisfied that it was not overtly giving the Palestinians an argument to seek revenge via more suicide bombings.

Israel limited its targets to those with a proven intention of performing a specific act of violence in the near future or to those linked to past acts of violence against Israel. Recognizing the sensitivity involved in targeting Palestinian leaders, Sharon insisted that he personally sign off on every targeted assassination [1].

For Israel, the tactic was comparatively easy to carry out. For the most part, the IDF or the police were used on the West Bank; only in the Gaza Strip was there an extensive use of air attacks because of the danger of inserting ground troops. No urgent escape routes had to be planned or executed.

For all the warnings that Palestinian terrorist leaders had been given, Israeli intelligence still figured out their hiding places. Upon acquiring intelligence of the target's whereabouts, Air Force helicopters—mostly the AH-64 Apache—were quickly dispatched, firing guided missiles at the person. At times, F-16 warplanes were deployed. One of those helicopter-borne guided missiles killed Sheikh Ahmed Yassin on March 22, 2004, as his bodyguards pushed him in his wheelchair after prayers at a mosque.

Sheikh Ahmed Yassin, founder of Hamas terrorist organization, flanked by two guards at his 1989 trial on terrorist charges, in the Gaza Strip. (*Credit*: Israel Government Press Office)

In 1989, Yassin had been arrested and sentenced to life imprisonment but was released from prison in 1997 as part of an Israeli arrangement with Jordan: Two Israeli Mossad agents were released following a botched Israeli attempt to assassinate Khaled Mashal, who eventually became the head of Hamas after the 2004 assassination of Abdel Aziz al-Rantissi, who was killed in a helicopter attack on his car a month after Yassin was assassinated.

Plotting the effectiveness of these targeted assassinations proved difficult. For one thing, the number of suicide bombings rose from 34 in 2001 to 55 in 2002. Still, the Israelis believed in their value. "Targeted killing is not only very valuable," Maj. Gen. Giora Eiland, chief of planning and policy in the Israeli military and one its most senior officers, said. "If we could not use this method in areas like Gaza, where we do not control the territory...we could not fight effectively against terrorist groups" [2].

"If we could not use this method in areas like Gaza, where we do not control the territory...we could not fight effectively against terrorist groups."

Whatever the effectiveness of the targeted assassinations, Israel was vilified by international critics for operating outside the rules of war that spelled out acceptable wartime behavior. Critics railed against the alleged deaths of innocent bystanders. Israel's argument that it had no alternative was not persuasive. The critics further argued that targeted assassinations did not reduce suicide bombings, but only encouraged new recruits to join terrorist cells.

Countering these claims, Israel described the tactic as a measured response to suicide bombings by focusing on the actual operatives who carried out these attacks. Weakening terror organizations and keeping their leaders and bomb makers on the run was sufficient justification in Israel's eyes.

Bolstering its case, the government and military were pleased to find support for the policy from two welcome sources: first, fully 90 percent of the population backed the assassinations, according to one poll. Second, the Israeli Supreme Court ruled that targeted assassinations were a legitimate form of self-defense against suicide bombers.

But it took time for the targeted assassinations to make a difference. And meanwhile, in early 2002, the suicide bombings continued apace. Israel came to believe that the time was coming when the IDF would have to be unleashed.

OPERATION DEFENSIVE SHIELD

At the start of 2002, the number of suicide bombings had increased from four in 2000 with no deaths to 34 in 2001 with 85 deaths. During the first three months of 2002, the number of suicide bombing attacks and deaths continued to be psychologically painful to Israelis, with 12 attacks and 37 Israeli deaths. But it was one particular event in late March that pushed Israel to decide on military action.

That overwhelming event was the suicide bombing of the Park Hotel in Netanya on March 27 that killed 30 people and injured 140 others. It was the most lethal attack against Israelis during the Second Intifada. The Park Hotel was holding a Passover seder (a festive religious meal) for its

250 mostly elderly guests in the dining area of the lower lobby. A former employee at the hotel, the bomber was disguised as a female wearing a woman's wig, pantyhose, lipstick and high heels.

The lobby was an open area, and fragmentation in the device shattered windows across the hotel. Most victims were 70 years old or over; some were Holocaust victims. Hamas claimed responsibility for the bombing carried out by Abdel-Basset Odeh, 25, from the West Bank town of Tulkarm. The assault, Hamas claimed, was meant to wreck a recently announced peace overture from Saudi Arabia. Israel arrested the mastermind behind the attack, Abbas al-Sayed, in May 2002; he was sentenced to life.

The Park Hotel attack was far too lethal and the Israelis were far too demoralized not to deal the Palestinian bombers and their sponsors a mighty military blow. After that incident, Sharon understood that he had to react. On March 29, 2002, Israel took the fight to the suicide bombers by launching a major military attack (Operation Defensive Shield) on West Bank cities, the largest Israeli military operation on the West Bank since the 1967 Six-Day War. It lasted 34 days, ending May 5.

Sharon explained that the main purpose of the action was to catch and arrest terrorists, confiscate their weapons, and destroy bomb-making facilities. But every Israeli knew that an equal goal was to force the terrorists to defend their homes instead of plot suicide bombings and other terror inside Israel.

The IDF called up 20,000 reservists, the largest number called up since the 1982 Lebanon War. The fighting began in Ramallah, with the IDF placing Palestinian leader Yasser Arafat under siege in his Ramallah compound. IDF soldiers moved quickly into five of the other large West Bank cities: Tulkaram and Qalqilya on April 1, Bethlehem and Jenin the next day, and Nablus on April 5.

For the next two and a half weeks, the IDF constrained civilian movement, imposing strict curfews and preventing outsiders, including journalists, from entering the West Bank. The Palestinians were taken by surprise. It had been widely assumed that the IDF would not enter Palestinian-controlled cities and refugee camps, out of fear of the potentially large number of soldiers who would die as a result of fighting in a dense urban environment, and international condemnation for allegedly breaching the Oslo accords.

The West Bank town of Jenin had proven the major hotbed for suicide bombers: Of the 60 bombers that had assaulted Israel in 2002, 23 came from

Jenin. Over 1,000 Israeli soldiers entered the refugee camp there, calling upon the 13,000 civilians to leave. When soldiers began sweeps through the Jenin refugee camp, they discovered 2,000 bombs and booby traps.

A combat bulldozer was brought in to detonate the bombs. Still not confident that soldiers were safe from the explosives, the army decided on a brief ground attack, under international pressure to end the fighting quickly. Soldiers went house to house, encountering stiff resistance, as army helicopters fired wire-guided missiles.

On day three, 13 Israeli soldiers were killed after accidentally wandering into a Palestinian ambush. Three bodies were captured. After that incident, the army, hoping to provide more safety to soldiers, sent in armored bulldozers to ram the corners of houses, creating large holes, thus avoiding the need for soldiers to enter through possibly booby-trapped doors.

Hoping for international help to stop the Israelis, the Palestinians said that Israel had conducted a massacre, claiming that 500 civilians had been killed. Israel countered that it had killed only 52 Palestinians: 47 terrorists and five civilians. Human Rights Watch, a nongovernmental organization devoted to protecting human rights, virtually confirmed the Israeli report by stating that 27 terrorists and 22 civilians and three unidentified people had been killed [3].

With no outside observers, especially journalists, on the scene to disprove the allegations, the massacre charge gained traction. But a United Nations (UN) investigation later proved the charges false [4]. A total of 497 Palestinians were killed, according to UN estimates; hundreds were captured and thousands were wounded; 29 Israeli solders were killed and 100 wounded. A total of 4,258 Palestinians were taken prisoner [5].

The IDF invasion was a major factor in diminishing the number of suicide bombings: Suicide bombings fell from a record 55 in 2002 to 25 the following year; Israeli deaths due to these bombings fell from 220 in 2002 to 142 in 2003. Occurring virtually weekly before Operation Defensive Shield, suicide bombings in 2003 dropped to about two a month.

With Operation Defensive Shield, Israel did not end Palestinian militancy, but it certainly eroded the capability of terror cells to send suicide bombers into Israel. With Yasser Arafat's Palestinian National Authority on the decline, Hamas gained new popularity.

The successful outcome of Operation Defensive Shield would take a while to be felt. Meanwhile, the Israelis searched for additional ways to keep the suicide bombers from reaching Israel. Its solution proved to be more controversial than the targeted assassination campaign; at the same time, the solution appeared to be Israel's most effective "weapon" in curbing suicide bombings.

THE SECURITY FENCE

The "weapon" was the building of a separation or security fence along and within the West Bank. Twenty-six feet high, with vehicle-barrier trenches and a 126-foot exclusion area, it was constructed largely in the West Bank and to some extent along the 1949 Armistice Line between the West Bank and Israel. Twelve percent of the West Bank is on the Israeli side of the fence.

The security fence near Baka al-Garbiya, an Israeli Arab community in northern Israel. (*Credit*: Israel Government Press Office)

Prior to the building of the security fence, terrorists had almost unhindered entry into Israel from the West Bank, since the area unofficially demarking Israel proper and the West Bank had no mutually recognized border or natural barriers. Putting a fence that separated Palestinian suicide bombers from Israel proper made great sense. Before the fence was installed, West Bank bombers had quick, easy access to a number of major Israeli communities that border the West Bank. Before the Second Intifada began (2000), Israel had erected a fence that surrounded the entire Gaza Strip. That fence explained why there were few suicide bombing attempts emanating from Gaza.

The Palestinians insisted that the West Bank fence was unilaterally creating a final political border with Israel despite Israel's claim that the fence was a security measure. The Palestinians also objected to parts of the fence that interfered with their rights of movement. On occasion, the Israel Supreme Court backed their claims and ordered the Israel government to reroute the fence at certain spots in order to meet Palestinian demands.

While the controversy simmered and went largely unresolved, the fence remained intact and led to a reduction in suicide bombing fatalities. While there had been 220 Israeli deaths from suicide bombings in 2002, the year prior to the start of the fence, the number dropped to 142 in 2003; 55 in 2004; 22 in 2005; 15 in 2006; 3 in 2007; 1 in 2008; and none in 2009 and 2010.

The fence led to a reduction in suicide bombing fatalities. After 220 Israeli deaths in 2002, the year prior to the start of the fence, 142 died in 2003; 55 in 2004; 22 in 2005; 15 in 2006; 3 in 2007; 1 in 2008; and none in 2009 and 2010.

Most bombers who succeeded in infiltrating did so in areas where the fence was not complete. Palestinian Islamic Jihad leader Ramadan Abdullah Shalah complained that the fence "limits the ability of the resistance to arrive deep within (Israeli proper) to carry out suicide bombing attacks, but the resistance has not surrendered or become helpless, and is looking for other ways to cope with the requirements of every stage of the Intifada" [6].

A fence such as the one Israel built would work in America as well. It would help prevent terrorists and illegal immigrants from entering the United States, particularly from the South. One burden the United States would have to bear would be the huge cost of building a fence that would stretch 1,989 miles along the U.S.-Mexican border.

Within Israel's security organizations—the IDF and the Shabak especially—a largely behind-the-scenes debate arose over whether Operation Defensive Shield, the fence, or excellent intelligence and cooperation among Israeli security agencies had been more important in reducing suicide bombers. In the end, no one could say for sure, but the point was moot: Fewer Israelis were killed in suicide bombings, and that was indisputable.

We now turn to the key players in the defense against suicide bombing—the first responders.

NOTES

1. *The Washington Post*, "Israel's Lethal Weapon of Choice," June 29, 2003.
2. Ibid.
3. *BBC News*, "MIDDLE EAST/'No Jenin massacre' says rights group," May 3, 2002.
4. *USA Today*, "U.N. report: No massacre in Jenin," August 1, 2002.
5. *Encyclopedic Dictionary*: Operation Defensive Shield (undated). http://www.zionism-israel.com/dic/Defensive_Shield.htm
6. *Al Sharq*, March 23, 2008.

Section V

Key Players

17

First Responders I
Police Officers and Bomb Techs

In this chapter we focus on first responders to suicide bombing attacks. For most of them, including emergency service technicians and firefighters, their basic task is to get to the suicide bombing scene as quickly as possible and, once there, to tend to and evacuate the wounded and to render the scene safe by checking for secondary devices.

IDF soldier and Israel police officer with guns ready searching for suicide bomber about to launch secondary device to harm rescue workers. (*Credit*: Israel Government Press Office)

But their other task is to gather as much information as possible, hopefully to prevent future suicide bombings. By identifying the bomber, they may then locate the cell that was behind the incident and eliminate it. By learning the inner makings of the bomb, first responders may help others develop techniques to defend against similar weaponry.

In some cases, first responders overlap in their responsibilities at the scene. Bomb squad technicians and forensics teams both search for evidence, whether DNA, fingerprint, or chemical residue, that will aid intelligence officers in identifying the planners of the attack. We begin our survey of first responders, in this and the next chapter, with law enforcement personnel.

POLICE OFFICERS

The police officer serves as the eyes and ears of the general public and law enforcement professionals, and so qualifies as a first responder. It is the police officer who serves as the primary guardian against potential suicide bombers. Stuck in traditional police thinking, the police officer must broaden his mind-set to take into account that, in addition to traditional crime (murder, robbery, rape, drugs), he might encounter a potential suicide bomber.

If he approaches a suspicious person, thinking him to be a traditional criminal, as he tries to put handcuffs on him or seeks to talk with him, he may be quite surprised at what happens next. Upon seeing the police officer approach, the would-be suicide bomber may well detonate his bomb prematurely, possibly killing or seriously wounding the police officer and others.

Therefore, the police officer requires up-to-date information that could help him identify a potential suicide bomber, particularly on those with radical, violent tendencies and a proximity to explosives. In New York City, pre-9/11, the police mind-set had centered on traditional crime, including those gangs resembling real-life street gangs like the "Jets" and "Sharks" of *West Side Story* fame or, more recently, the "Bloods" and "Crips." But for years an Israeli police officer has had to think beyond mere street gangs; his focus has had to be on Hamas and the Islamic Jihad.

One Israeli police officer whose mind had focused exclusively on a potential traditional crime did not take into account the possibility of a

In New York City, the police mind-set has centered on traditional crime, including those gangs resembling real-life street gangs like the "Jets" and "Sharks" of *West Side Story* fame.

suicide bombing; he paid dearly for his misstep. On February 22, 2002, Israel encountered a female suicide bomber, Dareen Abu Aisha, age 22, at the Maccabim Junction near the Israeli town of Modi'in. An Israeli police detective assigned to chasing drug dealers received a tip that a drug deal would occur near the junction. Upon arriving at the junction's checkpoint, he was approached by a soldier who informed him of a suspicious car nearby.

Sitting in the front of the car were two Israeli Arab men. In the back seat sat Abu Aisha, dressed like an Israeli prostitute, reeking of cheap perfume. The men spoke Arabic and Hebrew and identified the woman simply as their sister; but she did not speak Hebrew and that should have raised the detective's suspicion.

Approaching the car, the narcotics detective did not imagine that the passengers would be Palestinian suicide bombers, even though a month earlier a women suicide bomber had blown herself up in Jerusalem. The detective decided to search the woman for drugs while soldiers took the men away. He told the woman to get out of the car. The detective's only thought was whether he could ask nearby female Israeli soldiers to carry out a body search of the woman. Deciding that he had no need for the female soldiers to search her bag, he turned to the woman and asked her to open it. But her "reply" was to turn around and, with her back to the detective, blow herself up. By turning her back to him, she "saved" his life; he was, however, seriously injured, as were two other Israeli policemen. She was no drug peddler; she was a female suicide bomber. Her body had turned into mulch. Her spine was found on a hill a week later. The two Arabs tried to run away, but were shot and wounded.

Our message: Police cannot let themselves get into a mindset that precludes the possibility of a suicide bombing attack. Of course a narcotics detective is on the lookout for drug dealers, but if a police officer wants to survive, he must think out of the box—and not assume that he will encounter everyday crime only.

Once a suicide bombing occurs, the police officer may be the first to arrive on the scene. His presence turns him into something of a savior. Until 1994, when the first Palestinian suicide bombing was carried out on Israeli soil, when any kind of explosion occurred, every police officer nearby raced to the scene as quickly as possible. As a result, the mere presence of so many officers at the scene became inefficient.

By the late 1990s, as the number of suicide bombings in Israel increased, when police commanders realized that not every police officer was needed at the bombing scene, protocols were set up that instructed policemen in patrol cars what to do and where to go in case of a suicide bombing. Those new protocols also delineated the lines of authority for the responding police units. Each policeman arriving at a bombing scene knew who his immediate boss was.

At the bombing site, one task of police is to be on the alert for secondary devices. Some police officers stand on car roofs to scan for a potential second attack that can come in many forms: a car bomb, as happened at the Ben Yehuda promenade in Jerusalem on December 1, 2001; or a shooting and a suicide bombing, as occurred on February 10, 2002. Two Israelis were killed in a shooting in the southern Israeli town of Beersheba while a nearby would-be suicide bomber was shot and killed before blowing himself up.

Sometimes two suicide bombers will blow themselves up at an interval of several minutes or so, standing thirty yards apart, hoping that first responders will fall victim to the second explosion. This tactic was used on January 22, 1995, when the terror group Palestinian Islamic Jihad carried out its first suicide bombing against Israel at the Beit Lid Junction near Netanya. As usual on that Sunday morning, the junction was crowded with thousands of Israeli soldiers heading back to West Bank duty after Friday–Saturday leaves. At 9:30 a.m., a Palestinian named Anwar Squkar approached a pay phone at the junction and dropped to his knees, pretending to be ill. Soldiers rushed to his aid, and as they did, Squkar reached into a bag and detonated a bomb.

Correction officers at the nearby Ashmoret Prison went into lockdown, fearing an attack against the prison to rescue Sheikh Ahmed Yassin, serving a life sentence at the prison on terror charges. As emergency crews arrived at the scene to start triage for the wounded, another Palestinian terrorist, Salah Shaaker, ran to the spot where the first bomber had detonated his bomb. He then set off a switch on his upper torso, setting off a second bomb. In the two attacks, 23 were killed and another 69 wounded. A third suicide bomber was at the site, but, apparently frightened of killing himself, ditched his bomb and fled the scene without blowing himself up.

Rather than work at the bomb site, some policemen were more useful trying to ease traffic jams so that other first responders could reach a suicide bombing scene. Some opened up traffic emergency lanes to allow the free flow of ambulances and other first responders. Some set up traffic control and security checkpoints within the perimeters leading to and from the bombing site to try to catch fleeing suicide bombing facilitators.

Once police officers and bomb techs are satisfied that there are no other suicide bombers or hidden bomb devices, they turn to the task of creating order in the midst of chaos (in police parlance, controlled chaos): They erect roadblocks to divert traffic away from the suicide bombing site to avoid gridlock that could hamper rescue work. They set up a perimeter and an entrance point that allows first responders to enter the "inner sanctum" of the site.

At first, officers set up a "breathing perimeter," allowing first responders as well as some others to enter the site. But soon this boundary is turned into a "solid perimeter" through which only necessary personnel enter. Once all the wounded are evacuated and there is a critical mass of first responders, a final fully sealed perimeter is created.

Police officers also try to keep crowds from disturbing first responders. Under the best possible circumstances, the crowd may be tense and angry. Officers labor to keep crowds from morphing into a politically charged demonstration that could lead to violence. On occasion, crowds at Israeli suicide bombing sites may shout "Death to the Arabs!" Allowing people to vent their feelings or protest has not been a problem in Israel, but it is possible, if enough terrorism erupts on the American scene, it could become an "American" problem. But, unless demonstrators turn violent, police should do nothing more than monitor them or, if they seem to be getting disorderly, ask them to move farther away.

With the continuing wave of suicide bombings drawing international media attention, Israeli police have to know how to handle the press, catering to its needs while not allowing journalists to interfere with the work of first responders. The French Hill Junction in northeast Jerusalem has been one of Israel's most popular spots for Palestinian suicide bombers because, to the north, it is minutes away from the West Bank and thus within close proximity to the bombers' homes; to the south, it is just up the road from Israel Police headquarters. While one might think that suicide bombers would prefer avoiding targets near police headquarters, the bombers may have enjoyed pulling off a mission so close, in effect tweaking their noses at the police. And the fact that quite a number of Israeli Arabs live in the area makes it easier for a would-be suicide bomber to fit into the surroundings.

As police spokesman for the foreign press, Gil Kleiman knew from experience where to place the media at a suicide bombing site: 50 yards from the bombing, assuring camera crews and photographers a clear line of sight, but far enough away not to disturb rescuers. The police kept an eye out for a secondary device that might harm the gathering crowds. Their task was to allow the media to do its job unhindered, and that included preventing secondary devices blowing up in the media's midst. The police of course were not patrolling the crowds only to protect the media; their job was to protect everyone from a secondary device.

FIREFIGHTERS AND EMERGENCY MEDICAL SERVICES

Within minutes of a suicide bombing, firefighters and emergency medical service personnel arrive at the scene. Firefighters seek to save lives by putting out fires, shutting down power lines, and shutting off gas mains. Emergency medical service technicians decide who among the victims needs urgent hospital attention—and who does not. Certain victims may be teetering between life and death and may require on the spot life-saving procedures from medical crews.

The police create a safe working environment as quickly as possible so that all other first responders—medical and fire teams, bomb squad technicians, investigators, and forensics personnel—can perform their tasks without concern of being harmed by a secondary device.

Emergency medical personnel in Western societies have not been accustomed to dealing with suicide bombings. As a result, they might be tempted to treat suicide bombings as if they were car accidents. Upon arriving at car accident scenes, emergency medical technicians immobilized victims in order not to worsen spinal injuries.

Yet, unbeknownst to the technicians, suicide bombing victims do not normally experience spinal injuries. Learning the hard way, Israeli medical crews at first treated suicide bomb victims as if they all had spinal injuries, immobilizing them on the spot; but that on-the-spot (and unnecessary) medical treatment interfered with bomb techs doing their jobs. Indeed, the scene needed to be cleared as quickly as possible of all civilians (medical crews as well as injured victims) because of the possibility of a secondary device.

Once the Israelis learned the lesson that it was vital to remove victims from the scene posthaste, their emergency medical technicians adopted the "scoop and run," procedure, i.e., performing most procedures en route to or at emergency rooms in nearby hospitals.

BOMB SQUAD TECHNICIANS

Bomb squad technicians respond to all terror acts, not just suicide bombings. They want to be as close as they can when terror occurs. Whatever kind of terror it is, the bomb techs want be on hand in case of a hidden bomb. In the early 1980s, Israel Police decided that bomb techs should patrol certain sectors of the country to provide an immediate response to any suspicious person or objects. While most Americans bomb techs respond from their headquarter buildings to calls and events and might have assignments when not on call, Israel bomb techs are on patrol and on the streets at all times, similar to regular patrolmen, but specifically there for bomb-related issues.

CATCHING A SUICIDE BOMBER ALIVE

In Israel, catching a would-be suicide bomber, explosives strapped to his chest, on his way to carrying off a suicide bombing, was rare, but on the occasions when it did happen, the bomb squad was called into action.

One example happened on March 24, 2004, when 16-year-old Hussam Muhammad Bilal Abdu from the West Bank town of Nablus entered the nearby Hawara checkpoint, carrying 18 pounds of explosives strapped to his body. Walking toward soldiers, who had guns pointing at him, holding the detonator switch in his hand, Abdu became startled, raising his arms in surrender without blowing himself up.

Soldiers instructed Abdu to raise his shirt; it was then that they saw his explosive belt. Yelling at everyone to back off and take cover, the soldiers called in a bomb disposal robot holding a pair of scissors that, when handed over to the would-be bomber, allowed him to cut the straps holding up the explosive belt. The teenager, who seemed mentally challenged, kept saying that he did not want to die. He fidgeted, seemed extremely nervous, and worried that he was indeed about to die. He seemed like a frightened child.

The teenager, who seemed mentally challenged, kept saying that he did not want to die. He fidgeted, seemed extremely nervous. He seemed like a frightened child.

The soldiers were willing to guide the would-be bomber so that he could extricate himself from his suicide bomb belt, but not at risk to their own lives. Talking to the would-be bomber in Arabic, a bomb tech specialist told him how to take off his clothes (slowly, carefully) and how to remove the suicide belt (even more slowly and carefully). The robot's most important function was bringing the scissors close enough so that Abdu could grab them.

At one point, Abdu pulled out some wires that apparently were bothering him. As a result, the wires dangled from his body, making the situation even more dangerous. The slightest touch of those wires together could cause an explosion. Eventually, the bomb techs exploded the suicide bomb belt off to the side.

For bomb techs, there is no such thing as a risk-free attempt to dismantle a suicide bomb. The bomb tech has to take into account that the detonator switch could be somewhere other than in the would-be bomber's hand: It might be in his pocket or on his stomach. Were the bomber to rub his stomach hard enough while lying face down on the ground, he could detonate the device.

Bomb techs keep one rule in mind: There are no rules for shutting down a "live" suicide bomber. One cannot assume that the bomber will do one thing and not another. Keeping an open mind to any possible move on the bomber's part can save the bomb tech's life.

In the early 1980s, Gil Kleiman was a bomb tech with the Israel Police. It would take another decade before suicide bombers unleashed their attacks in Israel. But once Israel invaded Lebanon in June 1982, occupying southern Lebanon and other strategic points, including the outskirts of Beirut, it seemed to Israelis rather naively as if a golden era of peace with one of its once-hostile neighbors might be in the offing.

One hopeful sign was the opening of the Israel–Lebanon frontier to Lebanese travelers wishing to visit Israel. Lebanese wishing to plant car bombs in Israel practically had an open invitation. One day, Kleiman was told to check out a suspicious car with Lebanese license plates near the Shalom Tower in downtown Tel Aviv, which at 34 stories was Israel's tallest building. The skyscraper was also, according to Israeli intelligence, a high-risk target of terrorists. According to an eyewitness, a car with Lebanese license plates was double-parked next to the Shalom Tower, and the driver was seen fleeing from the car.

All signs suggested a car bomb: The car was parked in a high-risk area; it had Lebanese plates at a time when the modus operandi of Lebanese terror organizations was to use car bombs; and the driver seemed to flee hurriedly, giving the impression that he might be leaving a car bomb behind.

Gil Kleiman could not know it at the time, but experiences such as this one served as training for Israeli bomb techs, many of whom would later face a series of almost daily suicide bombings unprecedented in the Western world. Once a suicide bomber was caught, a bomb tech would be expected to dismantle the suicide bomb.

As Kleiman drove to the scene, he and his fellow bomb techs were assessing the need to close off the area within 200 yards of the suspicious car completely. If all phone calls to the Israel Police, warning of a possible bomb, were treated as genuine, and police shut down the risky site to nearby traffic, no Israeli would ever reach his destination on time.

Israeli life would have been so disrupted that the terrorists would have succeeded in one of their objectives—disturbing Israeli society through terror acts—without planting even one bomb. Therefore, the Israeli bomb squad developed a protocol that found the correct balance between treating the suspicious object as real and allowing the cadence of life to continue at its normal pace. The bomb squad's motto was: work fast and safely. The decision to close a site was given due consideration each time.

The bomb squad's motto was: work fast and safely.

To allow themselves to work fast and safely, Israeli bomb techs wore bomb suits that were far less cumbersome than those worn by other Western bomb techs. The Israeli suits allowed for easy maneuverability and for the bomb tech to suit up as often as 20 times a day during an eight-hour shift. American and Canadian bomb techs suited up much less often because their countries experienced far fewer bombs and bomb threats than Israel did.

Lighter than American and Canadian bomb suits, the Israeli suits did not carry the full protection of the heavier U.S. and Canadian suits. The Israeli suits, however, permitted Israeli bomb techs to operate freely inside the confines of a car trunk or when crawling under a bus seat.

It could take 90 minutes at least for a bomb technician to disarm a bomb. So, Kleiman and his fellow bomb techs had to weigh between assuring total safety and giving terrorists free reign to disturb society. In this case, the tip seemed genuine and Kleiman decided to close a wide area near the bomb.

Arriving at the scene, an adrenaline rush kicked in because soon Kleiman knew that he would be at center stage, the key actor for the many curious nearby civilians, oblivious to the possible danger. Someone was about to search for a bomb and perhaps take it apart, risking his life—high drama with the end uncertain. All bomb techs sensed this drama.

After the wave of suicide bombings in Israel in the mid-1990s, Kleiman concluded that for bomb techs, dismantling a car bomb was easier than preventing a suicide bombing. While the would-be suicide bomber had the ability to change direction and search out a new target at the last minute, a car bomb, essentially an inanimate object, had no such flexibility. As he approached the suspicious car, Kleiman did not have to worry that the car might suddenly run toward him, or that the car would wait for him to approach and then, upon his arrival, blow itself up, as a suicide bomber could do.

Kleiman only worried that the timer would get to zero at the precise moment that he reached the vehicle. That indeed would have been bad luck. But no bomb tech believes that bad luck will befall him. If he did, bomb disposal would have been the bomb tech's last choice as a career.

A concern of bomb techs, when facing a possible car bomb, is whether to wear a protective suit. The tech has to take into account that the suit might hamper his movements crawling inside a car where a bomb may have been planted. According to police protocol, a bomb tech would suit up only when he suspects there is an actual car bomb. Fearing an actual car bomb, Kleiman suited up.

An argument existed for suiting up before approaching a suspicious object that was not in a car. It was a safe assumption that an unattended object would not contain as lethal an amount of high explosives as a car bomb would. If the bomb tech had the bad luck of an unattended object blowing up as he approached it, the suit could still save his life. But, if a car bomb with its ton or more of explosives went off as a bomb tech approached it, no suit, helmet, or any other protective gear would help him.

Kleiman put his helmet on carefully, following police procedure; but, violating police procedure, which is to keep his visor down in order to protect his face, he left the visor up so that he could assure complete peripheral vision. Then he walked to the suspicious car, slowly and deliberately. Hoping to sound in control, he spoke into the police radio unhurriedly. Quickly reviewing his step-by-step checklist, he began his search by looking into the front passenger area, checking for suspicious wires, electrical tape, anything odd on the dashboard.

He did not see any explosive device on or under the seats. Crawling under the car, he could not have been less comfortable—or more anxious. His nose was three inches from the gas tank. His feet felt the heat coming off of the asphalt. He tapped the gas tank to figure out if it contained a bomb. Kleiman hoped that he would hear the dull, hollow sound of a full tank of gas and not the dull, solid thud that indicated a gas tank filled with explosive.

His nose was three inches from the gas tank. His feet felt the heat coming off of the asphalt. He tapped the gas tank to figure out if it contained a bomb.

For the first time as a bomb tech, he realized that he could die in the next few seconds. Seeking some comfort, he told himself that, should a blast occur, he would be so close to it that he would not know what happened. He would feel no pain as he was instantly disintegrated.

He told himself over and over: "It won't bother me if it goes off, it can't hurt me." To his good fortune, he found no bomb, not in the gas tank nor in any other part of the car. The car had belonged to a Lebanese Jewish family who were visiting relatives in Tel Aviv while Kleiman was searching for the explosive device.

WHEN A SUICIDE BOMB EXPLODES

When a suicide bomb goes off, police headquarters alerts patrolling bomb techs, who, using their computers, note the location of the bomb and race to the scene.

In Israel, numerous bomb tech teams show up at a suicide bombing site, spending up to four hours there. They operate in the midst of controlled chaos: Wounded are screaming, some unable to move; others walk around in a daze. Other first responders are shouting, too, trying to impose order, save lives, bring a sense of calm.

In those first few moments, bomb squad technicians search for telltale signs that a suicide bombing has indeed occurred. The bomb techs might see smoke billowing out of the back of a bus, indicating an explosion. But an explosion without billowing smoke could be the result of a bus tire exploding and not a suicide bombing.

If bomb squad technicians do believe that a suicide bomber has indeed launched the attack as opposed to someone using a timed or remote-controlled device, other first responders deploy their resources toward catching the sponsors rather than the bomber, since he (the bomber) is dead.

Bomb techs begin their work by joining police officers searching for possible secondary explosives that might harm first responders. Next, the bomb techs take on the role of investigators, searching for remnants of the bomb and the bomber. Determining where the suicide bomber stood or sat when he blew himself up may help the bomb techs locate a second bomber about to unleash a suicide attack.

Once they locate the remains of the bomb, they try to find bomb fragments, wires, and bomb residue that were used, gathering evidence for further investigation. The suicide bomber's body is of special interest to bomb techs. Looking at what remains of his body, they hope to learn what type of bomb he used and how the bomber carried it. Armed with that information, the bomb techs hope to uncover the identity of the bomber's terror cell as well as the bomb maker.

To locate the bomber, bomb techs search for specific body parts. By being the closest to the blast, the bomber would be the only one with certain bomb-related features: a severed head, legs separated from a torso, hands lying far apart from one another—all indicating that these belong to the bomber.

Nabil El Halbia, 35, after blowing himself up in Jerusalem on December 1, 2001, left an ID card behind because he wanted personal credit for the mission. (*Credit*: Gil Kleiman photo collection)

By identifying where and how the bomber's body absorbed the blast, a bomb tech can figure out how the bomb was carried. If the bomb had been placed inside a bag on the floor of a bus, the explosive device would have separated the bomber's torso from his legs; if a suicide bomber had a ready-to-explode bomb on his chest, the worst damage would be to the upper portion of his body.

The tech can also tell if the bomber was holding the bomb in his right or left hand by noticing which hand is mangled, and which is not. He can tell which way the bomber was facing by noticing the positioning of his hands: If the right hand had been hurled to the east and the left hand to the west, the suicide bomber would have been facing north.

Bomb techs sometimes perform a kind of autopsy on the bomber, not trying to determine what organ caused his death, but rather seeking whatever bomb parts—switches, battery parts, wires and the like—were embedded in his body.

CHECKING FOR THE "SIGNATURE"

It is also the responsibility of bomb squad technicians to determine the bomb's ingredients and the "signature" of the bomb maker. Every bomb has a signature, i.e., those unique characteristics that are exclusive to a certain bomb maker: a certain type of explosive, fragments, battery, suicide belt, wiring, masking tape, or a chemical; or a certain kind of camouflage:

a bag, a suitcase, or the canvas used for the bomb vest. Finding out what type of bag was used could lead investigative officers to identify the factory that sold the item to the terrorists. Certain distributors carry exclusively a specific battery or a special kind of an "on–off" switch. The way a wire is soldered, the kind of stitching used on a suicide bomb belt, or the color or type of electrical tape, all can be part of the bomb's signature.

Why would a bomb maker repeatedly use a specific signature, making it easier for the enemy to identify and seek him and his cell out? Perhaps he has no other option easily available. Most likely, having discovered how to make a bomb safely, feeling confident in the ingredients he has used in the past, the bomb maker does not want to tempt fate and risk producing a less safe bomb. Or, perversely, he just may want to take credit for the bombing, his way of helping to raise funds for his terror cell.

When two suicide bombings occurred the same day on September 9, 2003, outside an army base in Rishon LeZion and later at Café Hillel in Jerusalem, bomb techs found fragments that led to the same West Bank bomb maker. Police kept that information a secret. As foreign press spokesman, Gil Kleiman had to keep photographers from filming the fragments at Café Hillel to conceal from the bombers' facilitators the fact that the police knew that the fragments at both sites were similar. That would have given the terrorists information that could have sent the cell into deeper hiding, making them harder to discover.

In the next chapter, we describe other first responders: intelligence officers, forensics specialists, and investigative officers.

18

First Responders II
Intelligence, Forensics, and Investigative Officers

INTELLIGENCE OFFICERS

Intelligence officers are the first responders charged with analyzing evidence as it surfaces at a suicide bombing site, checking it for its significance, and then taking action to deter further suicide bombings. These intelligence officers are particularly interested in finding out the identity of the bomber's cell and then catching its members.

Intelligence officers do not passively wait for evidence that other first responders gather before taking action. To learn who was behind a suicide bombing attack, intelligence teams want to know whether the bomber left behind a vehicle with a license plate or perhaps a cell phone with cell phone numbers that would prove invaluable. They will check whether a suicide bombing sponsor might have been given a parking violation for his car near the bombing site. If he did, a car license and other information would be immediately available to intelligence units.

To produce results, intelligence accumulated at the bombing site must be quickly shared among intelligence agencies and even filtered down to professional security guards. Otherwise, the intelligence can be wasted. In the past, Israeli intelligence agencies were reluctant to share information with each other, and only intelligence directors would share information with their counterparts. Often, the information did not filter down to those most in touch with what was happening on the streets—police officers and detectives, the most likely people to notice suspicious would-be suicide bombers. By the time the top brass of the Shabak and the Israel Police allowed information to filter down the chain of command to the actual end user—the detective or the policeman in the street—it was too late.

The system was time consuming and inefficient, and it needed revamping in light of the new wave of suicide bombings that arose after September 2000. The Israelis decided that once information comes in to intelligence agencies that a suicide bombing is in the planning stages, decisions have to be made about sharing that information.

They realized the value of getting actionable intelligence first into the hands of the local police officer and then of private security companies as quickly as possible, eager for these firms to filter the intelligence to their security guards. The intelligence was given to the private security firms because Israeli law stated that the police and Shabak must "advise and guide" certain security establishments. The more sensitive the target, the more intelligence was given to security guards. Guards at government offices received more intelligence, guards at small stores, less.

Israeli intelligence agencies realized that they needed to share intelligence with those at the worker level in both the police and Shabak. It turned out that field-level end users of intelligence—the Shabak operatives and police detectives and lower-level police officers in the field—were meeting often on a day-to-day basis at suicide bombing sites, becoming familiar with one another; they soon began swapping intelligence on the spot.

Sometimes the information would be very specific: what kind of car to look out for or whom to look for. Many times the intelligence was watered down to avoid compromising intelligence sources, but under the new system, intelligence flowed up and down the chain of command with a new sense of urgency.

This new system saved a lot of time and many lives. One Israeli police commissioner noted that, in earlier days, a commissioner would have been embarrassed and annoyed that one of his field sergeants had learned certain intelligence from the Shabak operative before the commissioner had. But it soon became apparent that, with so much terror aimed at Israel, the new system was the only way to disseminate important intelligence quickly.

Should new intelligence be shared with local politicians? The answer almost always is no. A politician might decide to talk openly to journalists, who would then publish stories based on the intelligence and in that way hamper the police investigation.

Should intelligence be shared with journalists? Yes, but only under certain circumstances. For example, perhaps the police have obtained information that mosques are being used to hide suicide bomb belts. For a police spokesman to say such a thing publicly might endanger a police informant. But leaking the information to the media was important in helping to familiarize the media and the public with the tactic of using mosques as terrorist hiding places. That alone justified the leak.

Should intelligence be shared with patrolmen and detectives? The rule has to be: Intelligence should be shared with those who are in a position to affect the outcome of the case. Clearly, that includes patrolmen and detectives. Intelligence information that remains inside a computer will not stop a suicide bombing.

INTELLIGENCE GATHERING AT LOCAL AMERICAN POLICE DEPARTMENTS

In the American context, if terror, and along with it suicide bombing, escalates, among the busiest first responders will be local police departments, especially detectives and patrolmen. In some ways, their jobs will be exceptionally challenging, if only because these departments operate under severe handicaps such as low budgets and limited personnel. Most American local police departments are small: 81 percent (11,015) employ fewer than 25 full-time officers, 42 percent (5,737) employ fewer than five officers, and 7.5 percent (1,022) rely on only a part-time officer [1].

> Most American local police departments are small: 81 percent (11,015) employ fewer than 25 full-time officers, 42 percent (5,737) employ fewer than five officers, and 7.5 percent (1,022) rely on only a part-time officer.

These departments may need whatever intelligence exists to thwart a suicide bombing, but they do not always have the means to acquire the intelligence on their own. Still, they will be the ones called upon to develop actionable intelligence urgently should they confront a possible terrorist plan. For that reason, we look now at how the counterterror capabilities of local American police departments are organized and how those departments might improve their intelligence gathering.

243

Police departments in major American cities often face this quandary: Do they rely on the FBI and other federal agencies to gather counterterror intelligence, or do they try to gather it on their own? Most local police departments tend to rely on the federal government, especially the FBI, to engage in the intelligence work that will identify and thwart potential suicide bombers. Nearly every large police department tends to rely on the feds as the lead investigators, with local police participation via the FBI's Joint Terrorism Task Force (JTTF). The New York City Police Department (NYPD) and the Los Angeles Police Department (LAPD) have their own counterterror programs, with the NYPD being the gold standard for the world's municipal police departments.

The FBI runs a Joint Terrorism Task Force (JTTF), a partnership among a number of American law enforcement agencies mandated to defend against terror. The agencies include the Department of Homeland Security, the U.S. Coast Guard Investigative Service, the U.S. Immigration and Customs Enforcement, the U.S. Customs and Border Protection, the Transportation Security Administration, the U.S. Secret Service, the State Department's Diplomatic Security Service, and most importantly, local police investigators, because they know their beats the best.

The JTTF deploys surveillance, electronic monitoring, and does interviewing as part of its investigations. But, as the NYPD example has demonstrated, police departments, whatever their size, can and should take on as much counterterror intelligence-gathering responsibilities as possible. These departments can argue that their towns and cities are too small to interest suicide bombers, but the Israeli experience indicates that terrorists found lower-profile targets more appealing than higher-profile ones.

This intelligence work is complicated because it entails identifying possible suicide bombing cells before an attack occurs. Very often, the planning of a terror attack occurs in small hamlets, with the target being a major city. It means that local police detectives in those hamlets have to acquire training and skills that will enable them to identify a terror cell and shut it down.

In the United States, most local police departments do not have separate intelligence units. Only major American cities such as New York City do. But almost every American police department has a detective squad that routinely performs intelligence and investigative functions with its own informants and its own forensics teams. That is a good start.

Depending upon the size of the department, local police detectives may do their own intelligence work: driving unmarked cars, dressing in plain clothes with guns bulging, working confidential informants, spending hours in a car on surveillance. In smaller police departments, undercover officers function as investigative officers as well, passing information on to detectives who may take the suspect's case to a prosecutor.

What most smaller police departments are still missing—and what must be addressed quickly—is making counterterror intelligence a top priority. Until now, a local detective or patrolman has thought of intelligence gathering as investigating traditional crime such as murder, rape, robbery, or drug dealing. But in the wake of 9/11, American police departments must learn that the likelihood of terror, including suicide bombing, occurring on American soil is increasing. As a result, all American police departments, large and small, must attach the same if not more importance to uprooting terrorists as they have given to thwarting traditional criminals.

We are all too aware of the budgetary constraints placed on local police departments, but what we are urging does not require added police personnel or equipment. Instead, what is needed is nothing more than an adjustment in training courses that broadens the mind-set of law enforcement officers to watch for terror cells as well as traditional criminals.

Getting intelligence from the feds does not preclude local police departments engaging in their own human intelligence using informants or undercover intelligence officers who can pass as one of the enemy. To perform that function, local police officers must know the enemy, his customs, religion, and language. Hence, depending upon the size of the police department, hiring a certain number of Arabic-speaking police officers is an important first step for local departments. With their language skills, those officers can serve on the front line in determining who is suspicious and who is not, monitoring Islamic Web sites, interpreting wiretaps, and interviewing suspects.

In giving new priority to the threat of suicide bombings, local police have to be aware of possible breeding grounds for radical elements. If there is a mosque in the community, with an imam who is preaching radical Islamic ideology and urging violence, police would do well to monitor the imam and to check whether the audience seems to hang on his every word. This would all have to be done, of course, within the constraints of the U.S. Constitution. Someone in that audience might well become a suicide bomber.

More can be done at the local police level. It would be prudent to ask citizens for help in passing along information about suspicious people or materials. Also, local police departments should gather intelligence through the local prison system. Prisons can become breeding grounds for future suicide bombers, and therefore those prisoners who may have overheard would-be bombers discuss their plans would be especially valuable to police officers.

Hoping to trade information that prisoners might glean from inside, prisoners are often willing to pass on sensitive information in exchange for an early parole. Local police should arm themselves with as much "signet"—signal intelligence—as possible. Signet is intelligence culled from anything electronic, including telephone eavesdropping, wiretapping, and radio interceptions.

One new approach to intelligence concerns the Internet. In the same way that an intelligence agent, acting undercover, can try to reach out to a suspected pedophile in an Internet chat room, law enforcement officers should be sensitive to talk of suicide bombings over the Internet. When monitoring chat rooms, these officers should not expect to hear a terrorist talk of specific terror plans, but he may inadvertently offer some useful hints of what kind of violence he would like to undertake or of his connections to other terrorists.

FORENSICS OFFICERS

Forensics officers, made famous by popular television series, may seem the least exciting of the first responders. Bomb techs dismantle bombs; firemen put out fires; Emergency Medical Services personnel save lives at the scene. But forensics teams are scientists who sift through evidence and send it on to laboratories. However unexciting their tasks may seem, these officers are among the most important first responders at the suicide bombing scene.

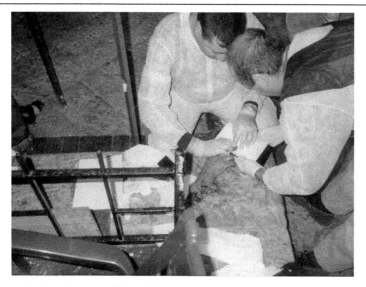

Fingerprinting of severed hand for victim identification. (*Credit*: Gil Kleiman photo collection)

Nabil El Halbia, 35, lies dead after blowing himself up in Jerusalem on December 1, 2001. Because his head was still attached and torso relatively intact, but half of his legs, hands and hips are missing, the indication is that the bomber was not wearing a vest; but was holding the bomb low down near his legs or in a bag on the ground. A detached head indicates an explosion near the upper torso. (*Credit*: Gil Kleiman photo collection)

They have two important tasks: While bomb technicians are searching for anything relevant to the bomb, Israeli forensics officers give priority to identifying the victims in order to give their families a sense of closure. The identification process is far more complicated than a traditional crime scene because of the far worse condition of the bodies at a suicide bombing, Once completed, the process allows the families to bury their loved ones quickly in accordance with Jewish law. For Jews, burying the dead quickly is very important. Jewish law requires that bodies have to be buried in the ground as soon as possible after death, usually within 24 hours. So Israel does not have refrigerator trucks waiting for pieces of flesh to be placed inside of them.

Burying suicide bombing victims as quickly as possible, and then getting back to normal, exemplifies one important way the Israelis combat terror. Gathering around the bodies at a suicide bombing, forensics teams take video footage and still photos of body parts and items that might have belonged to specific victims. The video footage and still photos are then turned over to the foreign ministry; only on rare occasions does the ministry use the footage, as when the then U.S. Secretary of State Colin Powell was shown still photos of a Palestinian suicide bombing in Israel. Israeli officials wanted to show someone at the highest level of American government what terrorists had done to unarmed Israeli civilians.

As a result of the explosion, the site is a mess. Unlike a murder scene where the victim's belongings are often near the body, victims and belongings at a suicide bombing site can be far apart. Even when forensics teams identify bags and other items belonging to the wounded, the items are left at the scene rather than taken along with the injured to hospitals. First responders want to avoid a situation in which a secondary bomb might have been placed in a bag that could be triggered by picking it up or in which a preset timing device in the bag is activated. Only if the wounded person identifies the bag and insists on carrying it will the bag be given to him or her. Hence, the forensics team does not have access to bags and other items that might have been used for identification, making their jobs that much more difficult.

Other methods of identification are available to forensics teams. If the suicide bomber blew himself up close to a victim, the victim's body may be so badly damaged that identification becomes almost impossible. A victim's face may be damaged beyond recognition. In that case, forensics scientists rely upon the victim's DNA that might match DNA found on personal belongings at the victim's home. After victims' families learn that a relative or friend might be a victim, a family member is asked to permit forensics teams to check the possible victim's home for DNA. Forensics teams may take hair from a hairbrush at a victim's home and cross-reference it with DNA found on bodies in morgues to get a firm identification. Such methods were used to identify the 9/11 victims.

To facilitate the work of forensics teams at the suicide bombing site, bodies are placed alongside one another at a nearby location called a roll call. In Israel's case, the actual official identification is carried out at the coroner's office at the National Institute of Forensic Medicine at Abu Kabir in Tel Aviv.

Within four hours, an Israeli forensics team is usually finished canvassing a suicide bombing site. After that, evidence may still remain on the scene, perhaps fragments that may not have been picked up. But forensics teams do not need every ball bearing. From a quick investigation of the bomb site, they will usually have a sufficient number of items to track down a terrorist cell. There is no need to find every ball bearing to catch the perp; he is dead.

Eventually the bomb tech team arrives at the lab, bringing evidence that will hopefully help in the identification process. The evidence is categorized and tested. It is at the lab where the actual work of bomb forensics is done.

American forensics teams, partly because they lack the experience of Israeli forensics teams, partly because they are almost always dealing with homicide, armed robbery, or rape, will keep a crime scene open for at least a day, sometimes more. But Israeli forensics teams feel compelled to shut down a suicide bombing scene as quickly as possible. They want to put to an end to any reminder of the deep scar that the suicide bomber caused, a scar that signified how on that given day terrorists disrupted Israeli life.

In a standard breaking-and-entry investigation forensics teams dust for fingerprints and correlate results to other fingerprints on record and then give evidence in court. With a suicide bombing, forensics officers will still have to give evidence at a trial, even though the bomber is already dead. The evidence is needed during a trial of a facilitator. The forensics officers use the prints to identify the bomber and then show a connection to the terror cell and those responsible. In the war against terror, however, the need to acquire intelligence information is far more important than acquiring admissible evidence.

Little bothers the Israel Police more in its work at the bomb site than not being able to identify a body. If word that there is an unidentified body gets on news broadcasts, their anger is even greater. The unidentified body means that some family has not been able to bury their loved one.

In fact, few Jewish victims at suicide bombing sites are left unidentified. Usually tourists or foreign workers cannot be identified because a family member cannot be located quickly or at all. Customarily, within 12 hours of the bombing, all of the dead are identified.

While Israeli first responders have had to deal with numerous dead bodies at suicide bombing sites, their American counterparts have for the most part not experienced or dealt with such agonizing scenes—other than at 9/11 and Oklahoma City. American forensics teams routinely deal with a single victim at a traditional crime scene, sometimes with two or three bodies, usually no more. The crimes, after all, are break-ins, murder, or rape, and the perp is not interested in wiping out large numbers of people.

As a New York City Police Department homicide detective, Mordecai Dzikansky helped to identify bodies in the aftermath of the World Trade Center attacks in September 2001. Until September 29, 18 days after the attack, work at Ground Zero had been a rescue and recovery operation, but after that, after all hope for finding additional survivors had disappeared, the sole task was the sad search for bodies and body parts.

Once discovered, the bodies and body parts had to be identified. Many had been pulverized beyond recognition; the chances of identifying their remains through photographs were slim. In addition to bodies, Dzikansky and others also searched for personal items and DNA that would confirm someone's presence at the site.

The Manhattan Medical Examiner (ME) established a tent city at the ME's office at 30th Street and First Avenue in New York; it brought together in one place most of the existing technologies used to identify victims' remains. On and off through December 2001, tent-city workers phoned the NYPD and asked a supervisor to round up five or so detectives to work two or three days a week at the improvised morgue.

On September 25, two weeks after 9/11, Dzikansky was sent to work at the tent city, the first of a number of stints that he did two days a week, 12 to 16 hours a day. He sometimes joined the security detail, which meant standing on rooftops to make sure that no one, especially paparazzi with their cameras, penetrated the perimeters. For those at the tent city, the site was holy, not a place to be photographed. Eventually, Dzikansky's main task was helping to process incoming remains and seeking to identify them, assignments that seemed on the surface tedious and hardly glamorous, but to him and others were of overwhelming importance, a practical act mixed with a touch of the sacred.

The process at the tent city seemed like an assembly line: Once remains had been identified, freezer trucks preserved the body or sometimes just body parts. Bodies and body parts as well as personal items moved through a series of stations, conveyor-belt style, where they were photographed and, if possible, fingerprinted. After proper paper documentation, specimens of any items that could be used for identification were then taken for DNA analysis. When remains were assigned to Dzikansky, his task was to escort them through the various stations. Everything done at a station had to be logged in and the results recorded.

In a normal homicide probe, some of these tasks would have taken weeks, but by increasing manpower and working round the clock, the ME's office produced results in hours. On any given day, Dzikansky might have had one assignment—or ten. It depended on the progress of digging at Ground Zero itself. Remarkably, most of the remains that passed through the tent city were identified.

INVESTIGATIVE OFFICERS

Investigative officers have overall responsibility for conducting the investigation of a suicide bombing. But other first responders take part in the investigation as well. Bomb squad technicians do investigatory work on the suicide bomber and the bomb. Forensics teams investigate the physical evidence. Intelligence officers gather evidence to help in tracking down the terror cell.

Table 18.1 is used to teach investigators to ask the basic questions that must be answered when they work a suicide bombing scene. It provides a basic comparison of suicide bombing events that occurred in Israel in 2004.

As he arrives at the attack, the investigative officer's first task is interviewing witnesses to determine whether a suicide bombing has occurred. If so, the investigator's job is easier than had it been a traditional crime like a homicide, an armed robber, or a rape. For those conventional crimes, he would have had to spend almost all of his time identifying and catching the perp. But, in a suicide bombing, the perp is dead. The investigator's job is to put together a complete, cohesive report or "package" with everyone's information to present to court. The investigators are the primary interviewers of witnesses, security personnel, victims, and the like.

It may seem difficult to distinguish the work of Israeli investigative and intelligence officers, so let's explain their different functions: Investigative officers gather information that will be used in court. Intelligence officers gather information to be used in the overall investigation of the suicide bombing scene. Their priority is gathering the information to help them

251

Table 18.1 The Basic Questions To Be Asked When Working A Suicide Bomb Scene

Event No.	Date	City	Location	Time	Casualties	Terror Group	Explosive Device	Characteristics	Bomber Gender	Profile	Security at Site	Attended Crime
1	Thursday, Jan 29	Jerusalem – Rechavia (near Prime Minister's residence)	Bus	0900	10	Al Aqsa	Bag	Powerful, a lot of fragmentation	Male	24-year-old Palestinian policeman from Bethlehem	None; bomber most likely entered bus at beginning of route. Detonated at rear of bus, opposite back door	Yes
2	Sunday, Feb 22	Jerusalem – Rechavia	Bus	0830	7	Al Aqsa	Belt	—	Male	23-year-old Palestinian from Bethlehem	Security guard got off bus one stop before the blast; detonated at center of bus	No, in USA
3, 4	Sunday, Mar 14	Ashdod	Seaport (Israel's busiest)	1630	9	Hamas & Fatah	Belt (grenades and other weapons found in container)	Double bombing, shrapnel	Male/Male	2 teenage Palestinians from Gaza	Subjects entered port in false bottom of container that originated at Karni Crossing in Gaza	No, in Madrid
5	Sunday, Jul 11	Tel Aviv	Bus stop	0715	1	Al Aqsa	Bag	Planted in bushes adjacent to a bus stop and was detonated by timer for maximum rush hour casualties; no fragmentation	n/a – device unattended	Unknown	None	Yes

| 6 | Wednesday, Aug 11 | Jerusalem | Checkpoint | 1520 | 3 Palestinian bystanders (6 INP MOS injured incl. lost limbs) | Al Aqsa | Unattended object detonated by remote control (possibly briefcase); device thought to be intended for suicide bombing in Jerusalem, prevented by checkpoint | Medium sized, contained fragmentation | n/a – device unattended | Transporter of device from Ramallah to Jerusalem | Checkpoint, heavily secured. High alert status; INP was roving at checkpoint and became intended target when transporter deemed it impossible to pass with device | Yes |
| 7, 8 | Tuesday, Aug 31 | Be'er Sheva | Buses | 1450 | 12 | Hamas | Belt | Simultaneous detonations; buses were 1 block apart from each other | Male/Male | From Hebron | Rear bus detonated approx. 30 seconds before second explosion, allowing driver to pull to side of road and enabling some passengers to escape from the bus | Yes |

Continued

253

Table 18.1 (continued) The Basic Questions To Be Asked When Working A Suicide Bomb Scene

Event No.	Date	City	Location	Time	Casualties	Terror Group	Explosive		Bomber		Security at Site	Attended Crime
							Device	Characteristics	Gender	Profile		
9	Wednesday, Sep 22	Jerusalem	Bus stop (most fortified in Israel since it was the sight of numerous attacks)	1350	2 (INP)	Al Aqsa	Bag	Small charge, contained fragmentation	Female	18 year old from Askar refugee camp in Nablus; dressed in full Arab garb	Booths at both ends of bus stop, each manned by 1-2 INP. All persons entering stop are scanned. There is also a border guard or security personnel roaming the length of the stop at all times	Yes
10	Monday, Nov 1	Tel Aviv	Outdoor produce market (large crowds)	1115	4	PFLP	Belt or bag	Small charge, contained fragmentation	Male	16-year-old Amar al-Far from the Askar refugee camp near Nablus	Minimal	Yes

get to the terror leaders and to eliminate the broader terror cell. Their focus is larger than the scope of a single attack, and they are not focusing on gathering evidence for a specific court case.

Investigative officers try to get intelligence information on the public record so they can take it into court. Intelligence officers don't want sensitive information to go public, as it might expose their sources. As a result, a constant tension exists between the investigating and intelligence officers with regard to what evidence may be used in court.

In Israel, the sharing of counterterror information between intelligence and investigative officers did not go smoothly at first, as both sides were wary of the other's intentions. Investigative officers feared that intelligence officers might "steal" their information in order to claim credit for its discovery. Intelligence officers, for their part, hesitated to show investigators certain information for fear that it would turn up in court against their wishes.

In this and the previous chapter, we provided a detailed look at the main players on the defensive side—the first responders who do their best to turn the chaos of a suicide bombing site into some kind of order, and who labor to prevent future suicide bombings. In the next chapter, we turn to another kind of first responder—the media—taking a careful look at the interplay between the media and the terrorists.

NOTES

1. Police: Organization and Management—The American System of Policing. http://law.jrank.org/pages/1668/Police-Organization-Management-American-system-policing.html.

19

Media

Creating Perceptions of Suicide Bombings

Various ways exist to defend against suicide bombers, including proactive law enforcement, deploying professional security guards, and hardening (fortifying) public facilities. None may be as important as the propaganda war that government public relations officers wage against the bombers and their sponsors for the hearts and minds of the international community. In this chapter, we focus on the international media and the global community, because the war against terror is waged largely on an international basis.

TWO AUDIENCES FOR SUICIDE BOMBING

It is worth keeping in mind that two audiences exist for suicide bombers and their sponsors. The first is the immediate domestic audience: What do the bomber's friends and relatives think of his act? How does his local community respond? After the action, will he be regarded as a hero with the following of a rock star or some idiot who has no appreciation for life? The second audience is worldwide: What do the leaders and populations of countries think of what the suicide bomber has just done? Do they consider him justified or not? How do the international media portray him and his mission?

With respect to his friends and relatives, the suicide bomber is confident that he will receive enthusiastic support, even adulation, from them. With respect to the international community, he cannot be sure of the response. The world media will determine that. That is why terrorist leaders and facilitators of suicide bombings compete in a propaganda war, a war of words, if you will, aimed at creating support for one side or the other.

The suicide bomber wants not only to kill and maim, a tactical objective; he also seeks a strategic goal, getting the international community to support his case. His enemy, on the other hand, wants to bend world headlines against the suicide bomber—to have him portrayed as some crazy fanatic who, valuing life so little, deserves condemnation.

TERRORISTS, MEDIA, AND GOVERNMENT

There are three prime actors in the media drama that gets played out after each suicide bombing: the first actor is the terrorists. To gain worldwide attention, they must get publicity to inspire fear and respect. As former British Prime Minister Margaret Thatcher famously said, "Democratic nations must try to find ways to starve the terrorist and the hijacker of the oxygen of publicity on which they depend" [1].

"Democratic nations must try to find ways to starve the terrorist and the hijacker of the oxygen of publicity on which they depend."

The second actor is the media. The media and terrorists share common goals: The terrorist feeds on media coverage, and the media enjoy great ratings from terrorist events.

Nothing is less appealing to the media than old news. Once it latches on to "hot news," the media wants to bolster reporting with dramatic coverage. For example, few who watched the Beirut-based June 1985 TWA hijack crisis will forget the staged photo of a terrorist holding a pistol aimed at the pilot's head as he spoke to ABC Television. (The terrorists loved the coverage too because of the wide reach ABC provided in focusing on their cause.)

The goals of terrorists and the media on occasion overlap, as they did when CNN obtained an interview with an obscure cave dweller named Osama bin Laden in May 1997, a time when few knew his name or the threat that he presented to the United States. Both the terrorists and the media rejoiced, but for different reasons. The terrorists were thrilled with the publicity; the media were delighted with being able to air a rare look at a terrorist financier and recruiter.

What would happen when members of the foreign media learn in advance that a terrorist attack is being planned? Are the media obligated, legally or morally, to inform the authorities? Or does the notion of "freedom of the press" give the media the right to withhold information that would appear likely to cause mass casualties?

Let us be clear. First, it is beyond imagination that a journalist would acquire specific information about a suicide bombing in advance of the action. Terrorists have been very careful to keep their future missions a secret. But more important, in the unlikely event that a journalist did possess such information, it is reasonable to assume that the journalist would turn the information over to authorities rather than becoming criminally complicit in the projected bombing and being labeled a terrorist. It is quite difficult to imagine a journalist claiming that he does not need to inform the authorities in the name of "freedom of the press." Accordingly, the authorities have little to worry that a journalist would cloak himself in a "freedom of the press" argument and not divulge what he knows.

In just the same way as attorneys have no obligation to report past crimes of a client to the authorities, nor are journalists required to divulge information concerning someone's past crimes. But we believe that a journalist has an obligation, just as any citizen has, to prevent future casualties.

The third actor is government, which, like the terrorists, also needs the media. The government wants global support to limit the damage terrorists do to society and to catch and punish the perpetrators of these awful acts. If it could, the government would keep terrorists from getting air time, in effect depriving them of the oxygen of publicity to which Margaret Thatcher referred. Realizing how difficult depriving terrorists of air time is, the government would be pleased to see as few stories as possible of terrorist relatives and friends extolling a suicide bomber as a martyr and a hero.

CAPTURING THE HEADLINES

To win international headlines, to spread the word, to become a global story, the suicide bomber has to "sell" himself and his story to the world media, to show that he brings something unique, hence newsworthy, to the table. His product, blowing himself up in a crowd, is indeed unique, for it flies against an individual's fundamental instinct of survival. It has a special brutality, aimed at unarmed, innocent civilians, flaunting the rule of warfare decreeing that only combatants can be targeted for death and injury.

Always ready to follow the traditional journalistic dictum, "if it bleeds, it leads," the media, especially television crews, are drawn to the story of the suicide bomber with its mass murder and suicide. It is too good a story to pass up.

Though earthquakes sometimes kill thousands of people, an earthquake will not garner as much media coverage as a suicide bombing that results in 10 or 20 deaths. The reason: Mother Nature, not a human being, has taken lives. The suicide bomber—acting so irrationally, frightening an entire population—brings the media to his doorstep.

FIGHTING A PROPAGANDA WAR

Nowhere is this "war of words" exemplified better than in the Israeli-Palestinian conflict, where each protagonist seeks to gain favorable international opinion. Both Israelis and Palestinians want an international seal of approval that their cause is just, and conversely, that the other side's is not. By capturing favorable world headlines, each side can define the narrative, distinguish the "good guys" (his side) from the "bad guys," (his enemy).

For both sides, capturing international headlines is not easy; other world events might, at a second's notice, override the continuing saga of suicide bombings. Or, without regard to other world events, too many suicide bombings or too few might erode international media interest.

On the surface, both the Israelis and Palestinians appear to have just causes: A number of "persecuted" Palestinians play the "occupation" card, arguing that they unleash suicide bombers to end Israeli occupation of their lands and Israeli persecution. Israelis counter that the Palestinians need not unleash suicide bombers to force Israel to end its occupation of Palestinian land; all they need to do is agree on secure borders for both sides, repudiate violence, and demonstrate a willingness to live in peace with Israel, putting these matters into a signed peace agreement with Israel.

To the Israelis, sending suicide bombers against unarmed Israeli civilians makes the Palestinian cause of ending the Israeli occupation and getting a state of its own less deserving.

Historically, Israel enjoyed massive support among the international media. From 1948, when Israel declared itself a state, to the late 1960s, the Palestinian cause gained little traction in the international media. The Israeli cause did. After the 1948 declaration of nationhood and the ensuing war, and especially after the Six-Day War, Israel became the darling of the global media. Its leaders were thought of as legendary, and their actions compared to the heroics of Biblical figures. With 650,000 Jews defeating 100 million Arabs in 1948, and with the IDF soundly defeating Arab armies in just six days during the Six-Day War, the Israeli were modern-day heroes who could do no wrong in the foreign media's eyes.

> From 1948, when Israel declared itself a state, to the late 1960s, the Palestinian cause gained little traction in the international media. The Israeli cause did.

For their part, all the while that Israel soared in the world media's view, the perception of the Arabs grew increasingly negative. They were no heroes; in fact, they seemed alien, unfriendly, and even dangerous. When Palestinians turned to terrorism, both the world media and citizens branded all Arabs terrorists, and many in the West grew uncomfortable being in their midst. The Palestinians did not seem bent on peace. They had no recognizable leaders; even fellow Arabs paid lip service in their support for the Palestinians.

It was not until the 1970s, especially after the hijackings of three commercial airliners on September 7, 1970, in Jordan and the murder of Israeli athletes during the 1972 Munich Olympics that the world media began to take notice of the Palestinians, becoming enraptured with their cause and providing them with headlines. Media interest in the Palestinians grew even more with the start of the First Intifada in 1987.

> It was not until the 1970s, especially the hijackings of airliners on September 7, 1970, in Jordan and the murder of Israeli athletes during the 1972 Munich Olympics, that the world media began to take notice of the Palestinians.

The growth of Palestinian support was as much due to the way the foreign media covered the Intifada (24-7), and to the development of cable television news, as it was to a newfound love for the Palestinians. Still, the Palestinians trumped the Israelis in the propaganda war and have remained on top since then.

THE PUBLIC RELATIONS OFFICER

We focus on the way the Israelis have used public relations to try to roll back worldwide media support for the Palestinian cause generally and for Palestinian suicide bombers specifically.

261

Palestinian terrorists believe that the more casualties they inflict upon Israelis, the more media coverage they will get. Still, whether three or 21 Israelis die in a suicide bombing, Israel's public relations officers need only convince the international community that Palestinians have no justification for employing the bombings. Because of the high stakes involved, the public relations officer defending civilians under attack plays a critical role in the ultimate defining of a suicide bomber as justified or not. It is his job to take control of the postattack public relations environment and to win the inevitable propaganda war that follows.

As suicide bombings are meant to alter public perceptions, to throw masses into a state of fear and uncertainty, the public relations officer seeks to convince the world media that despite the carnage and tragedy, the negative impact of a suicide bombing on citizens will be temporary.

Though the public relations officer is not strictly a first responder— rushing to suicide bombing scenes in order to help save lives—he qualifies as a de facto one. His role is crucial and must be undertaken at the suicide bombing site, just as in the case of other first responders.

The lack of a good paramedic may cost lives; but the lack of a good spokesman may cause the loss of the propaganda war that could lead to demoralization that could lead to the loss of the overall war. The public relations officer's work begins literally in the first 30 seconds after he receives notice that a suicide bombing has occurred. He releases that information to the media and then dashes to the scene of the attack as reporters, cameramen, and photographers rush to cover the event, frequently arriving earlier than some first responders.

Throughout the 1980s and 1990s, the Israel Police saw no need to supplement its spokesman for the Israeli press with a fluent English-speaking spokesman for the foreign media. Much of the work of the Israel Police concerned domestic issues such as crime, organized or not, burglaries and robberies, and drug cases, hardly any of which would interest the foreign media. Accordingly, when necessary, the police relied upon an English-speaking spokesman who worked for the Ministry of Police, but who primarily worked for the minister, not for the police itself.

The Second Intifada, with its high level of violence, including suicide bombings and its continuing international criticism of Israel, led the police to consider hiring its own spokesman for the foreign press. Since the Israel Police were directly responsible for curbing the Second Intifada violence, the need for a police spokesman for the foreign press became compelling. Still, senior police officers debated whether to retain the practice of local commanders serving as police spokesmen for terror incidents on their turf, or to hire one spokesman to handle all foreign press matters.

Eventually, the argument began to tip in favor of finding a fluent English-speaker, preferably American; a British, South African, or Australian accent might be hard for an American television audience to understand. The new police spokesman would face the immense challenge of getting American "soccer moms" and "workaholic dads" to focus on the Israeli–Palestinian issue even for a ten-second sound bite.

The new police spokesman would face the immense challenge of getting American "soccer Moms" and "workaholic Dads" to focus on the Israeli–Palestinian issue even for a 10-second sound bite.

And, though many in the spokesman's audience would be unable to distinguish Israelis from Arabs easily, he would need to convince his audience that he was an Israeli who represented Israelis and spoke on their behalf; and that he was not an Arab representing and speaking on the Arabs' behalf.

Aware of these awesome challenges, when appointed the new police commissioner in 2001, Shlomo Aharonishky studied the issue carefully and in time favored hiring the police's own spokesman. He found a Renaissance man within police ranks, an 18-year veteran who had been a bomb tech, a homicide detective, an attorney, and a security-training instructor with the added advantage that he had been born and bred in Brooklyn. His name is Gil Kleiman.

To the new commissioner, Kleiman spelled out his vision of the job: Credibility was crucial. Given the confusion and complexity of a suicide bombing, the public needed to see and hear one person, providing information and explaining the event. Too often Kleiman had cringed at watching spokesmen representing emergency services or forensics or the bomb tech squad speaking at the same news briefing, some exhibiting clarity, some not, some radiating credibility, some not.

Kleiman also emphasized to the commissioner that he did see his task as burnishing his reputation or that of Aharonishky and his senior colleagues. Getting their names on the front pages of the *New York Times* was of no importance to Kleiman; convincing the single mother in Des Moines, Iowa, that the Israelis were the good guys, was.

The international media up close at suicide bombing site on April 17, 2006, at the Shwarma Rosh Ha'ir restaurant in Tel Aviv. (*Credit*: Israel Government Press Office)

DEFEATING THE ENEMY: GETTING BACK TO NORMAL

Gil Kleiman took up the post of Israel Police spokesman for the foreign press in June 2001. His goal was to convince the foreign media that Israel had weathered the past seven months of suicide bombings and would continue to do so. His message would be: We are the good guys; we are morally superior to these Palestinian suicide bombers. Good will triumph.

SPEED IN GETTING OUT THE NEWS IS CRITICAL

To gain credibility, getting word of the suicide bombing to the world media speedily is vital. Like the other first responders, the public relations officer has to rush to the scene of the attack and gather as much information as possible.

Because of their need to preserve secrecy surrounding their findings, intelligence officers and bomb techs make a point of not talking to the media at the scene. That was Gil Kleiman's responsibility. Because certain information has to be concealed from the public, Kleiman had to confer with senior police brass to learn what he could say, and what he could not.

He knew he must make contact with and brief the foreign media as quickly and as often as possible. Why is speed and updating so important to the media? It is because cable television channels such as CNN, Fox News Channel, Sky News, and BBC World, on the air 24 hours a day, have an insatiable appetite for breaking news. Television executives have learned that the more a channel can put updates of breaking news on the air, the more likely that viewers will stay tuned.

"Feeding" the foreign media quickly and often, to Gil Kleiman, was the best way to take command of the story and the overall narrative—before the terrorists could present their version. With two versions available to the media, journalists would have to decide which was more plausible, which spokesman more credible, which version should be given priority in their reports. The version given priority is usually the one that the public views as the more credible.

If Kleiman presented his facts first—the number of dead and wounded, what he knew about the identity of the suicide bomber—and he sounded credible, the Israeli side would be given priority. To ensure that he had access to the media, Kleiman convinced his superiors to let the media come as close to the suicide bombing site as possible. The closer television camera crews and still photographers were to the site, the more graphic their coverage would be. And the graphic nature of their coverage helped Israel show the evil represented by suicide bombings.

Kleiman refused to wait to release information until a final count of the dead and wounded existed, which could have taken three to four hours. He "hogged" the air, knowing that he had to prove to journalists that he was their fastest, most reliable, accurate, and accessible source. More than anything else, it was his presence at the scene and quick response time once there that gave him continuing credibility.

Other so-called spokesmen for first responders from the emergency medical services and other units tried to establish rapport and credibility with journalists, but because these spokesmen were not on the scene, the media paid little attention to them. Journalists could tell that their information was secondhand, late, and hardly updated or reliable.

Again to ensure accessibility to journalists, Kleiman answered as many calls on his cell phone as he could. He could not afford to have a journalist phone him and get a busy signal. Reporters were routinely hooked up to his pager system. Each time a terror incident or suicide bombing occurred, Kleiman sent news of the event on his beeper system at once to his journalist subscribers.

Gil Kleiman's advantage in the battle to gain credibility was that he was allowed access to the "inner sanctum" at the suicide bombing scene, while most others were denied any such close access. Having worked as a bomb technician and investigator, he knew first responders who gave him immediate, continuing entry to the inner sanctum. Only once—at a suicide bombing in the Jerusalem market—was Kleiman asked to leave. When the local bomb squad commander objected to his presence, Kleiman informed the Jerusalem district commander, Mickey Levy, of his expulsion; Levy immediately told everyone: "Gil has access to everything."

After standing where the suicide bomber stood, after looking at corpses and the wounded, then clearing with intelligence officers what information he could release and what he could not, Kleiman walked over to the media standing on the other side of the ropes and provided them with a brief synopsis of what had happened, including the latest casualty count. Thus the reporters were getting firsthand information every 30 to 40 minutes from someone who three seconds earlier had been an upfront eyewitness to the horror. Kleiman basically became the only source of information regarding the suicide bombing for the world's media.

On one occasion, terrorist leaders released the age of a female suicide bomber as 16, but Kleiman reported that she looked like she was in her 20s. The leaders wanted the public to think that she was younger, making her seem more heroic. But Kleiman's report was taken as truth.

In contrast with Kleiman's accent on speed, the Israel Defense Forces (IDF) did not believe in disseminating incomplete information about violent military incidents quickly. Acting speedily, the IDF believed, could mean that mistaken information would be given to the public, and that could damage the IDF's reputation, making it unable to control the narrative.

Kleiman knew, however, that the perception that formed within the media in those first few minutes or hours after the attack would hold sway. When the IDF stormed the West Bank town of Jenin as part of Operation Defensive Shield in March 2002, the Palestinians issued news that an Israeli "massacre" had occurred and that the Israeli Deputy Chief of Staff had been killed. In fact, there had been no massacre, and the Deputy Chief of Staff was unharmed. But the IDF waited hours to release its own version of events, surrendering the propaganda field to the Palestinians, giving them a "victory." Once the world media began circulating those Palestinian reports, it was too late for Israel's refutations to gain much media traction. The damage was done.

Kleiman refused to slant the story overtly in favor of his country. He would slant the story, but subtly. While Kleiman was emphatic about giving the facts of the suicide bombing, he always sought to slip in the one message that he felt Israel should try to get across: Israel is good, the Arabs are bad.

Immediately after 9/11, reports arose that Arabs in East Jerusalem were handing out candy to celebrate the attacks that day. "Reporters asked me if the reports were true. I decided not to use that question as a platform to show how bad Arabs were. All that I chose to say was that there had been certain instances of Arabs distributing candy, but it was not a widespread phenomenon. I feel that honesty is always the best policy. It is better to underplay than to overplay your hand. That will give you a lot more credibility as a spokesman" [2].

Kleiman was often asked, when a suicide bombing occurred on a bus, how many children were killed. Rather than emphasize that gruesome number, he tried to be subtle: He noted that the front part of the bus—the likely location of the suicide bomber—was far more vulnerable; since older people, not children, tended to sit in the front, more elders were killed than children. He was honest, making sure to mention the children on the bus, but to put the children's presence in a perspective that journalists would understand and appreciate.

On August 11, 2004, a suicide bomber showed up at the Kalandia checkpoint between Jerusalem and the West Bank town of Ramallah, but realizing that the police were on heightened alert, ditched his bomb and remotely detonated it.

Soon after the event, spokesmen for both the Israelis and Palestinians were debating what had actually happened.

The Palestinian version was that the suicide bomber's target was the checkpoint, and his mission was to kill as many Israel Police stationed there as possible.

In the Israeli version, the checkpoint was not the original target of the suicide bomber; rather, the bomber planned to carry out his action in Jerusalem. Gil Kleiman observed that great police work at the checkpoint had prevented the bomber from blowing himself up; the bomber was forced to detonate his explosives prematurely. Hence, the incident was a failure for the Palestinians, who continued to insist that the bomber's target was the checkpoint.

Kleiman showed the press proof of what he had said: Though the Palestinian planners insisted the attack had been prearranged, Kleiman noted that the Palestinians could not possibly have planned in advance an attack on the checkpoint, for the Palestinians had no way of knowing that numerous Israeli police would be there. After hearing Kleiman, journalists confronted terrorist leaders, who admitted that indeed what had transpired was a failed suicide bombing attack that was supposed to be a high-casualty event in Jerusalem.

By attacking the checkpoint, the bomber killed two and injured another 18 including 12 Palestinian bystanders. The terrorists backed down from their version because they did not want to get caught in a lie in public, fearing it would damage their credibility.

TESTING A SPOKESMAN'S CREDIBILITY

Gil Kleiman pondered whether it was worth trying to change the agenda of certain media, especially in Western Europe, that had an already established anti-Israeli bias. Many Israelis believed that it was possible through superb public relations to change the agenda of a news organization, converting it from an anti-Israel to a pro-Israel stance. Kleiman disagreed. He knew that any attempt Israel made to show the human face of an Israeli soldier walking an elderly Arab across a street would backfire; any attempt to point out how much benefit the Israel government had brought to Israeli Arabs would boomerang. Such efforts would not change the opinion of a newspaper already holding an anti-Israeli bent because such newspapers were prospering from their pro-Arab stance.

With so many unfriendly television outlets, what was the point of trying to get one's message across on television? Kleiman acknowledged that the only thing one could do was get "face time" on television and hope that one's point of view was aired. As long as the spokesman was quoted, that was the best that could be expected.

But how does a spokesman get face time? He must make sure that he has something to sell and, most importantly, that he has credibility with the media. On one occasion, Kleiman's credibility saved Israel from a possible public relations disaster. Such was the case on a Friday, March 8, 2002, when the Israel Police had fresh intelligence that a suicide bomber was on his way to Jerusalem to carry out an attack. Finding the would-be suicide bomber before he could blow himself up, the police wrestled him to the ground, pinning his hands to his side. In the struggle the police found a suicide belt wrapped around the bomber's chest. The bomber was held face down by police officers while a bomb technician moved toward the bomber, planning to dismantle the device.

Though caught, the bomber remained intent on carrying out his mission, even while lying on his stomach, pinned down by Israeli police; he kept trying to rub his chest on the ground in an effort to detonate the on-off toggle switch. As the bomb technician approached the man, a police commander some distance away was observing these events. Deciding that the bomb tech and several other police officers were in danger, a senior police officer ordered another police officer to shoot the bomber in the head, which he did, killing him. The bomb belt was then successfully dismantled with the aid of a police bomb disposal robot.

Though Palestinians automatically accused the Israelis of cold-blooded murder, the senior police officer and the shooter had undeniably acted in self-defense. That was the story that Gil Kleiman gave to the press. Two days later, a French television reporter wanted to know if Kleiman would go on camera and repeat what he had said two days earlier. Kleiman agreed. The reporter asked Kleiman if he would also respond to new still photographs the TV reporter possessed. What photos, Kleiman asked? It turned out that the French television channel had received still photos of the event from a bystander who had filmed the entire scene, from the time that several police officers held down the suicide bomber to the moment when the police officer shot the suicide bomber.

Worried that these photos might become a public relations catastrophe for Israel by showing its police as murderers, Kleiman was also bothered that these photos could very well become the signature photograph of the Second Intifada for the Palestinians; he could not help but recall that Eddie Adams's Pulitzer Prize–winning Associated Press photo had come to symbolize America as the bad guy in the Vietnam war; the Adams photo showed South Vietnam General Nguyen Ngoc Loan executing a Vietcong prisoner, Nguyen Van Lem, on a Saigon street on February 1, 1968, during the opening stages of the Tet Offensive.

Trying not to get tripped up, Kleiman said he would respond to the film, telling the same story he had told the media on Friday. He then asked to see the photos, and the reporter complied. Kleiman's heart sank as he looked them over. While confident that the commander had acted in self-defense, he understood that anyone looking at the photos might conclude otherwise. Kleiman knew he would have trouble explaining and justifying why an Israeli policeman had shot and killed a seemingly unarmed suicide bomber after he had been taken into custody.

No reporter would take into account that the suicide bomber still had a bomb belt attached to him and was still trying to detonate it. Kleiman waited for the international media to report, based on the photos, that Israel had been caught carrying out a cold-blooded killing of an "innocent" Palestinian youngster. But no reports appeared in the media, and finally Kleiman phoned a *Boston Globe* reporter based in Jerusalem. "What am I missing? Why isn't the media giving me a problem?" Kleiman asked.

"It's not a story," the reporter said with little excitement in his voice. "On Friday, two days ago, you explained what happened without the photos. Your story fit the photos. I guess every journalist believed that even with the photos that the policeman was acting in self-defense.

RELEASING GRAPHIC SCENES TO THE MEDIA

To some first responders, allowing television crews and still photographers to roam freely near suicide bombing scenes, to photograph the victims during moments of utter personal tragedy, seems inappropriate, disrespectful, and degrading. True, publishing such horrific images can help demonize the suicide bombers and their terror groups, but for the most part, Israeli decision makers have kept TV crews from showing the most gruesome scenes.

Israeli officials were concerned that Palestinians would feel empowered, knowing that millions were watching their deeds, with some even expressing understanding or support. The Israeli officials, by not showing the gore, wanted to project the view that they were superior to the "barbaric" terrorists. Israeli officials also worried that audiences would become numbed by what they were seeing and would demand even more graphic footage.

And so the Israelis hesitated to allow the portrayal of the gore at suicide bombing sites. One argument Israelis made was that exhibiting dead Israelis in public could easily backfire. What if Israelis engaged in similar acts that others described as brutal against Palestinians and those acts were aired in the media? As Gil Kleiman observed:

If you are using cheap propaganda tools in showing mangled bodies, it is hard later to play the noble act when you do something reprehensible. You can't then say: "Well, at least we don't do suicide bombings," or "Well, at least we don't use our children as human shields." Israel cannot act morally one day but not another day. [3]

And so the Israel Ministry for Foreign Affairs simply held back the film it had acquired from forensics teams each time a suicide bombing occurred—until the attack on the Park Hotel in Netanya on March 27, 2002, when 30 Israelis were killed. The death toll was so high that Prime Minister Ariel Sharon decided to send his soldiers into the West Bank soon after the attack to weed out suicide bombers. To make sure the world understood the reason for the planned Israeli invasion, Sharon decided to allow the graphic outcome of the Park Hotel suicide bombing, permitting television crews inside the hotel to film the carnage.

But in all other suicide bombings after that, once the Israel police forensics team completed its filming at the scene, it routinely sent the raw footage to the Foreign Ministry knowing full well that the ministry would keep the film from being aired. Every reason existed to believe that the Foreign Ministry would follow its practice on January 29, 2004, when a suicide bomber exploded a bomb while standing in the back of a Jerusalem bus, killing 11 and wounding another 50 people, 13 seriously. The bombing occurred quite near Sharon's official residence.

The person in charge of the ministry's Internet site took advantage of his boss being away. After receiving the usual film from that day's bombing, he decided this time—against Israeli policy—to release film footage and put it on the ministry's Web site. It was the first time that Israel "officially" released such footage to the public. When senior Israeli public relations officials saw the footage on the Internet, they went ballistic and insisted that the original policy be followed in the future.

The January 2004 suicide bombing was not the only time that a Palestinian suicide bombing was shown in public. For their own purposes, Palestinians released footage of suicide bombings on Palestinian television and the Internet. Proud of their operations, the Palestinians wanted to show the world what they had done. At one suicide bombing at French Hill in Jerusalem, an Arab television station obtained highly graphic footage of the postattack scene with bodies still burning.

The long-standing Israeli policy of not showing horrific carnage was modified on March 11, 2011, after a Palestinian terrorist used a knife to stab to death five members of an Israeli family living in the Jewish settlement of Itamar near Nablus. Horrified by the senseless, brutal killings, the Israeli government released photographs of the murdered members of the Fogel family: Udi, his wife Ruth, and three of their six children, Yoav, age 11, Elad, age 4, and Hadas, three months old. "We have never done anything like this before," said Israel's Minister for Diaspora Affairs and Public Diplomacy Yuli Edelstein, "but only these horrific pictures can make the world realize who Israel is dealing with" [4].

Thus far we have devoted much space to what first responders to suicide bombings do and why they do it. In the next chapter we take a close look for the first time at what being at suicide bombing sites can do to their mental health.

NOTES

1. http://www.brainyquote.com/quotes/quotes/m/margaretth162424.html#ixzz1EzKq5EeJ.
2. ..." Gil Kleiman, in a conversation with Mordecai Dzikansky and Robert Slater, November 17, 2010.
3. Ibid.
4. http://llphfreedom.blogspot.com/2011/03/israel-moves-to-release-graphic-photos.html.

20

Mental Health
When Too Much Is Too Much

Until now we have discussed suicide bombing and how law enforcement officers working in Western urban environments can defend their societies against this phenomenon. We have portrayed the victims: the person eating a meal in a restaurant, the passenger on a bus, the customer shopping in an open-air market. But another victim exists: the first responder who visits suicide bombing sites on a repeated basis—and eventually becomes another "victim" of these attacks. Not every first responder becomes a victim, but enough do to warrant our attention.

These first responders do not suffer any physical harm. But they do suffer from the constant observation of the carnage: the blood, gore, charred bodies, disengaged heads, and split torsos; as well as of the horrible detritus left behind: the baby carriages, toys, pocketbooks, and water bottles.

For a long time, what these first responders suffered from had no medical name because doctors did not think that their symptoms constituted a disorder. In the early 19th century, military physicians described war-weary soldiers as suffering from "exhaustion." The sole treatment was to bring the afflicted soldiers to the rear lines for some rest, then return them to battle. By World War II, the disorder still had no name, but the symptoms were present in at least 10 percent of American soldiers hospitalized for mental disturbances between 1942 and 1945. It has only been since the 1970s and the experience of American military veterans of the Vietnam War that a true appreciation and understanding of posttraumatic stress disorder (PTSD) dates.

THE SYMPTOMS

Without describing the collection of symptoms as a specific disorder, doctors started to understand certain similarities in the way soldiers and law enforcement personnel were reacting to particularly stressful events. The symptoms followed a traumatic event or series of events and began at once or after a few weeks or months, but no later than six months. If, during the first six weeks after a traumatic event, the person feels less distress about the event, he may not be suffering from a mental disorder, but may be simply going through a normal process of adjustment. But if the symptoms last more than six weeks, the symptoms qualify as a disorder, and the person is routinely advised to speak with a physician.

Among the symptoms is reexperiencing the original trauma through flashbacks or nightmares. The flashback or nightmare can seem so real that it feels as if one is living through the experience again. Another symptom is hypervigilance; the person feels compelled to be on guard, to remain on alert all the time; there is no time to relax. This makes it hard for the person to sleep, causing him to be jumpy and irritable. A victim typically feels emotionally numb, especially toward loved ones and close friends.

THE TRAUMATIC EVENT

What kind of traumatic event can cause such personal distress? It may be a violent and/or sexual assault, torture, being taken hostage or a prisoner of war, involvement in a violent car accident, getting a diagnosis of a life-threatening illness. The most traumatic events are sudden and unexpected, and the symptoms of trauma last a long time, giving the feeling of being trapped, unable to get away.

Someone experiencing such trauma can feel depressed, grief-stricken, guilty, angry, or anxious. Many so-called normal people experience such symptoms without having a specific disorder, making diagnosing the disorder that much more difficult. But over time, the way a person handles enduring traumatic events reveals whether or not he has a clear-cut medical issue.

Why are traumatic events so terrifying? They undermine our sense that life is fair and our lives are safe and secure. The traumatic experience reminds us that we can die at any time, even when we are young.

Through most of the 20th century, until the 1970s, all forms of the psychic pain that traumatizes some first responders were grouped under the phrase, "nervous breakdown" or the even more vague: "He's just burnt out." But physicians began to understand that biochemical changes accompanied the person's acute trauma: an overactive adrenaline response, which creates neurological brain patterns.

GIVING THE DISORDER A NAME

Doctors discarded the phrase "nervous breakdown" and started to describe traumatized soldiers' and first responders' symptoms as a specific disorder: posttraumatic stress disorder (PTSD).

No one knows for sure why someone gets the disorder. Some argue that a hormone called adrenaline is produced in our bodies when we are under stress, and its presence signals the onset of the disorder. Adrenaline helps the body prepare for forthcoming stress. When the stress disappears, the level of adrenaline returns to normal. But with PTSD, the graphic memories of the trauma keep the adrenaline high.

Many recover from PTSD: The patient knows he is improving when he can think about past stress-related events without becoming distressed, when he no longer feels under continuing threat. For others, however, the emotional scars might remain for some time, even permanently. No one can predict who will suffer from this disorder and who will not. Some speculate that someone who seems edgy and under stress will be more prone to suffer from PTSD than others. But that is nonsense. Bomb techs are no more likely to pick up PTSD than emergency service workers.

One can predict accurately that, when there is a spate of suicide bombings, some first responders will be afflicted. But not all will be impacted, as some units witness more PTSD than others do. Twenty percent of the Israel bomb squad was diagnosed with PTSD. Most of the forensics teams were diagnosed as well. This is not surprising. Bomb techs and forensic scientists spend much time at suicide bombing sites. It seems logical that PTSD would appear during a wave of suicide bombings, but the opposite is true. It is only when lulls in the action occur that the symptoms of PTSD begin to appear.

Acquiring the disorder has nothing to do with having a so-called weak psychological profile. All Israeli bomb tech personnel who suffered from PTSD had been vetted carefully by psychologists and had to pass a tough battery of tests before qualifying for their jobs. Their psychological profiles were high.

New treatments, both psychological and physical, have been developed to help someone with PTSD recover quickly. Those psychotherapies for PTSD that work concentrate on the traumatic experiences, and not one's past life. The goal is to think more healthily about the experiences and about one's life.

There are different kinds of psychotherapy: cognitive behavioral therapy (CBT) is a talking treatment that tries to help patients understand how habits of thinking can make the PTSD worse, or even cause it. There is group therapy that may help patients speak more freely when meeting others who have been through similar experiences. And there is anti-depressant medicine that may be taken for as long as 12 months.

THE FIRST RESPONDERS BECAME VICTIMS

Both Mordecai Dzikansky and Gil Kleiman suffered from posttraumatic stress disorder. Both men understood that the only way they could do their jobs successfully was to drop everything, jump into a car, and rush to a suicide bombing site the moment they heard of the incident. Both visited numerous suicide bombing sites: Kleiman visited 48 suicide bombing sites in Israel. Dzikansky attended 21 suicide bombing scenes in Israel and five elsewhere. The two men met constantly and soon became great friends.

They had a lot in common. Both were born and raised in Brooklyn; they knew every street, every part of the Brooklyn culture and every "good guy" and every "bad guy" there. They appreciated each other's sense of humor. Both liked to gossip about the old neighborhood and its residents. Once in Israel, they loved to gossip about the many first responders they had met at suicide bombings.

In the early days, both men did their jobs with total devotion. They observed the carnage, gathered information from specialists, and then disseminated that information as quickly as they could, winning praise from their superiors for their zeal and reporting skills. At each event, Dzikansky and Kleiman behaved with clinical detachment.

They were professionals who could not afford to display their emotions. Expressing their emotions might have led their superiors to think they were not suited for the kind of work they were doing. But clearly they were on edge. They knew on the way to a suicide bombing what they would find, and still they went time after time until, in each of their cases, a day came when they knew that they had seen too much. Here then are their stories of battling with their demons.

GIL KLEIMAN'S STORY

For Gil Kleiman, early signs of PTSD appeared in the 1980s, but he did not know it at the time. Once, on April 2, 1984, Kleiman, then off duty, was present at his first mass-casualty terror incident: A terrorist shot civilians on Jaffa Road in Jerusalem; the terrorist was killed and 60 others were wounded.

Kleiman remembers stripping down the terrorist to see if he had any explosives attached to him and then smoking a cigarette with the terrorist's blood on the cigarette. He was stoical, too stoical, he remembered much later, for that lack of emotion was an early sign of the PTSD that eventually seized him. For the next 21 years, he saw hundreds of suicide bombing victims, and he continued to numb his emotions. The numbness, however, turned into a cumulative trauma that led to his full-blown PTSD in 2005.

While the Second Intifada, with its wave of suicide bombings, was in full force, Kleiman worked as foreign press spokesman for the Israel Police at feverish pitch. When first visiting suicide bombing sites, Kleiman went into an automatic mode where he paid attention to his job—not to the dead bodies or the severely wounded. But in time he felt that those visits were leaving psychological scars on him: "What I saw was something that people shouldn't have to see. It wasn't natural. There was no question that I was seeing things that were having an effect on me" [1].

During that time, Kleiman experienced what he described as "small moments," moments of short outbursts, unexpectedly breaking into tears on his way or departing from a suicide bombing site. He called these moments "small" because he could control them, sometimes for months at a time.

For Kleiman, the major symptoms of PTSD burst out suddenly. As the symptoms mounted, he began to realize that he had reached some kind of critical state, visiting one too many suicide bombing sites, reaching a point where it was inevitable that he would crash.

The middle part of 2002 was the worst period for suicide bombings during the Second Intifada. Kleiman grew increasingly depressed. Approaching a friend from his bomb squad days, he explained, "I need someone to talk to. I am on the verge of a breakdown." The friend replied: "Sounds serious. Guess we have to make tea." Though he does not recall what they talked about, Kleiman does recall that the conversation "charged my batteries" for two years—2002 to 2004—and apart from one incident in the fall of 2003, he was coping.

At that incident his crying became uncontrollable. He had difficulty talking for fear that tears would flow. One memory was especially vivid. The date was September 9, 2003. A suicide bombing had occurred at 4 p.m. that day at Rishon LeZion, opposite a major army base and hospital, killing nine and wounding 30. During the hour-long drive to the scene, he thought about the bombing and the dead. He shed a few tears, but "nothing serious."

Returning home six hours later, he followed his usual routine: He placed his clothes, perhaps contaminated with chemicals or flesh, into the washing machine. "You don't bring parts of dead people" into your home, he recalled. He started to relax for the first time that day. The phone rang once again. It was a *Chicago Tribune* reporter. The reporter explained to Kleiman that the reporter's wife had been on Emek Refaim Street in Jerusalem's German Colony and had just heard an explosion. The reporter's next sentence floored Kleiman: "You have another one."

Verifying the news with Israel Police headquarters, Kleiman began calling reporters to update them on the second suicide bombing incident that day, where seven were killed and 50 wounded; he then rushed to the scene. While at the site, he went through his usual routine. By 4 a.m. he had been working frantically for 12 hours. "I was handling it—two suicide bombings in one day. I had done that before." He was about to be interviewed by CNN on the Café Hillel bombing when a medic approached him with horrible news: "Gil. Don't tell CNN, but one of the dead is David Appelbaum" (a well-known physician whose daughter, Nava, was killed in the bombing as well; she was due to be married the next day). Kleiman had to make sure not to mention on air the two as deceased, since the family had not yet been notified.

For Kleiman it was full circle: At the 1984 incident—his first experience at a mass-casualty event—David Appelbaum had been present as a medical first responder; and now on this night in 2003, the physician and his daughter had died in the German Colony suicide bombing. Kleiman had a very special personal link to Appelbaum: Rabbi Manny Appelbaum, the physician's father, had officiated at Kleiman's wedding: "It suddenly hit me. I broke down. I walked across the street. I got behind a car. I cried for about five minutes. I needed that relief."

By the start of 2005, suicide bombings in Israel had gone down in number from two or three a month to less than one a month. The adrenaline charges that Kleiman had experienced were fewer. He had more time to think about himself and what he had gone through. But then, on February 25 at 10 p.m., his phone rang, informing him that a suicide bombing had happened at the Stage Club on the Tel Aviv promenade along the Mediterranean beach. Detonating his explosives, the suicide bomber had killed five, including members of a reserve army unit waiting outside the restaurant. Another 51 were wounded.

Kleiman rushed to the suicide bombing site and suddenly felt a "psychological fog" descend on him. It was this incident that pushed him over the edge—when he understood for the first time that he had gone from "small moments" to something far more grave. He could see and hear everything, but it was as if all the usual adrenaline he had previously felt at these suicide bombing scenes had surged out of his body: "I arrived at the suicide bombing. I had done this many times before. So I knew the routine. I knew what I was supposed to be feeling and I wasn't feeling it. I felt nothing."

"I arrived at the suicide bombing. I had done this many times before. So I knew the routine. I knew what I was supposed to be feeling and I wasn't feeling it. I felt nothing."

> If you had hooked me up to a computer and checked my brain waves, you would have thought I was meditating or sleeping. I had no feelings. I wasn't feeling good. I wasn't feeling bad. Nothing. I turned to a policeman [Mordecai Dzikansky] I was with, a friend of mine. I told him that I felt like a soda without bubbles. I felt nothing.

Dzikansky will always remember that Friday night. It was at that Stage Bar bombing site that he noticed signs that Gil Kleiman, by then his closest friend and colleague in Israel, was suffering from posttraumatic stress disorder (PTSD).

TECHNICAL ANALYSIS OF STAGE BAR SUICIDE BOMBING

Mordecai Dzikansky

NYPD

Date: February 25, 2005

Time: 23:00 hours

Location: Queue outside Stage Night Club, Tel Aviv beachfront

Victims: 5 killed, 51 injured

Bomber's position at detonation: Bomber within the crowd with his back to the nightclub, facing victims; because security guard was wanding all people entering the Stage, bomber blew himself up outside in crowd.

Camouflage: Vest, with explosive on the bomber's chest (covered by jacket)

Explosive material: High improvised explosive; 5 kg; fragmentation

Explosive effect: Bomber's body—from above knees mangled; head found approximately 30 meters from the site of explosion.

Damage to cars and stores in the nearby vicinity from explosion and fragmentation.

Dzikansky looked at Kleiman carefully and felt that he wasn't himself. As usual, Kleiman was trying to help Dzikansky as much as possible, giving him complete access and complete information. Dzikansky noticed that Kleiman's shirt was out of his pants and he did not look right. He did not have his usual alert and commanding appearance. Something seemed very wrong. Back home, Kleiman slept for two hours but awoke from a dream in which he was back at the suicide bombing scene.

For the next week, Kleiman had no memory of the suicide bombing or anything else from the previous week, for that matter:

I found myself in my office crying. I couldn't stop crying. A door had opened, and everything that was behind that door came out, a nonstop flooding of tears. Once I broke down, once I wasn't able to control it anymore, I knew I needed professional help. If you think at that stage you can continue working by yourself, you're making a big mistake. People don't understand.

Collecting himself, he phoned a police mental health officer. "I need to see you," he said softly, with a desperate tone. The officer proposed to come in the following week. "I need to see you sooner than that," Kleiman pleaded, and the mental health officer fit him in earlier.

Meanwhile Kleiman saw his family doctor, who referred him to a psychological trauma unit in a nearby hospital, and he also gave him calming medicine. The family physician asked him what he should write in his report. "The truth," Kleiman responded. "I have nothing to be ashamed about. I am not to blame. I have done nothing wrong."

When he began therapy, Kleiman had no idea how long it would take to return to "normal." Again, in his words:

> It took about two months before I was nearly able to function again. I couldn't talk. Every time I talked to somebody, whatever he did reminded me of something that happened. I had seen hundreds of people dead. It was as if everybody else needed seven days to mourn one person, but in my case, someone was telling me: "You haven't mourned for four years—now you are going through intensive mourning for hundreds of people. Start to mourn now for them and eventually you will stop crying." I didn't know it would take two months.
>
> That's the way it was. There's a certain secret that's going on that no one is talking about: First responders—policemen, firemen, forensics scientists, and bomb technicians—hundreds of people like them have been exposed to these terrible scenes and they're holding it in because they refuse to admit to themselves that they suffer from a mental disorder.

By March 2005, Kleiman decided he would try to resume duties as the foreign press spokesman for the Israel Police. But once he appeared at police headquarters, Kleiman knew that he had not completely recovered. He could watch as people spoke to him, but he did not understand what they were saying. It was as if they were speaking in a foreign language. When his wife, Ilanit Kleiman, heard that her husband might return as foreign press spokesman, she phoned Kleiman's boss: "You are responsible for him, and look what happened. Now I am here to take care of him. And he's not going to back to work at the police anymore."

Kleiman's boss assigned someone else to the spokesman's post. He offered Kleiman some other undefined "cushy" job. Kleiman was livid. It was all happening way too fast—the obvious ending of his 24 years with the police. Returning to his office, he began crying. He couldn't breathe properly for ten minutes. "I got it all out. Then I took a deep breath. I wiped my face." He remembered an expression from his days in Brooklyn: "We don't get even; we get better." He vowed that he was going to get better.

It was a strange time for him. Each day he showed up for work, went to his office for four or five hours with the door closed. Told not to use the phone and to do no police work, he spent hours on the Internet. He finally retired from the police in February 2006.

Though no longer a police officer, Kleiman continued to spend almost daily time with his close friend, Mordecai Dzikansky. On April 17, 2006, they were driving to Tel Aviv to meet several off-duty Israeli police officers for dinner. Dzikansky's beeper went off, telling him of a suicide bombing. He knew he had to race to the site. Kleiman quickly responded: "I can't go. Drop me off." The suicide bombing had occurred during the Passover holiday at the Rosh Ha'ir restaurant near the old Central Bus Station in Tel Aviv: 11 people were killed and another 60 wounded.

Dzikansky, who was driving, was torn between his responsibilities to the NYPD and his sympathy with Kleiman's condition. He knew that he could not ask Kleiman to join him at the site. Dzikansky came up with a compromise. He asked Kleiman to help direct him to a point near the site. Dzikansky would then proceed to the site on his own.

Kleiman replied: "I have PTSD. I am shell-shocked. I can't do this for you." Finally, Kleiman relented and gave directions. "Only for you," he said to Dzikansky. "No one else." Arriving just 15 minutes after the attack, while bomb techs were still scouring the place for secondary devices, they got to the perimeter, and Kleiman made sure that Dzikansky reached the "inner sanctum." Kleiman could not avoid looking at the dead bodies. He could not believe he was at yet another suicide bombing scene; speaking to his wife on the phone from the site, he listened as she urged him to leave at once.

While recovering from PTSD, Kleiman was startled to realize how ill-prepared the Israel Police had been to deal with his disorder: It turned out that he was forced to turn to private medical psychiatric help. In the meantime, police spokesmen told journalists with straight faces that the police had psychologists available for handling PTSD.

Once suicide bombings tapered off and cases of PTSD began to surface, the police hired clinical psychologists and sponsored programs for resilience training for officers and their families, but that help had not existed for Kleiman. It was hard for him to fathom why he could not get more help: "The police provided flak jackets to the police to protect against metal fragments, but they gave us no psychological flak jackets."

After retiring from the police at the age of 47 in 2006, Kleiman was recognized as a disabled veteran with benefits that included psychological treatment for PTSD. One benefit allowed him to obtain an instructor's degree in Tai Chi from the Wingate Institute in Netanya. In the summer of 2011, he was teaching Tai Chi to traumatized war veterans as well as regular students.

MORDECAI DZIKANSKY'S STORY

Though no one diagnosed Gil Kleiman as having PTSD that evening at the Stage Bar suicide bombing, Mordecai Dzikansky sensed that his friend had gone to one-too-many suicide bombings; he wondered if he too might have become similarly afflicted [2]. Meryl Dzikansky, his wife, had constantly suggested to her husband that he was too personally involved in the Israeli–Palestinian violence. But he could not detach himself from his assignment for even a moment.

It was sometimes hard to realize that one was suffering from PTSD. Busy with work, one simply did not have time to dwell upon one's personal mental health. But by 2005, the number of suicide bombings had fallen to seven, and Dzikansky had to respond to bombings over much greater intervals, giving him the unwelcome opportunity to dwell on his previous interactions with suicide bombings.

He visited the sites of two suicide bombing sites in 2005, both in Netanya at the Sharon Mall, the third attack at the same location in four years. At the first visit, on July 12, five were killed and 90 wounded; at the second, on December 5, five were killed and more than 50 wounded. Sandwiched in between those two events, Dzikansky began to feel increasingly burnt out.

No specific event triggered this feeling. In the past, the pressures of getting to a suicide bombing site quickly, of scooping up all the details, and of reporting to the NYPD as soon as possible had been mitigated by his adrenaline high as well as by the continuing praise he had received from the NYPD, Police Commissioner Ray Kelly, and the media. While on that roller coaster, he had been obsessed with his work, as he waited for the beeper to go off, not taking a day off, morbidly curious over whether this might be a day when he again would be looking at dead bodies and listening to the screams of the seriously wounded.

As 2006 arrived, the quiet times continued for him, but he remained obsessed. The only difference was that now he had plenty of time to think about his obsessions. For the past three years or so he had been coolly clinical at suicide bombing sites. But he now realized that his career, his obsessions, his uncertainties had become his entire life, and he could do nothing about it.

The grisly images of human flesh, blood, body parts, and mangled strollers came into sharper focus, and his spirits dampened. He began to sense that he was suffering from a serious psychological ailment, but he ignored the signs of that ailment for as long as he could. He tried to convince himself that he was too absorbed in his work to take time off and give the signs and symptoms the proper medical attention.

Meanwhile, his health was deteriorating. His blood pressure was high. He became obese, ballooning from 250 pounds in January 2003 to over 300 pounds three years later. Frustration over the pressures that he had once lived with calmly, but that had now taken over his life, drove him to eat—and eat and eat.

A social drinker his whole career, he started doing the wrong kind of drinking. Like many American police officers, he liked the fact that social drinking led to positive bonding, a camaraderie that emerged from a few beers. But instead of the joyous social drinking that was a constant for police and that helped them unwind, Dzikansky now looked at drinking as something that he needed to do on his own, hoping that it would help him deal with his mental problems.

He did not drink that often, but when he did, he drank too much, and used alcohol as a crutch, a way to numb himself. He rationalized, as did other alcoholics, that he knew how to keep from getting drunk. Even if he had taken one too many, he would know how to keep from injuring himself or anyone else. He never thought that he needed Alcoholics Anonymous. But he knew that drinking was no longer fun.

He resisted giving up his work even though he knew that the time had probably come. He resisted because the adrenaline rush continued, as did the feeling that he was still making a difference. And yet, the warning signs that he was plunging into his own hell were all too apparent. His obsessions and demons were getting the better of him. Once he drove behind a bus and saw an advertisement on its outer side for a children's festival. His natural instinct should have been to look at the dates so that he could take his kids to it. But the only thing that went through his mind was the fact that the festival would be a vulnerable spot for a terror attack.

He supposed that he was simply burned out from the job—nothing more serious. But, in fact, he was obsessed with his work, so obsessed that as his workload diminished, he grew even more gripped, entering his own isolated world: His relationship with his wife and children suffered. He might be at an event with his wife and children, and he could not enjoy the moment. While they were in the United States in August 2006, he took his wife and children to Disney World in Orlando, Florida.

But he was simply not there, too preoccupied with dark thoughts of events that he had witnessed and that might be recurring at this very moment thousands of miles away.

Dzikansky was dissociating from the once normal life that he had led, even as a New York City homicide detective. At least he had his wife's strong support: Though very much aware that his situation was difficult for the family, she understood his plight. Dzikansky assumed that Meryl believed that he would one day simply "get better"; that the job would end one day; that with a lessening of terror in Israel, he would return to normalcy. That's what she had hoped for, but it was going to be a struggle to get back to a good place.

With the obesity and the drinking, and the continuing pressures from the job, he could not enjoy anything. He could not free his mind of his work; he could never turn it off. Still, he began to feel that he needed some professional help, perhaps even medical. He had not been to a doctor for a general checkup in several years. In the fall of 2006, a doctor ran a series of tests and found nothing of any worrisome nature, but he did warn that if Dzikansky did not take off weight, he would face serious medical issues. That visit was a wakeup call, and Dzikansky got the message. The doctor made him look in the mirror—a crucial experience that brought him back to Earth.

Dzikansky's conclusion, apart from believing that he had to lose weight and ease up on the drinking considerably, was that he had to end his assignment in Israel soon. When he was deep into his malaise—what he thought of as his dark period—he began to confide in Gil Kleiman, who had been burdened with many of the same symptoms that Dzikansky had endured, and for many of the same reasons.

When Kleiman began describing his own situation as PTSD, Dzikansky refused to believe that he had the same disorder, similar as their symptoms were. He felt that he did not suffer from a specific medical disorder. One reason was his recollection of NYPD detectives, himself included, routinely going to crime scenes in the 1980s and 1990s, and their constant exposure to unnatural deaths.

"Dear God," he thought, "If these guys, with their almost daily contact with horrific scenes of both death and injuries, don't have PTSD, or they're not claiming to have it, how dare I claim to have it? Many of us had been at 9/11. Everyone has seen terrible things."

Dzikansky had seen hundreds of bodies. He had been to hundreds of crime scenes. He had seen every conceivable kind of death—from a newborn with SIDS (sudden infant death syndrome) to an elderly person dying peacefully in her sleep to people who had been run over by trains. He had seen it all: suicides, murders, shootings, stabbings, and too many autopsies to count. He had even come across a beheading in New York: a jumper who had committed suicide and was beheaded on his way down when he collided with sharp metal support rails in the midtown Marriot Hotel's atrium. He was a very considerate jumper. His last booming words were: "Look out below."

Dzikansky's ailment was PTSD. Somehow, the emotions that he was experiencing were easier for him to absorb once he learned that his situation had a rational explanation. It was all so ironic. His job had been to be the voice of authority; his tasks had been to make sure that the awful scenes that he witnessed would never happen again. He was supposed to witness these horrific events, stand back, report on them, and move on to the next event; and yet he had become one more victim.

As much as Dzikansky had tried to convince himself that he was not suffering from PTSD, he knew deep down that witnessing suicide bombing sites had most likely affected him emotionally in ways that did not happen to the police officers at New York crime scenes or autopsies. He remained on the assignment, looking into any possible connection between people and potential terror cells in Israel and New York City, waiting for the next attack. The tension that he had always felt remained, but his life became far less dramatic.

In 2007 there had been "only" one suicide bombing. From conversations that Dzikansky had had with his NYPD colleagues at that time, he realized that they believed it was time for him to turn over his task to someone else. In October 2007 he ended his Israeli assignment.

Later, one sign that he was recovering from PTSD was his willingness to acknowledge that, indeed, he had suffered from this illness. Yet the burnt corpses and the screaming wounded at a suicide bombing could still tug at his heartstrings in a more profound way than did victims of a robbery, jealousy, envy, or greed.

To recover fully, Dzikansky had to disengage himself from the second-to-second pace that he had lived through in recent years in tracking suicide bombings around the world. He could feel himself improving even while still focusing on terror issues because monitoring terror events was no longer the main driving force of his life. He focused more on taking care of himself—spending time with his family and exercising.

He found sharing his up-and-down tale with others quite cathartic. After stepping down from full-time police work, he picked up the slack nicely by giving public speeches in which he urged others to maintain vigilance with regard to terror. Once he had integrated himself back into a day-to-day routine with his family, he knew that he was getting closer to a full recovery.

Having described the phenomenon of suicide bombing and the various ways that can be deployed to defend against it, we spell out in our final chapter the "take-away" that law enforcement professionals can get from this book.

NOTES

1. Gil Kleiman, in conversation with co-authors Mordecai Dzikansky and Robert Slater, November 17, 2010.
2. Mordecai Dzikansky in conversation with Gil Kleiman and Robert Slater, November 21, 2010.

21

Battling the Suicide Bomber
Our Recommendations

Now that we realize who the suicide bomber is—what he or she can and cannot accomplish—we can say almost certainly that the bomber and his terrorist organization are unlikely to bring down a government, not that they don't want to; they just can't. They may threaten governments; they may kill civilians; but they are unlikely to force a government to surrender. However zealous radical Islamists are, only rarely have they actually replaced existing "infidel" regimes with Islamic states that abide by Islamic (Sharia) law.

Radical Islamists imagine a day when infidel states will crumble one after the other and Muslims will rule the world. Their success on 9/11 buoyed such hopes. Thus far, only five states in the Muslim world have become Islamic republics: Pakistan (1956), Mauritania (1958), Iran (1979), Afghanistan (2001), and Iraq (2006). Suicide bombings have occurred in all five states. With its conservative religiosity and its penchant for provocation (witness its threat to build its own nuclear weapons), Iran has been the most controversial of these Islamic republics. It became an Islamic republic in April 1979, three months after the shah had left Iran and gone into exile. At the same time, Ayatollah Khomeini, returning to Tehran, was welcomed home by several million Iranians. On February 11, the royal regime collapsed after guerillas and rebel troops defeated troops loyal to the shah in armed street battles. A national referendum was held in April, with Iranians voting to turn their country into an Islamic republic, to create a new theocratic constitution, and to make Khomeini the supreme leader of the country starting in December 1979.

As for the most bombastic goal of radical Islamists, replacing one state after another with Islamic states until they rule the world, that turn of events seems most unlikely. As radical Islamists such as Hamas attempted to replace the State of Israel with a radical Islamic one, the militarily powerful Israel found suicide bombing a painful nuisance, but not a serious threat to the existence of Israel.

How effective has the suicide bombing tactic been in Western urban environments? One is tempted to say—not very. Yet, if it has not succeeded strategically (i.e., toppling governments), suicide bombing has had a devastating effect on the populations it targets.

Though 9/11 was the most dramatic suicide bombing in history, Osama bin Laden failed to achieve his goal of forcing U.S. troops to leave Saudi Arabia. He could argue that 9/11 caused the United States to engage al-Qaeda in wars in Afghanistan and Iraq, and that al-Qaeda remained functioning, however weakened by bin Laden's death in May 2011.

But Palestinian suicide bombers, though killing 543 Israelis in suicide bombings from 2001 to 2008, did not succeed in forcing Israel to abandon the occupied West Bank. Israel yielded control over the Gaza Strip on September 12, 2005, but its jet fighters continue to attack terrorist targets in retaliation for Hamas's firing of rockets against Israeli communities.

Given the fact that terrorist leaders cannot pin much hope on using suicide bombing to overturn governments, they are forced to regard the bombings less as a game-changer and more as an ongoing form of barbaric torture that, by terrorizing the enemy, slowly weakens it. Each suicide bomber can only inflict limited physical harm, but he can cause much psychological damage. Each time a suicide bomber kills three people, or six, or 20, he terrorizes the entire community; he disrupts economies and the personal routines of thousands, sometimes millions. And that is where the suicide bombers and their facilitators have found the most success.

It is small comfort to governments under attack from suicide bombers to know that they will not be forced to surrender to the bombers. The very fact that suicide bombers can inflict so much psychological harm is reason enough for everyone from political leaders to law enforcement officers to other first responders to remain vigilant. Israel learned that lesson the hard way, increasing its watchfulness while suicide bombers constantly carried out attacks. Unlike Israel, the United States has the luxury of preparing for the next wave of suicide bombings before that wave begins.

To help Western nations—especially the United States—prepare for that next wave, we offer a set of recommendations arising from our lengthy hands-on experience. If these recommendations are followed, they will go a long way toward foiling suicide bombings, but should bombings occur, these recommendations will help mitigate casualties.

LESSON 1: LEARN HOW TO REDUCE THE IMPACT OF SUICIDE BOMBINGS

The most important lesson is that one can draw lessons from suicide bombings and can take steps to reduce their impact.

Years ago it was customary to discount terrorist events as inconsequential to America if they occurred in faraway lands. Those events had nothing to teach us, so it was believed: They were thousands of miles away, and they were happening to non-Americans. Even after 9/11, it was hard to argue that terrorism around the world carried significant lessons for American law enforcement. But one lesson was perfectly obvious: If a terrorist can blow himself up outside a railroad station in Israel, another terrorist can decide to imitate that tactic and blow himself up near the Rockefeller Center ice skating rink or inside Grand Central Station in New York City.

This is our message: It is smart not to relax, because terror is definitely occurring, and it may occur soon enough, if not at your doorstep, then close enough to impact your life directly.

LESSON 2: DO NOT FEEL HELPLESS

Another highly significant lesson: If terror does occur in America—in its large cities or small—we are not helpless. We might not be able to prevent suicide bombings, but we can take security measures that will reduce casualties in advance of the bombings. By the time a suicide bomber has carried out an attack, it is too late, too late for the dead victims, too late for the wounded, too late to stop the terrorist physically from setting off his explosives.

Terrorists have an advantage over security forces. They possess the element of surprise; they can, under the right circumstances, insinuate themselves stealthily into large crowds simply because they are ready to die as part of the attack. And they possess a remarkable devotion to carrying out the most irrational deed imaginable. So catching them in advance or as they approach a target is very difficult. But it is not too late for Americans and others in the West to learn valuable lessons that can reduce the amount of dead and injured in the future, if and when suicide bombers strike.

Mordecai Dzikansky and Gil Kleiman noticed that some suicide bombers had inflicted massive casualties, some much less. It was clear to them that this differing number of dead and wounded had to do with the measures that security officers took near the target, sometimes weeks before the attempted attack, sometimes seconds.

LESSON 3: CREATE A PLAYBOOK OF LESSONS LEARNED

As Mordecai Dzikansky scoured suicide bombing sites in Israel, he kept in mind that, while the Israelis had the most counterterror experience, not all of their security measures might work well for American law enforcement. Therefore, he felt a special obligation to look for lessons from Israeli-based suicide bombings that could be applied to New York.

He proposed that the New York City Police Department (NYPD) create a playbook based on lessons learned from suicide bombings in case terrorists begin zeroing in on New York City's public places. With his reports and those from other foreign liaisons, the playbook would be in place at the proper time.

If faced with a spate of terrorist attacks in New York, the NYPD would not have to start from scratch. It would have a roadmap for becoming proactive. Merely responding to terror events was clearly not enough. There were too many lessons to be learned, too many to put into practice. The NYPD adopted Dzikansky's idea at once.

The playbook was a compilation of reports generated by Dzikansky and other foreign liaisons attending overseas terror (including suicide bombing) attacks. Sometimes, after getting information from one of the liaisons, changes in day-to-day operations were implemented immediately. For example, after Dzikansky learned that the Madrid bombers assembled their devices a distance from the target, the NYPD expanded its security perimeter surrounding New York City public transportation hubs and increased the presence of police officers.

LESSON 4: SECURITY MEASURES MATTER

This lesson is crucial to reducing casualties even if a suicide bombing should take place: Take as many security precautions as possible in order to mitigate the harmful effects of a suicide bombing. The better the security measures, the fewer the casualties; the looser the security measures, the larger the number of killed and wounded. As Gil Kleiman taught security officers in Israel:

> Remember that it is extremely difficult, if not impossible, to have 100% protection. When no immediate threat exists, it can be difficult to get even 10 percent (since funding dries up as the threat decreases). Therefore, a security officer must rely upon himself to determine the level of threat and what type of tactics a terrorist might use.

That lesson exhibited itself negatively when Hanadi Jaradat struck the Haifa restaurant Maxim on October 4, 2003. The number of dead (21) and wounded (51) was especially high because of the security guard's failure to detect the fragment-laden explosives the terrorist was wearing. For whatever reason, the guard's metal detector was not at the restaurant entrance; it was elsewhere in the restaurant.

Had the terrorist realized she would have to go through a metal detector, she might not have entered the premises; or she might have exploded her device at the front door, undoubtedly killing the security guard and a few people nearby; or she might have chosen another target. But with no metal detector at the door, she was able to enter the restaurant, causing a much higher casualty rate.

Kleiman taught security officers that "terrorists are predators searching for the weakest prey." The job of security personnel is to make it as difficult as possible for "the terrorist predator to kill near your watering hole." The security officer succeeds if he forces the terrorist predator to hunt somewhere else.

"Terrorists are predators searching for the weakest prey."

Another suicide bombing occurred outside the Kfar Saba train station on April 24, 2003, when a Palestinian Arab attacker blew himself up during morning rush hour. He killed a security guard and wounded 10 others. Only one person (the security guard) died in this attack. Why were there so few casualties?

The answer: As dictated by Israeli law, a private security agency under government supervision had trained security guards to work at sensitive locations such as the Kfar Saba train station. The guard had established an aggressive presence outside the railroad station, identifying and confronting the bomber, not permitting him to move one step closer to the train station. The suicide bomber had no other choice but to explode his device at a time and in an area where few people had gathered. Thanks to the Kfar Saba security guard's training from the agency, his professionalism and heroism resulted in only one death—his own.

Completely professional and prepared for various threats, these security guards were in their 20s and had recently completed a three-year stint in the Israeli army in combat roles. They were skilled but not particularly well paid. However, their dedication was unquestioned.

Security measures matter. The question is how long should a nation or a major city keep security guards outside entrances to public places? The answer is simple: for as long as the threat of suicide bombings exists. By March 2011, Israel's aggressive security measures, defending against the suicide bombing and other terror during the Second Intifada had become a distant memory: After February 2008, there had been no suicide bombings for three years, justifying in the eyes of small business establishments their cutting back on security.

Few places got rid of security guards entirely, but many guards seemed less vigilant and professional. While Israelis reduced the quality of their guards in the absence of suicide bombings from 2008 onward, it was a risky step to take.

Israeli security officials kept guards at all sensitive public locations: government offices, public transport, public malls, and large private gatherings. The vigilance of guards at railroad stations, government offices, and buses remains high. However, lower down the food chain—at small supermarkets, small restaurants, and the like—the quality of the guards is not as high, and that is not how it should be. Once guards are in place, they should be kept in place. People will naturally let their guard down in seemingly calm times, but it is the responsibility of the government or private security to maintain vigilance to protect this calm.

After 9/11, New Yorkers were convinced that more such mega suicide bombings might occur in their city; residents remained on a high state of public alert. Law enforcement officials did not go as far as Israel did during its wave of suicide bombings: They did not require all public places to place security guards at entrances, nor did they insist that all packages be searched electronically. They did institute random searches in the New York City Transit System on July 21, 2005.

Our wish would be for residents of communities who have been or may become a target of suicide bombings to remain on high alert at as many public places as possible. New York City has maintained a high level of security despite the perceived calm, and it has been very successful.

It is a challenge to keep security guards at a high alert when threat levels remain low. Security officers must constantly maintain their vigilance, thus allowing the public to live their day-to-day lives safely. We realize how tempting it is during quiet periods to lower one's guard, but as long as a realistic threat exists, security officials must realize that where security gaps exist, terrorists will rush in to exploit those gaps.

On October 21, 2010, three armed Army National Guardsmen, dressed in full battle attire, stood against a wall inside New York City's Grand Central Station, looking for anyone suspicious. Yet, no security guard had been posted at any of the station's entrances; that "security gap" allowed anyone wearing a suicide belt to walk through the door unexamined, position himself in a large crowd, and detonate an explosive.

It was fine for the army personnel to be posted inside Grand Central Station; their visibility may serve as a deterrent to a potential suicide bomber, and one soldier might spot someone suspicious and take action against him. Still, placing soldiers in full battle dress, rather than assuring passersby, may project a sense of armed siege, hardly the feeling of security they were meant to convey. Still, it is always good to see uniformed, armed guards protecting the population. Their presence, in full battle dress, may make people edgy at first, but they will adjust and appreciate the protection.

LESSON 5: BE AWARE OF SUSPICIOUS OBJECTS AND PEOPLE

Perhaps the hardest lesson to implement throughout America is the importance of maintaining a high state of alert for suspicious objects and people. This is not a lesson that is easy to get across to the general public, especially to New Yorkers. Most people's response to anything out of the ordinary—a suspicious person, a brawl in the street, the largely naked "Singing Cowboy" frequenting Times Square—is not to take notice of such events. Almost everything imaginable goes on in New York, and nothing seems out of the ordinary. Still, the message to stay alert needs to be taught.

The lesson was learned painfully in Israel when ultra-Orthodox Jews traveled on a bus from the Western Wall to their homes in the community of Mea She'arim in August 2003. Because Ultra-Orthodox Jews on a bus make a habit of not staring at others for reasons of modesty, and would certainly not look at a differently clad person, the suicide bomber, dressed in ultra-Orthodox garb, was able to hide in the crowd. In that suicide bombing, 21 people were killed.

The lesson to be learned for anyone on the bus, ultra-Orthodox Jew or not, was to pay attention to suspicious people on the bus or any place with crowds and not to avert one's eyes, as had been the practice of these passengers. The need for constant high alert is a lesson that has to be drilled home on every possible occasion, if only because it is abundantly clear that one could save lives if security forces and citizens are on continuing high alert. The corollary of this lesson is that the less the public is alert, the greater the likelihood of high casualties in terror attacks.

The need for constant high alert is a lesson that has to be drilled home, because one could save lives if security forces and citizens are on continuing high alert.

Being in a state of alert depends little on financial or human resources. It only requires the authorities, both in the police and city government, to issue constant reminders to their citizens in speeches and advertisements, and to maintain a media barrage warning the public to be on the lookout for suspicious people and objects.

It also requires educating children from a young age by adding security awareness to their curricula, as is done in Israel. Again, we caution that a proper balance has to be maintained between turning every citizen into a whistle-blower (even when unfounded) and someone who reports authentic suspicions to the authorities.

LESSON 6: HIRE PROFESSIONAL SECURITY GUARDS

We strongly recommend that only professionally trained individuals be used as security guards at public places. They form the bulwark of protection against potential suicide bombers, but they will only be effective if properly trained. Because private security personnel may not be trained, we strongly suggest that major American cities develop a corps of security guards, providing training courses for them. This lesson is one learned from Israel: According to Israeli law, the police are required to set and monitor the training criteria for private security that includes differentiating between higher- versus lower-risk locations. The same legislation should be enacted throughout the United States.

New York City, with its population of 8 million, is far too large to possess the manpower required to place trained security guards at all public places and to guard each and every establishment. Accordingly, while we would like to see a trained guard outside every entrance to a public place, we, more realistically, suggest posting guards at as many sensitive public places as possible. We propose that the "hard drive" of these guards be shifted to focus more on potential suicide bombers and terrorists rather than on loss prevention.

> New York City, with its population of 8 million, is far too large to possess the manpower required to place trained security guards at all public places and to guard each and every establishment.

Not only must the guard spot the suspicious person, but he must also do so in time to keep the person from entering the premises or from blowing himself up outside the entrance where a line of people may have formed to enter the building. To do his job properly, a security guard does not need to do a thorough check of everyone waiting to enter the premises. But he does need to separate in his mind those who look or act suspicious (based on criteria described in chapter 13, e.g., the kind of clothes a person wears, his degree of nervousness, and the like) from those who do not. Israel, despite its small size (7.7 million, less than that of New York City), has had the capacity to station guards at all of its sensitive public places and to train guards to identify suspicious people before they can cause harm.

The City of New York might be able to establish a force of security guards that matches the quality of Israeli security guards, but the city lacks the automatic staff replenishment that Israel has been able to draw upon. Both Israel and the United States have available pools of young men and women with military experience. But American soldiers, unlike their Israeli counterparts, who are willing to work for smaller compensation, require a higher pay scale.

Every year Israel "graduates" a fresh class of 21-year-olds from the Israel Defense Forces, willing to work comparatively (to the United States) cheaply as civilian security guards for several years. Those "graduates" with actual, professional guarding experience are usually hired by high-end, government-sanctioned programs for a few years or longer, but many other "graduates" take on guarding temporarily as a way of financing a part of their schooling. (Israeli youth attend universities after serving in the army.)

The job of the Israeli guards, on its face, does not seem particularly dangerous. They have to be on alert for suicide bombers, but, with thousands of public targets around the country, the odds were and continue to be low that any one security guard might actually confront a suicide bomber. Israeli guards were killed or wounded in suicide bombings, but that fate befell few of them.

To strengthen the bond between private security personnel and law enforcement officers, we suggest upgrading cooperation between private security companies and law enforcement agencies along with legislation establishing a minimum qualification for private security guards. New York City's Shield program provides private security professionals with the latest information regarding terrorist threats and should be emulated nationwide in America.

LESSON 7: PROVIDE VIGILANT GUARDS
AT PUBLIC TRANSPORT

Public transportation—airplanes, trains, subways, and buses—is a favorite target of suicide bombers, for good reason. Every day large crowds, moving swiftly from one place to another, thereby reducing the ability to spot suspicious people, use public transport.

We believe that stationing security guards inside a bus or a train will not be effective in stopping would-be suicide bombers. Israeli buses had guards stationed on them, but not a single guard stopped a suicide bombing. If a suicide bomber succeeds in getting on a bus, it is too late for a guard on the same bus to foil the bomber, unless the guard can shoot or tackle the bomber. Our recommendation is that guards be stationed outside entrances to train terminals and bus depots.

The first ring of security should include an outside perimeter, checking for countersurveillance against the target, and, as the Spanish police organized in response to the Madrid attack, an expanded perimeter. An outside perimeter is set up in the immediate area of the target to discover if someone is doing surveillance on the target.

An expanded perimeter is a distance away from the target (it varies depending upon location) where other actions leading to the attack may be staged; the device may be assembled or a sponsor may drop off attackers.

The next ring of security should be guards within the bus and train stations, roaming both in uniform and in plain clothes. The next security ring is placing police on the trains, buses, and airplanes.

We also recommend that random checks for suspicious bags be instituted and publicized aggressively. It is remarkable to us that so much attention has been placed on airport security while train security is so neglected.

LESSON 8: "HARDEN" OR FORTIFY PUBLIC PLACES

You must "harden" or fortify your location as much as possible. Fortification of schools should be a top priority. Suicide bombers could strike at institutions in different ways: Explosives could be placed in a vehicle, with the suicide bomber trying to get as close to the target as possible before setting off the explosive device. Suicide bombers could seek to penetrate the location and detonate the explosives they are wearing at a point where there would be maximum casualties. The least likely kind of suicide bombing would be a chemical or biological assault, because that requires the most sophistication.

Hardening or fortifying a building includes doing background checks on all employees; it includes doing searches and/or ID checks of people coming into your building. Security personnel should install a good camera system that photographs both inside and outside a building to determine if someone is engaging in surveillance around the perimeter of the building. Professional personnel should view monitors and recordings regularly. Any unusual or suspicious activity should be relayed to law enforcement.

When and if possible, building managers should put in place physical barriers, such as planters or cement blocks, that can block an explosive-laden vehicle from getting close to its intended target. The barriers will almost certainly minimize casualties and building damage.

Building managers should pay attention to windows. There are many ways of doing this. One of them is applying blast-resistant film or putting up blast curtains to mitigate shattering from the blast effect of explosives. If the building, especially a sensitive one, has a garage, cars entering should be checked, including trunks, to make sure that they are not carrying explosives. Authorities should also limit the size of vehicles permitted to enter a garage. A large truck packed with explosives could take down the building.

Security and building maintenance officials need to be aware of the building's heating, ventilation, and air conditioning systems, as terrorists may try to place chemical or biological agents inside of them. Make sure access to these systems is limited and controlled. All exterior doors and operable windows should be alarmed and have a system that reveals if someone has tampered with the doors or windows. Panic buttons should be installed in key locations, especially in schools. But, panic buttons only work if someone at the other end can provide an immediate armed response.

A gate or fence should be installed along the perimeter of a school (as Israelis require at their schools) or of any other building where applicable. Youngsters should be taught safety practices against suicide bombings from an early age; they must be warned not to pick up anything from the ground. It might be an explosive. In Israel, such instruction begins in kindergarten. It's never too early.

Following our advice will get you off to a good start but there are many other ways to fortify premises against terror. In the end, with your budget in mind, you will have to make the final evaluation, reacting to conditions as you find them.

LESSON 9: MAKE SUICIDE BOMBINGS A LAW ENFORCEMENT PRIORITY

American law enforcement officers, in large and small cities alike, no longer have the luxury of treating counterterrorism, including suicide bombings, as an unimportant part of their work. Prior to 9/11, it was understandable that law enforcement officers focused exclusively on catching common criminals. But post-9/11, terror cells have sprouted up in a number of American cities, among them Buffalo, New York; Columbus, Ohio; Albany, New York; Aurora, Colorado; and Lodi, California. Those who have plotted terror, and sometimes suicide bombings, in the past decade, have focused on major American cities, mostly New York City. But nothing is to stop a cell outside Denver from switching a suicide bombing target from New York City to Denver or some outlying suburb of that city.

Accordingly, law enforcement officers must be trained not to disregard the possibility of terrorist plotters in their midst. These officers must, upon entering someone's premises, be trained to look for not just the usual drugs and firearms, but for signs of a possible suicide bombing in the making and of possible terrorist connections: bomb-making materials, including written instructions on how to construct an explosive device; other terrorist literature including radical Islamic writings; perhaps a photo on the wall of a suspected terrorist about whom your superiors have alerted you.

We strongly recommend that local law enforcement not wait for federal authorities to inform them of possible terror threats in its community. You, the local police officer, know your territory better than any other law enforcement officer elsewhere. You know your community and its inhabitants and transients. You know which public places are the most vulnerable; you know where crowds are likely to gather; you should take the initiative and watch for anyone suspicious. You must wear two hats and think about both terrorism and traditional crime.

We strongly recommend that local law enforcement not wait for federal authorities to inform them of possible terror threats in its community.

What does thinking about terrorism mean?

1. Be aware of what devices are available to protect targets in your vicinity; read brochures; attend security trade fairs.
2. Identify the most vulnerable spots in your area; draw up a list of those spots as possible targets that a terrorist might attack. Do not hold back: Even take into account the proverbial "dirty bomb in a briefcase" scenario.
3. Examine the list carefully and decide which of these targets a terrorist may be capable of attacking. If so, ask yourself if you can protect against this threat. Realistically, because of budget limitations, a threat may exist. Let's say that, because you have skyscrapers in your town, a terrorist could crash a plane into one of them. Your community is unlikely to be able to afford to purchase a ground-to-air missile system, and so you will be unlikely to stop the air attack. But you can limit the damage, should there be such an attack.
4. You can create evacuation plans for large-size buildings and run practice drills. You can prepare local firefighters as well as first aid and rescue teams; you can make sure equipment is maintained. You can ensure that fire escapes are kept up and that lighting within these targets is maintained.
5. You should buy what you need and can afford and will actually use. Purchasing an expensive "toy" like a top-of-the-line X-ray machine that cannot be manned is wasteful and a bad decision for you.

It will be tempting to exaggerate your counterterror needs to obtain a budget for equipment and manpower, but be realistic. There is no point in purchasing a $200,000 sophisticated bomb detector robot if you lack the resources to run it and maintain it.

Finally, law enforcement personnel should constantly monitor terror events around the world to stay on the alert for anyone in the U.S. trying to imitate such an overseas event on American soil. The best way to undertake such monitoring is to keep abreast of local news reporting in international trouble spots.

These, then, are the nine vital lessons to be learned in defending against and trying to mitigate the lethal, tragic effects of suicide bombing:

Lesson 1: Learn how to reduce the impact of suicide bombings.
Lesson 2: Do not feel helpless.
Lesson 3: Create a playbook of lessons learned.
Lesson 4: Security measures matter.
Lesson 5: Be aware of suspicious objects and people.
Lesson 6: Hire professional security guards.
Lesson 7: Provide vigilant guards at public transport.
Lesson 8: "Harden" or fortify public places.
Lesson 9: Make suicide bombings a law enforcement priority.

We hope that the wave of suicide bombings that you are preparing for will never happen. We suspect that it will. Nothing sums up our attitude better than that well-worn expression, "Better to be safe than sorry." That is pretty much what we ask: Be safe, be alert, be prepared. Then you can at least take heart that you have done all you could.

INDEX

For Product Safety Concerns and Information please contact our EU
representative GPSR@taylorandfrancis.com
Taylor & Francis Verlag GmbH, Kaufingerstraße 24, 80331 München, Germany